INTERNATIONAL SERIES IN EXPERIMENTAL SOCIAL PSYCHOLOGY

Series Editor: Michael Argyle, University of Oxford

The
Mass Media
and
Social Problems

by

DENNIS HOWITT

PERGAMON PRESS

OXFORD · NEW YORK · BEIJING · FRANKFURT
SÃO PAULO · SYDNEY · TOKYO · TORONTO

U.K.	Pergamon Press, Headington Hill Hall, Oxford OX3 0BW, England
U.S.A.	Pergamon Press, Maxwell House, Fairview Park, Elmsford, New York 10523, U.S.A.
PEOPLE'S REPUBLIC OF CHINA	Pergamon Press, Qianmen Hotel, Beijing, People's Republic of China
FEDERAL REPUBLIC OF GERMANY	Pergamon Press, Hammerweg 6, D-6242 Kronberg, Federal Republic of Germany
BRAZIL	Pergamon Editora, Rua Eça de Queiros, 346, CEP 04011, São Paulo, Brazil
AUSTRALIA	Pergamon Press Australia, P.O. Box 544, Potts Point, N.S.W. 2011, Australia
JAPAN	Pergamon Press, 8th Floor, Matsuoka Central Building, 1-7-1 Nishishinjuku, Shinjuku-ku, Tokyo 160, Japan
CANADA	Pergamon Press Canada, Suite 104, 150 Consumers Road, Willowdale, Ontario M2J 1P9, Canada

First edition 1982
Reprinted 1983, 1985, 1986

Library of Congress Cataloging in Publication Data

Howitt, Dennis.
The mass media and social problems.
(International series in experimental
social psychology; v. 2)
1. Mass media—Social aspects. 2. Social
problems. I. Title. II. Series.
HM258.H63   1982   302.2'3   AACR2   81-19971

British Library Cataloguing in Publication Data

Howitt, Dennis
The mass media and social problems.—(International
series in experimental social psychology; v. 2)
1. Mass media—Social aspects
I. Title II. Series
302.2'3   HM258

ISBN 0-08-026759-9 (Hardcover)
ISBN 0-08-028918-5 (Flexicover)

Printed in Great Britain by A. Wheaton & Co. Ltd., Exeter

Introduction to the Series

MICHAEL ARGYLE

SOCIAL psychology is in a very interesting period, and one of rapid development. it has survived a number of "crises", there is increased concern with external validity and relevance to the real world, the repertoire of research methods and statistical procedures has been greatly extended, and a number of exciting new ideas and approaches are being tried out.

The books in this series present some of these new developments; each volume contains a balance of new material and a critical review of the relevant literature. The new material consists of empirical research, procedures, theoretical formulations, or a combination of these. Authors have been asked to review and evaluate the often very extensive past literature, and to explain their new findings, methods or theories clearly.

The authors are from all over the world, and have been very carefully chosen, mainly on the basis of their previous published work, showing the importance and originality of their contribution, and their ability to present it clearly. Some of these books report a programme of research by one individual or a team, some are based on doctoral theses, others on conferences.

Social psychologists have moved into a increasing number of applied fields, and a growing number of practitioners have made use of our work. All the books in this series have be some practical application, some will be on topics of wide popular interest, as well as adding to scientific knowledge. The books in the series are designed for advanced undergraduates, graduate students and relevant practitioners, and in some cases for a rather broader public.

We do not know how social psychology will develop, and it takes quite a variety of forms already. However it is a great pleasure to be associated with books by some of those social psychologists who are developing the subject in such interesting ways.

Contents

Part One

THE HISTORICAL AND
THEORETICAL BACKGROUND TO
THE DEBATE ON THE MASS MEDIA
AND SOCIAL PROBLEMS

1

Introduction

OUR view of the world outside of our own work, family, and friends is often distressing. Although we may sit contentedly in a warm glow of love, companionship, and affection, beyond that encircles a world of danger, discomfort, and disaster. We are cocooned in a cosy, comfortable world, but outside we see mass starvation, disease, poverty, unemployment, violence, death, theft, crime, unprovoked violence, mob violence, oppression, deprivation, squalor, brutality, injustice, war, civil disturbance, racism, sexism, exploitation, and unrest. This outer world is known to us even if we never experience most of it directly. It is a world which makes little sense to us but threatens us by surrounding us. We hear things, see things, read things from this outside world but these build up our fears rather than reassure us.

This outside world is delivered to our doorsteps by a newspaperboy or relayed by friendly people on radio and television, but the newspapers, radio and television seem no better at coping with it than we are. They cannot understand violence either. The outside world will not go away but neither can we master it. How can we explain what is going on? Soon we wonder whether we have been tricked. The media do not simply bring the outside world to us; they seem obsessed by conflict, violence, and force. Instead of being mere messengers from the outside world, they actively propagandize on its behalf. After all, as far as we can tell, the outside world is made up of people very much like ourselves with families and friends. Is it then the mass media which create this mayhem? What most of us see of violence is not in the street but on television.

The mass media have made us instantly aware of the outside world. We are used to knowing what happens hundreds or thousands of miles away within moments of its happening. It may have taken weeks or months for the news that Livingstone had been found to reach home a century ago but we have looked over the shoulders of moon explorers from our living rooms. The outside world is no longer an unknown mystery but it is bewildering. What has mass communication done to society? Society must have changed in many ways with the advance in communications technology. Has the change always been for the better and can the media be blamed for the terrible things going on in the outside world which they bring to us so eagerly? Could we use the mass media to change the outside world to make it a less dangerous, less horrifying place?

But more frightening realizations are to come. The mass media are not just changing the outside world but they appear to be undermining our inner world. Divorces are more common, our children are becoming unmarried parents, people are swearing and blaspheming in our living rooms (albeit 'on the box'), people are not going to church any more. We cannot blame ourselves for this; things were not the same in our pre-mass communication days. What further harm can the media inflict on us?

The main function of the mass media is entertainment but research into the process and effects of mass communication has neglected this. The favoured topics include ways in which information about the state of society is processed and received; ways in which the mass media have a bad effect on things that happen in society; and ways in which the mass media have a beneficial effect on things that happen in society. The mass media are seen as tools to reconstruct society. Harnessing the mass media for the good of society has been a dream, an ideal, which underlies much of the research and argument reported in the rest of this book. Research into the process and effects of the mass media has never been motivated primarily by purely academic concerns. Mass communication research has been the product of a desire to help change the world, alleviate misery and suffering, and maintain social ideals. Indeed, the mass communicator and the mass communications researcher are working with very much the same pragmatic goals in mind.

The history of research into the mass media has been dominated by two themes. The first is the concern over the power of communication to change society and the second is political involvement in financing and initiating mass communication research. Most research has emphasized the role of the mass media in causing crime, violence, civil disturbance, educating those whom the education system has failed, and so forth. In short, the research is social problem oriented rather than academic and theoretical. One consequence of the applied orientation has been that mass communication research was slow in developing a coherent body of theory. The earliest mass communication research by psychologists was probably the Lashley and Watson (1922) study of the effects of an anti-venereal disease film. This was foremost a pragmatic enterprise directed at a social problem, inclined towards a social engineering philosophy, and stemming from no particular theoretical interest at all. This first study in mass communication was prophetic of the style of many later studies.

The role of politics, our second major determinant of the shape of mass communication research, is easily seen. Research costs money and someone has to pay for it. Whoever pays the piper calls the tune in research as much as anything. The role of political forces has been largely in the provision of funds for the research which has shaped much of the mass communications literature. In the late 1920s and early 1930s the Payne Fund published several book-length accounts of research they had commissioned from several famous psychologists and social scientists (Blumer, 1933; Blumer and Hauser, 1933; Cressey and Thrasher, 1933; Foreman, 1935; Peterson and Thurstone, 1933; Shuttleworth and May, 1933). During the 1940s the American Army used Carl Hovland's research skills to investigate the effects of army propaganda on the morale of U.S. troops (Hovland, 1954; Hovland, Lumsdaine, and Sheffield, 1949). During the 1950s in Great Britain the Nuffield Foundation provided funds for research into the impact of television on children's education, attitudes, and behaviour, partly as a response to the introduction of commercial television into the country (Himmelweit, Oppenheim, and Vince, 1958). In Great Britain in the 1960s, the Home Office persuaded commercial television to provide funds which led to the establishment of a television research committee as a response to the feeling that delinquency was increasing due to television. In the U.S.A. the Eisenhower Commission into the causes and prevention of violence included a section on Television Violence as a possible contribution to the urban violence associated with demonstrations and riots (Baker and Ball, 1970); in 1969–70 the United States Surgeon General spent about two million dollars on research into the effects of television violence, and about the same time the American Presidential Committee into Obscenity and Pornography initiated and reviewed research (Commission on Obscenity and Pornography, 1970). Throughout the 1970s money was available for research into the use of the mass media in social policy research of one sort or another.

Although obscenity and pornography, violence, and delinquency have attracted the most attention from the public *and* researchers, many other problems have been blamed on the media: materialism, racism, antifeminism, poor industrial relations, abuses of welfare, abuse of welfare claimants, illiteracy, innumeracy, divorce, short sight, obesity, skinniness, the decline of high culture, the decline of the theatre and cinema, the breakdown of the family, disrespect of politicians, drug abuse, mugging, football hooliganism, the hijacking of aeroplanes, and so on, almost interminably. The media are also thought responsible for good things: contributions to education, information, leisure, and culture are frequently mentioned. However, most of the more vocal claims about the good and bad effects of the mass media are mere assertions based on opinion rather than scientific evidence.

In deciding which social problems to discuss, their coverage in the literature was an important guideline. There are a number of social problems which could not be covered because researchers have largely ignored them. Despite this, and despite the clear tendency for mass communication research to dwell on certain pet themes, the spread of issues is quite impressive and reflects many key issues. The need for variety in the sort of arguments and ideas has also been important in making the final choice. Most social problem areas are thematically similar in their treatment in the media, and research tends to follow similar patterns. In order to avoid endless repetition as much as possible, the themes which are best highlighted by a particular social problem are discussed mainly in that context. Some may find the selection of social problems a little glib, perhaps concentrating on the more sensational and familiar examples. If so then this partly reflects a desire to keep close to the sorts of topics researchers have chosen to investigate.

This book could not be restricted to the contributions of a single discipline. While written from a psychological viewpoint, much of what is discussed has its origin in sociology and political science. Many of the authors whose work is discussed would not recognize themselves as mass communication researchers. Their primary interests lie in areas which only fleetingly led them into communication research. For example, some may be practising social workers whose professional needs had created an interest in the mass media. Although not confined exclusively to a single discipline, it was felt that the contributions of those working from a psychological viewpoint have been given relatively little attention in recent years. Sociological ideas have tended to dominate. The imbalance is partially rectified in this book. Latterly mass communication research has moved towards being an intellectual specialism in its own right. It remains to be seen whether it becomes less dependent on the major social science disciplines for its inspiration and ideas.

2

Three Models of Mass Communications Research

THREE models recur frequently in the mass communications literature. They are: (1) the Effects Model (sometimes known as the hypodermic approach or the stimulus–response approach). (2) the Uses and Gratifications Model, and (3) the Cultural Ratification Model. There are others, much as one would expect, but these have little bearing on the psychology of mass communication. The order in which they are listed above is the same as the order of their emergence and, to some extent, their dominance. All three models coexist fruitfully although each has come under critical scrutiny by proponents of the other approaches.

The Effects Model

This, as the name suggests, concentrates on the direct influence that the mass media have on the audience *en masse*. Basically the question posed by the model is whether a particular event transmitted through the mass media has a particular effect on the audience. The sorts of question asked are simple: Can the incidence of venereal disease be reduced using propaganda? Does television cause delinquency? Did a particular programme enhance a politician's image? Can people be educated through television? In other words, just *what do the mass media do to people?* There is nothing particularly wrong with this model in itself and quite clearly it reflects precisely the sort of concerns about the mass media which politicians and public alike seem to want to be dealt with. Its other name, the hypodermic model, draws attention to the analogy on which it is based. The idea is that the mass media *inject* into the audience a dose of persuasive communication which has a fairly uniform effect on the audience. The assumption is that persuasive communication in the mass media operates *directly* on the

7

audience. Nothing intervenes between the two. This is just like a syringe entering flesh directly. Perhaps the brutality of the needle and the vulnerability of the patient are also intended as part of the analogy. To call the model a stimulus response (SR) model is to allude to a tradition in psychology from which some of the early mass communication researchers came. The stimulus response model is a strategy for studying behaviour in which a stimulus is applied to the organism and the behavioural response to that stimulus noted. The parallels to the crudely expressed model of mass communication effects are clear. The SR model, largely adopted by the Behaviourist School in psychology, is based on the philosophical idea that what is in the mind is scientifically unknowable and consequently worthless. Only what can be observed is of any value. Although never a universal in psychology, Behaviourism became closely associated with the use of the experimental method, particularly laboratory experiments in the study of people.

This emphasis on the experimental method placed great store on net shifts in behaviour in response to the stimulus. Individual differences between people are hidden by considering only overall changes in groups. The response of the mass of individuals was what mattered, not how individuals differed in their responses. This had a curious parallel or analogue in sociological writing and social criticism. The nineteenth century and early part of the twentieth century had demonstrated the power and fury of so-called mass movements. The French and Russian Revolutions, trades unions, communes and other 'mass' movements could be seen, whether accurately or not, as the actions of uncontrolled and uncoordinated mobs undermining social order. Likewise the growth of the mass media promoted the idea of a mass audience easily swayed by the arguments of the press. The First World War saw both the upheaval of millions and the possibility of propaganda directed at a huge audience. All of this was reflected, albeit on a much smaller scale, in the model of media effects which dominated early mass communication research.

In itself the effects model of mass communication research has no particular theoretical allegiances. It does however tend to make, by implication rather than explicitly, assumptions about the nature of mass communication which are not without drawbacks. The first difficulty stems from the assumption that there is a simple pattern of influence which starts with the mass media and ends with the individual member of the audience being affected, persuaded, or changed in some way. This conceptualization makes it possible to undertake small-scale laboratory experiments to study the effects of the mass media. Assuming that the media act directly on the audience, we can show a film in a psychological laboratory, measure its effects on our experimental subject, and claim that we have discovered an effect of mass communication. Although some psychologists, including most importantly Hovland (1954), have pointed to the disparities between these skeletal reconstructions and the richness and complexity of the mass communications process in real life, many adhere to the unstated view that real-life and the psychological laboratory are as one.

A second drawback of this model is that it narrows down our attention to a very limited idea about mass communication—its effects. Unfortunately the effects of the mass media cannot be fully understood without reference to their contents. That is, why the images transmitted by the media are what they are. Such concerns lead to questions of who owns the media, who controls the media, who recruits media personnel, what sorts of personnel are recruited, how programmes are produced, how content is determined, how stylistic factors influence the output, what effects pressure groups have on programmes, amongst others. But we can criticize donkeys for not being race horses too much. Since no one has yet discovered a way of investigating the totality of the human experience in one fell swoop, at worst the effects model can only be blamed for diverting attention to questions that some researchers find relatively uninteresting.

The third drawback of the effects model, while not absolutely inevitable, is that net changes brought about by the mass media are emphasized in preference to considering the many different though conflicting effects the media may have on people. The mass media may influence everyone but produce no net changes because the changes cancel each other out.

Finally, the overwhelming drawback of the effects model is the unwarranted assumption, long encouraged by critics of the media, that the mass media's effects are of almost cataclysmic proportions. The rub is that if effects research fails to unravel such effects of the mass media it risks destruction through its own success. Demonstrating that most media effects are comparatively minor undermines effects research as a pressing concern.

It would be superfluous to give detailed examples of the effects model in this section. Later chapters in the book are replete with examples since virtually any question asking about the effects of the mass media on people relates in some way to this model.

As we will see, some mass communications researchers and theorists have tended to reject the effects model. This is partly because the model gives a rather incomplete conceptualization of the role of the mass media in society, but also because it tends to demand the highest levels of empirical proof which cannot be fully met. In outline, the major methodological problems facing the mass communications researcher interested in media effects are:

1. The most rigorous standards of proof of causation come from care-

fully controlled laboratory-style experiments in which the effects of competing, non-media variables are reduced to a minimum. Unfortunately the laboratory environment lacks many key features of the social world and cannot be seen as equivalent. Therefore laboratory style research may not fully answer questions about the mass media as they actually function in society.

2. When studying the effects of the mass media in natural settings without manipulating events (i.e. the field study) important questions of causality arise. For example, if it was found that people who read the Bible commit fewer crimes than those who do not read the Bible what should we conclude? That the Bible makes people good? That not reading the Bible makes people bad? That good people naturally gravitate towards the Church and as a consequence are more likely to read the Bible? All of these would be possible conclusions from the original research data. In addition, it is possible that a third factor has to be taken into account. For example, we know that young people tend to commit more crimes than older people and that older people tend to be more frequent Church attenders than young people. Thus the association between Bible reading and not commiting crime might simply be an artifact of age rather than demonstrating a causal influence of Bible reading on standards of conduct or vice versa.

3. Another methodological problem is that of voluntary exposure. Most field research does nothing to alter the mass media consumption patterns of the audience. However, most experimental research deliberately changes the media usage patterns of the audience and demands fairly careful scrutiny of the films, programmes, etc., used. There is therefore the distinct possibility in experimental research that one studies the effects of material that people would normally not view or hear or read. In addition, experimental methodologies—by demanding careful scrutiny of filmed materials—produce results radically different from what would be expected in more normal circumstances in which people perhaps just flick through newspaper headlines, watch the television and hold conversations at the same time, and so forth. The effects of the same material in the experimental setting and in real life might be radically different.

4. Finally, there is the fundamental problem that often the mass media and other social influences are difficult to separate. That is, the media and other social forces seem to be pushing the individual in identical directions. This makes it very difficult to evaluate the relative influence of the mass media compared to the school, family, peers, and other important social groups. Furthermore, sometimes different

forces to change in society may be acting in conflicting ways so confounding the picture even more.

The Uses and Gratifications Model

This is in part a reaction to and explanation of the failure of the effects model. But it also has quite distinct intellectual roots and a life independent of the effects model. The first papers published in the 1940s laid down the essentials of the methodology and the problem (Herzog, 1944, 1954; Warner and Henry, 1948) which have scarcely changed since. Underlying the uses and gratifications approach is the idea of *function*. To ask for what purposes do people use the mass media is as an illuminating a question as what effects do the mass media have on the audience. No single simple set of functions of the media could be expected to emerge from the wide range of mass communications which exist. The early work concentrated on the gratifications gained from listening to day-time serials (largely intended for the housewife audience) on radio. More recent research has kept up this tradition (Blumler *et al.*, 1970). The research methods too have remained constant. Basically the audience is asked what they get out of a particular programme. For the fictional programmes like soap operas two main categories of gratifications emerge, although the list put forward is long and potentially as varied as the audience. The major functions are described by Klapper (1960) as *emotional release* (feeling better, for example, because their own personal troubles are shared by the characters in the serial) and *school of life* (some women claimed, for example, that they felt they learned how to deal with their own lives from such programmes). One of the classic early uses and gratifications studies was that of Bereleson, on the consequences of a newspaper strike for the daily habits of the newspaper reader. A daily newspaper serves a minor but useful function in the life of the reader; its absence causes some disruption in daily routines (Bereleson, 1948).

Much of the early research was centred around researchers directly or indirectly connected with the Bureau of Applied Social Research at Columbia University, New York. Its director, Paul Lazarsfeld, a Jew, had left Austria early in the 1930s for the United States. This was a move precipitated by the rise of fascism. Although Lazarsfeld was associated with the Psychology department in Vienna, in the American and British context he is better described as a sociologist. The Bureau itself was established and initially financed by a philanthropic foundation. However, much of its research programme needed supplementary funds which sometimes came from advertising and market research. Despite this commercial base the Bureau produced much work of significance to the academic study of the mass media.

Lazarsfeld was primarily a methodologist whose research had considerable influence on mass communication theory. One of his inventions, the panel study, provides a method of studying social change over time. Essentially, a 'panel' of people volunteer to be interviewed several times over a considerable period. Lazarsfeld used the panel method to study changes in voting behaviour during an election campaign. The research (Lazarsfeld, Bereleson and Gaudet, 1948) into the effects of the 1940 presidential campaign was the first satisfactory study of this phenomenon. Residents of Erie County in Ohio were asked their voting intentions in May preceding the national conventions and later on in October. Most people did not change their voting intentions by one jot: only about 5% switched their political allegiance. A later study by Bereleson, Lazarsfeld and McPhee (1954) produced a very similar conclusion. The presidential campaign of 1948 converted a mere 8% of the sample. Much the same emerged in later studies. For instance, Butler and Stokes (1969) found as few as 2–3% of voters switching. Persuasive communication persuades— but only just. Political campaigns did more to keep the partly faithful in line than to produce radical shifts.

Evidence like this led Joseph Klapper, who had been associated with Lazarsfeld's Bureau and was eventually Director of Research for the Columbia Broadcasting System, to argue that the 'phenomenistic' approach gave more hope of understanding the mass media (Klapper, 1960). For phenomenistic read 'functionist' or 'uses and gratifications'. Therein lies the key to understanding the importance of the new emphasis. People, it seems, use the mass media to maintain things as they always were. Propaganda hardly affects them as they actively reject what they do not want to accept. The crude effects model is undermined by this. Klapper had in fact both spearheaded an attack on the older effects model and, by meshing together effects and uses and gratifications research, kept the effects tradition alive. Although the older effects model became for a while an Aunt Sally (the slogan 'It's not what the mass media does to people that is important but what people do with the mass media' seemed to catch on) its demise was more apparent than real. Klapper's reformulation was in its turn vulnerable to research showing that the mass media affect their audiences directly.

With some justice, the Klapper book is regarded as a watershed. This is not because it signalled the demise of effects research, which in fact gained strength in the 1960s. Paradoxically, Klapper's glorification of uses and gratifications research marked its sudden demise. The phenomenalistic approach promises much greater revelations than it actually provides. The uses and gratifications model resurfaced early in the 1970s in rather different geographical settings. It became more central to European mass communications research than American. Intellectually however, the leader of the European tradition, Elihu Katz, was a former associate of the Bureau of Applied Social Research in the 1950s. Having moved to Israel, he became involved in the resurgence of the uses and gratifications approach. The old concern with soap opera also resurfaced. *The Dales* and *Coronation Street* were amongst the British examples that were studied (Blumler *et al.*, 1970).

Uses and gratifications research has been a crucial and formative influence on thinking about the mass media. Over and over again we are guided to consider the audience as active users of the mass media rather than passive absorbers. Despite this the actual research emerging from this approach tends to be banal, stifled by the limitations of method. While this is not the only approach, researchers usually ask their respondents *why* they watch a particular programme or read a particular part of the newspaper. Thus the respondent, not the researcher, has the responsibility for (a) theorizing about why he consumes this media fodder and (b) producing from his experience of his own behaviour the empirical support for the theory. It is not at all certain that people are capable of doing this effectively. Psychologists might be right in thinking that the uses and gratifications approach is crypto introspectionism, disguised phenomenology. Let us take an example: imagine we wish to understand why a dirty old man in a raincoat pays substantial sums to see an obscene or pornographic film; if we ask him why, he might reply: 'I like to see vaginas twenty feet high' (as one of the American Commissions found). Now this may be the best insight he can come up with to explain his behaviour. The trouble is that although it may adequately reflect the content of the film he has just seen, one feels cheated in the sense that any understanding achieved lacks real substance. We do not know why this man should need this material at all, only that he likes what he sees. What are the origins of such needs? The same dissatisfactions will probably emerge if you attempt to explain your own viewing behaviour in this way.

Uses and gratifications research tends to concentrate on developing typologies of needs satisfied by different sorts of programmes. One example of this (Blumler *et al.*, 1970) is the fourfold classification of functions as:

1. Diversion (escape from routine, emotional problems, and other problems),
2. Personal relationships (companionship and social utility),
3. Personal identity, and
4. Surveillance.

Others have come up with similar, perhaps slightly longer or shorter, lists. The approach, despite being couched in terms which emphasize the individuals understanding of his social world, is statistical, relying on methods rather than substance to impress. This is a little unfair in that some researchers (e.g. Dembo, 1972, 1973; Howitt and Dembo, 1974) have attempted to lend more substance to the functionist approach by relating the social and psychological characteristics of the individual, objectively measured, to his media usage. Such an approach is quite promising since it has been well documented that different sorts of people have distinct programme preferences and newspaper choices. Advertisers often capitalize on this in order to aim their advertising at selected sections of the audience. Beer and razor blade advertisements are probably well placed during sports programmes since the number of males watching is thereby maximized. Men obviously like sports programmes, but we would explain this as a product of many interrelated cultural forces rather than in terms of gratifying needs.

In summary, the most important drawbacks of the approach include:

1. Since social and psychological needs cannot be effectively defined, the list is infinitely expandable to meet the characteristics of different audiences and different content of mass communication.
2. Although the approach is based firmly in the psychology of the individual, and implies a fairly deep, complex, and thorough understanding of human experience, the research technique used often results in a very crude and superficial understanding.
3. It assumes that mass media usage is purposive but fails to establish the generality of this claim. At least some media consumption is unplanned, unintended, and accidental. The risk is that the model is undermined by pushing it too far.
4. Despite the success of Klapper in using the functional model to clarify the process and effects of mass communication, later writers seem to have made little progress towards amalgamating the two paradigms into a fully coherent point of view.

The uses and gratifications approach has a certain intuitive appeal. It seems to give the audience a new dignity: they are seen as active and self-determining rather than passive absorbers of mass communication. Instead of being manipulated the audience is the manipulator. The uses and gratifications approach is not a fully unified body of theory and research. It is a loose conglomerate of particular types of research questions and methodologies. Clear formulations of the aims, purposes, and objectives of the functionalist approach are difficult to find. There are plenty of reviews but they leave the limits and intents of the approach very loosely stated (e.g. Blumer and Katz, 1974; McCron, 1976). Let us take a simple example. Does the uses and gratifications approach try to explain *why* people use the mass media or does it try to say what the individual gained from his mass media experiences? These are, of course, very different questions. If the uses and gratification theorists are trying to understand the former, then there is very little evidence in their favour; if the latter, then it is difficult to even conceive of any evidence which could disconfirm their point of view. Virtually all evidence used by uses and gratifications theorists comes from self-reports of viewers about their motives and rewards in the viewing situation which usually have to be taken at their face value. Only rarely, as in the studies of media deprivation, does any other sort of evidence appear.

Goodhardt, Ehrenberg and Collins (1975) present evidence which suggests that the viewing selectivity required by the uses and gratifications model does not exist. Some viewers, it would be argued, need to watch soap operas because, for example, they provide ideas about how to cope with the stresses, problems, and trauma of their lives. This implies that there should be a special type of viewer for a special type of programme. According to the data of Goodhardt, Ehrenberg, and Collins, this is not the case. They found very little or no evidence in favour of the view that certain programme types attract a special type of viewer. The probability that any programme will be watched is largely determined by the popularity of that programme, rather than any specific element in the programme. They propose the *duplication of viewing law*. Essentially the problem is as follows: What is the likelihood that the viewer of a play will watch another play screened later that week compared to the probability that that viewer will watch a completely different type of programme such as a light entertainment programme? Following uses and gratifications principles, one would assume that the viewer of one play will be more likely to view another play than a light entertainment programme. The data suggests otherwise, the likelihood that the viewer will watch another play or a light entertainment programme is virtually completely determined by the popularity ratings of these programmes. So if the play is more popular (that is, watched by more people) than the light entertainment programme, our viewer will be more likely to watch that; if the light entertainment programme is more popular then our viewer is more likely to watch that. Thus programme type has little bearing on viewing whereas popularity ratings have an enormous effect. The authors explain their law as follows:

'. . . the duplication of viewing law', states that the size of the audience common to two different programmes on different days depends on the ratings of the programmes and the channels on which they are shown, rather than the content of the programmes (p. 19).

Others have been very critical of the uses and gratifications approach. Particularly vulnerable to attack is the notion of psychological needs which can be satisfied by the mass media. Elliott (1974) offers a thorough critique of the gratifications model. Some researchers (e.g. Dembo and McCron, 1976), although obviously impressed and influenced by the approach, find that its conception of needs and motives require revision.

The Cultural Ratification Model

Although this has some links with the uses and gratifications model, it is best dealt with separately because its dominant intellectual roots are different. The basic principle of the cultural ratification model is that the media, along with many other social institutions, act as agencies of the political control of society. That is, the mass media are so allied to the power structure of society that it is inevitable that they serve to support and maintain power structures and dominant ideologies. The mass media, in particular, present a world view to members of society which regenerates continually and pervasively the ideological structures that are required for the maintenance of the existing power structure.

It can also be seen as a variant of the effects model since it states that the output of the mass media has the effect of preventing radical change in the attitudes, values, beliefs, perceptions, etc., of members of society. Although it does not propose that the media have the effect of changing things, it does proclaim that the media prevent change. But even the uses and gratifications model says something similar: the user is seen here as treating the media in such a way as to prevent his own attitudes from changing. The difference is clear though. The cultural ratification model assumes that the media manipulate people (exactly as with the effects model) but (exactly as with the uses and gratifications model) people tend not to change.

The empirical evidence for this model is virtually non-existent. Certainly there is no direct evidence for the idea that the media maintain 'correct' beliefs in society. The evidence usually quoted is confined to content analyses of the media. These show distinct limits to the range of ideas that the mass media are prepared to present. The ideas tend to be consensual and reject 'extreme' viewpoints. Examples of this are Golding and Middleton's (1978) analysis which suggests that welfare is treated with hostility by the media, Hartmann and Husband's (1971, 1973, 1974) presentation of race news, and Halloran, Elliott, and Murdock's (1970) discussions of the press's treatment of an anti-Vietnam War demonstration in London in the 1960s. The consensus in the media emerges in many areas. The treatment of strikes and industrial relations in all the popular media tend to be uniformly anti-union (Glasgow Media Group, 1976). Even in the treatment of politics the range tends to reflect the views of the dominant political parties with comparatively little or even no attention being given to more 'extreme' groups.

The cultural ratification model has no great currency among psychologists interested in mass communications. It deserves inclusion for the sake of completeness and because it appears in later pages in various guises. It lacks a clear allegiance to empirical evidence which in itself makes it less attractive to psychologists. In addition, it tends to be favoured by those of more Marxist or left-wing political beliefs. In many ways its inadequacies are a combination of those of the other approaches to the mass media.

Conclusions

We should not be over-eager to select one of these three models as the best. Each of the models complements and supplements the others and there is no sense in which criticisms of one really promotes satisfaction with the others. They represent quite distinct traditions in the literature and have rarely, if ever, been successfully integrated into any one research project. Nevertheless, in later chapters, the different approaches will be freely amalgamated.

3

Important Concepts in
Mass Communications Theory

THE three models of mass communication outlined in the previous chapter serve to focus attention on certain major strategies in the study of the mass media. In themselves they provide little by way of explanatory principles for what is observed. A number of concepts have been developed in the mass communication literature which are an invaluable framework with which to analyse the role of the media. It would be an overstatement to describe these as a formal theory of mass communication. In no way are these explanatory concepts proven facts and should not be assumed to operate in a particular context without further proof. The selection is culled fairly widely from the mass communications literature.

The Structure of Communication

It is convention to analyse the communication process using the following simple guidelines:

Who says *what* to *whom* through *what channel* with what *effects.*

One merely substitutes more concrete phrases for those italicized above. This is just as useful for analysis of the mass media (e.g. The *Democratic Party* says *vote for our candidate* to the *American public* on *television* and the *audience switches to another channel*) as for any other form of communication (e.g. The *dog trainer* says *walkies* to the *dog speaking loudly and firmly* and *the dog obeys*). This sort of structural breakdown is important since it draws our attention to the need to analyse a particular communication in its context and implies that the same content may not have the same effects if read in a newspaper as if seen on television. That is, it is wrong to conceive the mass media as a single entity. Our attention is thereby shifted from global questions such as 'What are the effects of the mass media', which yield no easy answers, to rather more specific and manageable ones.

In other respects it is rather misleading when applied to mass communication rather than direct person-to-person communication—not misleading in the sense of leading to the wrong conclusions but in focusing our attention too narrowly on one aspect of the mass communication process. Too much is ignored and it tends to suggest that mass communication is a singularly one-way process. No explanation is given of why certain people have access to the media or even why the audience are prepared to listen. Of course, in the real world the audience is capable of affecting the content of the mass media (e.g. by not watching, thus affecting viewing figures).

But this division of the mass communications process into five elements—no matter if further analysis demands more or more subtle divisions—at least points to the need not to assume that all of the mass media are much the same, that all messages are equally persuasive, that different sources of communication are equally credible, and so forth.

Gatekeepers

The term gatekeeper means literally what it says. A gatekeeper decides what should be allowed to pass through the channels of mass communication. In the world of broadcasting any number of individuals may act as gate-keepers—programme controllers, members of boards of governors, directors, producers, news editors, programme researchers, and others. In newspapers, they include reporters, sub-editors, and editors. Although it is tempting to assume that there is only a single gatekeeper (an attitude encouraged by the fact that the original gatekeeper studies tended to be of particular individuals such as news sub-editors), this is a little too simplistic. Certainly some individuals are in a better position to allow the passage of information through the mass communication system than others, but this is too autocratic a conception of what happens. Some people may act as gatekeepers in the day-to-day running of a media organization (e.g. sub-editors of a newspaper), but others may only fulfil the function for more crucial decisions. Thus the proprietor of a newspaper may choose to influence the content of the news on rare occasions when it suits his purpose while having no influence at all on its day-to-day running.

The concept of gatekeeper was about the first major theoretical idea developed to explain the way in which media organizations operate and function. In recent years studies of the so-called 'production process' have become rather common. These attempt to understand why the product of the mass media is what it is. Production studies take various forms. These include attempts to explain how a particular programme came into being (e.g. Elliott, 1973), explorations of patterns of ownership of the mass media and their bearing on their content (e.g. Murdock and Golding, 1974), investigations of how the news is produced, selected, and presented (e.g. Chibnall, 1977; Tunstall, 1971), the effects of the geographical distribution of news gathering provisions (e.g. Golding and Elliott, 1979; Tunstall, 1977), and the role of government in shaping the media (e.g. Tracey, 1978).

Such studies take us far away from the simple elegant concept of gate-keeping, though they tend to lack the power of the original concept. In these studies the processes described become more and more intangible, more subtle, and more specific. The ideology of the newsman or producer or any other gatekeeper is nowadays more likely to be used as an explanatory concept. The phrases 'news values' and 'production values' are quite common: they merely refer to those elements of the news or a programme which are considered to produce 'good' stories or 'good' television pro-grammes. Thus excitement and human interest are highly valued features of news items. Usually the individual personality of the occupant of the gate-keeping role is assumed not to matter. To some extent this may be fair but there are occasions when the character of the particular occupant of a position is a key feature.

The Social Environment of Communication

The notion that the mass media cannot be studied in isolation from the social context in which they operate is restated frequently. It is, of course, perfectly acceptable. The features of the social world within which the mass media operate can be as vital to the understanding of the role of the mass media in society as more myopic examinations of the effects of a particular programme. Although this formulation itself seems totally reasonable, it proves a little too glib to be of much significance. It is virtually impossible to study any social phenomenon in entirety—one has to be selective and reduce research to a manageable size. No area of research outside of mass communications research achieves such a total view and often a quite limited understanding of a problem is sufficient to make research worthwhile and satisfying. On the other hand, a broad overview is helpful and in many instances greater clarity of understanding will come from exploring the mass media's links with the rest of society.

One early and important concept with which to analyse the mass media as a part of a social system is *opinion leadership*. Opinion leaders are individuals who latch onto new ideas, products, and fashions the soonest and who have a formative influence on other people's decisions about adopting these innovations. Research (Katz and Lazarsfeld, 1964) shows that for some innovations certain people were more likely to be early adopters and to influence others to make similar decisions. As might be expected, opinion leaders are influential within relatively restricted spheres. Some are opinion leaders in fashion but for nothing else, while others may be opinion leaders for domestic appliances but nothing else. In some respects opinion leaders differ from followers, but how they differ depends on the sort of innovation in question (e.g. Katz, 1961; Katz and Lazarsfeld, 1964). The development of the idea of opinion leaders leads directly to the concept of a *two-step flow of communications*. A one-step flow of communications exists when the influence of the mass media is directly on the individual—in fact the classic assumption of mass communication affects research. The two-step flow of communication inserts the opinion leader as a sort of intermediary step or link between the mass media and the person influenced. So the process is one in which the mass media influence the opinion leader, who then influences a second party. Of course, there is absolutely no reason why there should not be a three-, four-, or five-step flow of communications or more. Likewise we may have just a single step flow but research suggests that cases of direct influence between the media and the individual viewer or reader are relatively uncommon. Furthermore, opinion leaders can serve merely to inform others about an innovation. Being informed about new developments, however, does not necessarily lead to their adoption. This conceptualization has bred a whole specialization in social sciences—the diffusion of innovation—which studies the way in which important innovations (contraception, agricultural methods, etc.) spread through society. It tends to concern itself more with the problems of modernization in Third World countries but obviously is by no means confined to this (Rogers, 1962).

The Obstinate Audience

Theories about the nature of the mass media's audience are both covert and overt. Covertly any assumptions about the power of the mass media to change, alter, or manipulate the audience imply something of the nature of the audience. If the mass media are powerful, the audience conversely must be weak. But more overt theorising about the nature of the audience for the mass media takes quite a different point of view. Such speculation has to begin to explain why the mass media are not the all-powerful persuaders that is sometimes assumed. Just why is it so difficult to change people's minds? The explanations of this are varied but only the more common ones will be mentioned.

Selective Exposure

The reader, viewer, or listener does not watch, read or hear every single item of the vast output of the mass media—he may not even pay much attention to that which he is nominally viewing or read everything in his chosen newspaper. The point is simple—people select which of the products of the mass media to use. This would be fairly banal but for certain research findings. People tend to expose themselves to mass media which present points of view which are most like their own. Republicans read republican newspapers, Democrats read democratic newspapers, and socialists read socialist newspapers. The theoretical basis of this is a little clouded. One suggestion would be, of course, a psychological abhorrence of ideas which conflict with one's own. Contradictory ideas are avoided because they are psychologically uncomfortable. This idea is strengthened by cognitive dissonance theory (Festinger, 1957), which suggests that individuals like to keep their psychological world balanced. Ideas which do not fit in with their belief system cause a psychologically unbalanced state which motivates the individual to correct the imbalance by whatever means he can. Thus, a Republican viewing a democratic party political broadcast would be in a psychological quandary. This might best be avoided by switching off. However, there is considerable doubt whether selective exposure is motivated by such a state of imbalance. People do not seem to find ideas which conflict with their own impossible to cope with. Freedman and Sears (1968; Sears and Freedman, 1967) reviewed the evidence on this and suggest that although there is a tendency for people to be exposed to ideas similar to their own, this is for reasons other than finding comfort in the similarity. These other reasons would include social class differences in attitudes and viewing or reading patterns. For example, most people do not read Marxist ideas because they do not read any books at all rather than because such ideas would necessarily cause them discomfort.

Selective Perception

The difference between this and selective exposure is that in the latter one chooses what to see and in selective perception one chooses how to interpret what one sees. In other words, selective perception is the tendency of the individual to interpret what he sees, reads, or hears in a way which supports his own viewpoint. The classic demonstration of this comes from the Cooper and Jahoda (1947) experiment in which they showed anti-racist cartoons to racists. Instead of being perceived as poking fun at racism, they were perceived by the racists as supporting their racist point of view. Such a tendency is readily observed in many settings. Arguments in bars, between politicians, and so forth often reveal that the same statistics, points and claims can be interpreted in many different ways.

Selective Retention and Recall

These refer to a tendency to recall things on a selective basis. That is, arguments which fit in with one's own point of view are remembered. The evidence for this is not very consistent (e.g. Greenwald and Sakumura, 1967; Smith and Jamieson, 1972).

All of the above ideas on selectivity refer to trends in the processing of information received via mass communication. In effect they are very similar despite their obvious differences. They all imply that the response to the mass media is an active and manipulative process. But it is likely that selectivity is far from being a complete explanation of the failures of the mass media to affect the audience. The failure to absorb a great deal of information from the mass media (studies have shown, for example, that recall of news items shortly after viewing is far from complete) is more likely to be because the news is of very minimal interest or because there is simply too much information to cope with. Although there is good evidence of a certain amount of selectivity, care is needed to avoid the glib assumption that it applies to every case where a viewer or reader fails to be affected by mass communication.

The Vulnerable Audience

It is obvious that the mass media do not influence everyone. No one claims that the mass media cause *everyone* to be violent, determine *everyone's* voting intentions, keep *everyone* abreast of the news, or educate *everyone*. There has been a tendency to claim that only *certain* individuals have a predisposition to be influenced by the mass media in some way. This is not a major personality characteristic—gullibility if you like—since there is no evidence pointing strongly to the ideas that some people are more persuasible than others no matter the subject matter (e.g. Hovland and Janis, 1953). Who the vulnerable individuals are is not made fully explicit. Presumably they include children, adolescents, and others in need of protection.

The idea of audience vulnerability does not come directly from empirical evidence or theory. Its origins are in the failure of research to consistently find major effects of mass communication. Dramatic cases reported in the newspapers sometimes suggest that television had a bad effect on some adolescent or child. For example, occasionally it is reported that a child dies accidentally while emulating, say, a hanging scene from a television programme. The easy way to explain this is that there is something special about this child—he was more vulnerable or impressionable than all the hundreds of thousands of others who had seen the same programme but did not copy it. This is plausible as far as it goes but it has proven notoriously difficult to find ways of distinguishing these vulnerable children from the rest. One important source of information would be carefully controlled experiments, but unfortunately these tend to suggest that virtually everyone is capable of being influenced by the mass media. Studies specifically designed to find the vulnerable have failed (e.g. Walters and Willows, 1968) or have been heavily criticized (Liebert, 1976).

The hoary idea of a particularly vulnerable audience is not particularly useful to the social scientist wishing to come to terms with the mass communication process in depth. The media executive may find it useful in circumventing criticism of programming policy.

Different Types of Media

Much experimental work in social psychology tends to assume that in important respects the different mass media are analogous. The experimenter tends to make no distinctions between films, television, radio, newspapers, clips of videotape, mimeographed pages, and the like. All are reduced to being mere persuasive messages. There have been certain attempts to rectify this. One comes from the uses and gratifications researchers who have studied the different media and found that they are not all functionally equivalent (e.g. Blumler and Katz, 1974).

The ideas of Marshall McLuhan are more widely known, especially their embodiment in the phrase 'the medium is the message'. He argues that some media impinge much more on our conscious experience and are experienced with a greater degree of examination than others. These media tend to be those which depend on a single sense modality but not exclusively so. These are called hot media. For example, the cinema is a hot medium because in the film theatre we attend carefully to our experiences of the film and examine our experiences more. In contrast there are the cold media. Television is a good example of this since we tend to view it with low levels of attention and not to examine our viewing experience as carefully as when we watch material at the film theatre. Such ideas are important in directing our thoughts wider than is sometimes allowed by the crushingly unimaginative research literature. Perhaps it is true that the ideas are too nebulous to be effectively transformed into social scientific theory or research. That, however, does not mean they have no place. To understand the social scientific research on mass communication requires an appreciation of its narrowness and failings.

Advertising Works so the Media must be Powerful

Although this would appear to be the most reasonable of statements it needs care. It might be questioned whether this really warrants inclusion in a chapter on the important concepts in mass communications research. The idea that advertising must be effective because companies pay for it (which means that the mass media are powerful persuaders) is used to discount any claims that the mass media are relatively powerless to produce social change. Of course this line of argument makes several assumptions which may be unwarranted. The first is that advertising can persuade us to do what we do not want to. This is something of a fiction. Most advertising campaigns are failures and the history of advertising is littered with products which could not be sold. Certainly there are some products which are brought to the attention of the consumer through advertising but this is a different matter and is no evidence at all that anything can be sold through clever advertising. The second assumption is that a product's success can be attributed to advertising. Advertising is merely one of many marketing ploys, which include special promotions, in-store advertising, competitions, and other strategies. Any or all of these could be contributing to the success of the product. The third assumption is that advertising increases the sales of a particular product rather than a particular manufacturer's version of that product. Most advertising is directed towards enhancing sales of one brand rather than selling more of a particular type of consumer goods. Relatively little advertising is aimed, for example, at selling more cars rather than selling more Rovers, Triumphs, Fords, etc.

Few studies of the effects of commercial advertising have been reported. There are various reasons for this. The first is that the commercial agencies which plan advertising campaigns for a fee have no vested interest in promoting research which might prove their work worthless. The second is that since advertising is rarely the only form of marketing strategy tried out at any one time it would not be possible to say what are the effects of advertising alone. The third reason is that manufacturers have no desire to publicize their failures. The fourth reason is that a company might feel the money that evaluation might cost could be better spent elsewhere, since it is already committed to the advertising.

Goodhardt, Ehrenberg, and Collins (1975) make the position very clear:

Advertising's role is seldom a very powerful one. It is not a matter of persuading or manipulating the ignorant consumer, since consumers of heavily advertised products are most highly experienced. They have usually already bought the product often and have used a wide range of different brands. No exceptional liking or 'image' needs to be induced in the consumer, because he knows similar brands to be similar and does not greatly care which he buys (which mainly matters to the *manufacturer*) (p. 134).

In later sections we will examine the effects of non-commercial advertising in social work and other areas of social concern. The muted picture of the effects of advertising applies to these also.

Conclusions

The ideas described in this chapter tend to be more specific to mass communications research than to any other area of the social sciences. This does not mean that they are a complete explanation of the mass media. General psychological theory, sociological theory, economic theory, and others may often be much more valuable.

4

Psychological Theory in Mass Communication Research

No psychological theory is limited solely to mass communication. Psychological theories are usually borrowed and applied to the media when appropriate. A wide range of psychological sources have been culled. So theories from such different fields as physiological and Freudian psychology make appearances in the mass communications literature. This electicism is due to two things:

1. Mass communication research has largely been a sideline to most psychologists who have written about it. Their primary interests are in other fields of psychology. They also move out of mass communications research very quickly. This lack of specialism enhances the chances of importing theories from other areas of psychology.
2. It is impossible to pinpoint differences between our experience of the media and other forms of psychological experience. To talk of vicarious versus real-life experience seems quite reasonable at one level but the dichotomy is hard to maintain. What is the difference between witnessing a car crash on television and in real life? We might be more upset by a crash in the street outside but this is a matter of degree rather than kind. If there is no crucial difference then no special theories are needed.

Nevertheless, it is easy to find differences of degree between mass communication and other forms of experience. For example, it is asserted that television has become a parent substitute, taking over the responsibilities of parents for socializing and educating the child. As a dramatic way of making a point this conception is not without merit but no-one would seriously contend that parents and mass media are exact equivalents. For

27

example, the relationship between parents and children is a much more interactive process than that between television and children. But we cannot say that non-interaction distinguishes the mass media from everything else. Many of our non-media experiences lack this interactive element. Sitting quietly at the back of a lecture theatre may be similarly non-interactive and in many ways analogous to our experience of the mass media.

However, some explanatory concepts tend to be particularly associated with the mass media. There may be relatively few of these, but selective exposure, selective retention, selective perception, gatekeepers and opinion leaders are all excellent examples of this and have been discussed already. In general, these refer to the ways in which communication flows from source to receiver and the factors which determine its influence and retention. Consequently they could be applied to any communication system whether or not involving books, newspapers, or broadcasting. Our inability to define the quintessential elements of mass communications does not imply that the mass media are on a par with everything else which produces change. There is one set of speculative ideas, though entrenched in research, which probably could be described as a psychological theory of mass communication. It is primarily a theory of the circumstances in which the mass media are likely to have effects. These proposals emerged from Klapper's (1960) study of the effects of mass communication. The ideas have recurred in the work of several authors (e.g. Halloran, 1967, 1970).

Klapper's Approach

Joseph Klapper (1960), more than anyone, articulated the revised views concerning the power of the media which were being forced on social scientists in the 1940s and 1950s. Quite simply it had been virtually impossible to find any research, other than simple laboratory experiments, which demonstrated a substantial change in the audience following exposure to the mass media. Public information (e.g. Star and Hughes, 1950) and political campaigns (Lazarsfeld, Berelson, and Gaudet, 1948) had yielded, at best, only minor effects on information and political attitudes. Since these were well-planned campaigns the resistance of the audience was remarkable. Research had effectively destroyed popular myths of media power. Klapper tried to explain why this should be so. He offers a number of 'guidelines' to suggest what the typical role of the mass media is in effecting change. These guidelines include:

1. In themselves, the mass media are not normally enough to produce *change*. In association with other influences and because of associations with other factors they might contribute to it.

2. Normally, the role of mass communication is that of *reinforcing* the *status quo*. That is, maintaining behaviours, values, and beliefs, etc., largely unchanged.
3. When the mass media produce *change* rather than *reinforcement* it is likely that other social factors normally producing reinforcement will be acting towards change and that some of the social forces resisting change will be inoperative.
4. The nature of the medium of mass communications, the nature of the persuasive message, the social climate into which the message is 'beamed', and other factors affect the degree to which change will be produced.

These principles are not really very powerful. That is, there is not much precise detail to tell us what is going to happen in any particular set of circumstances with any particular message. But this may not matter since the importance of Klapper's ideas is in allowing a more subtle and mature appreciation of the media's role in society than the almost hysterical view that the mass media produce social change simply and easily.

Other 'theories' of mass communication originated by recognised psychologists tend to be narrow in scope. Stephenson's *Play Theory of Mass Communication* (1967) is a rare exception. Stephenson focuses on the mass media as entertainment (most research concentrates on the mass media as agents of social change). Play theory applies to many institutions—the church, college, factory, or home—as well as mass communication. Apart from reminding us that mass communication is not primarily 'mind control' but entertainment in our culture, the theory has little to offer our discussion of the issues raised in later chapters.

Psychological Theories in Mass Communications Research

An overview of all the ways that psychological theory has contributed to understanding the media would make tedious reading. Often there is just one article or book available which makes any reference at all to a particular psychological theory. But some indication of the various ways in which psychological theory has been incorporated into thinking about mass communication may be of help. Our approach will be to look at the input of such branches of psychology as Physiological and Developmental Psychology to mass communication research. As will be seen, and as might be expected, some fields of psychology have rather more to offer than others.

Physiological Psychology

The most common physiologically based theory mentioned in the mass communication literature is the general arousal theory of Tannenbaum (1970, 1971) and Zillman (Zillmann, 1971; Zillman *et al.*, 1973, 1974). In outline the argument is that a heightened state of emotional arousal increases the likelihood that some form of activity will take place. This idea has its origins in the work on emotion by Schachter and Singer (1962) which demonstrated that general arousal combined with environmental cues concerning what emotion is appropriate determines the particular emotional state which is experienced. General arousal theory applied to communications research retains some of these features. Firstly the film creates a state of emotional arousal. Its specific content does not matter— the film can be violent, sexy, frightening, or even athletic—so long as arousal occurs. Secondly, the consequence of this physiological arousal is increased probability that some form of behaviour will occur. This may have no relationship with whatever produced arousal in the first place. Thus theoretically it is perfectly possible that the sexual content of a film increases the viewers' aggressive, humorous, sexual, or any other behaviour given appropriate environmental contingencies. There is a growing amount of empirical research to back up these theoretical ideas.

The more acceptable general arousal theory becomes, the more it undermines the position of the experimental psychologists who advocate it (Howitt and Cumberbatch, 1975). The reason is that it makes nonsense of any demands for the censorship of the specific content of the mass media based on arguments about their effects. Wishing to censor films because it is believed that sexy scenes cause rape is one thing, but censoring films because they are interesting and exciting adventures (which according to this theory will increase the likelihood of rape) is a totally different matter. Essentially it is a recipe for dull, boring television and films which will depress physiological arousal and thereby decrease the probability of any consequences desirable or otherwise. Advocates of dull boring television are not commonplace.

In a totally different vein, though still physiologically based, Emery and Emery (1976) write about a tendency for television to blunt the higher mental processes. They describe television as a dissociative medium—one which turns the viewer away from involvement in life. Research evidence on the effects of television viewing on the electrical activity of the brain (brain waves) suggests how this 'turning off' may occur. One type of brain wave (alpha) tends to be present only in the absence of processing of visual materials by the brain, that is, when the eyes are shut and no visual images are being constructed. So it is possible to argue that the appearance of alpha waves indicate a state of dissociation. Through a process of habituation, television which is 'a simple, constant, repetitive, and ambiguous visual stimulus gradually closes down the nervous system of man' (p. 82). This produces symptoms similar to those caused by physical destruction of parts of the brain.

Evidence from Krugman (1970) is cited which suggests that alpha waves occur very readily once the individual begins viewing. Emery and Emery argue that the brain wave pattern during viewing is closest to that of people who have been subject to several days of sensory deprivation! In sensory deprivation research the subject is placed in an environment lacking physical sensations—floating in water, in complete darkness and soundlessness, usually with touch sensations minimized as far as possible, and so forth. Television causes sleep rather than stimulates the intellect. The other media of communication do not necessarily have the same effect. Reading, in particular, is quite different. McLuhan's claim that different media have different characteristics—that television is a 'cool' medium—finds some support in this.

In physiological terms this theorising has some plausibility. It suffers a little since it is difficult to provide behavioural evidence that television has turned people off—that their involvement in life has declined.

Developmental Psychology

Given that a major focus of concern has been the influence of the media on the behaviour of the developing child, it would be expected that theoretical ideas would be imported from child or developmental psychology. What is a little surprising is the limited extent to which this has happened. This may be because developmental theory is too specific to be generalized to mass communications research. Perhaps one should not expect any discussion of, say, language development in relation to the mass media, despite this being a highly theoretical area of developmental psychology. Rarely, if ever, has it been argued that the mass media make a special contribution to language development. Children have mastered the basics of language before they are capable of using the mass media.

Piaget's theory is obviously relevant for three reasons: (1) it is important in developmental psychology, (2) it deals with the origins and processes of cognitive developments, and (3) it is clear that a child's ability to deal with the media changes markedly over time. The 18-month-old and the 18-year-old are not at all the same media consuming animals. One commonly known aspect of Piagetian theory is the idea that the intellectual (and moral, for that matter) development of the child passes through distinct stages which must be mastered before the child proceeds to more advanced levels. Although research has tended to modify this picture quite considerably most of the ideas are still sufficiently current to make them attractive to mass communication researchers.

Grant Noble (1975) is one media researcher who uses Piagetian theory. He explains how the thinking of the youngster is different from that of adolescents and adults. As adults we can readily understand the thinking of the adolescent. He is capable of both very concrete and abstract thinking—transcending time and space. But as adults it is far more difficult to understand the younger child whose response to problems tends to be in the here and now, incapable of dealing with time and space.

Noble suggests the following characteristics typify media use during Piagetian stages in development.

Stage of Pre-operational Thought (18 months to 7 years)

In this stage the child tends to perceive everything from his own point of view (egocentrically) and in an all or nothing manner. Thus viewers in this age range structure perceptions of characters as either completely good or bad; they tend to believe everything they see is true; they tend not to comprehend the story in a holistic way with a beginning, middle, and end, so when the action is interrupted by a commercial break this is seen as completing the story; and they imaginatively include in the programme fragments from their own lives.

Stage of Concrete Operations (7 years to 11 years)

At this stage the child becomes able to deal with things which are not necessarily in his immediate purview. He begins to see the world through the eyes of others—that is to say that he is no longer completely self-centred in his thoughts. During this televiewing period the child becomes able to deal with the media in new ways. For example, he becomes far more capable of comprehending the plots of stories, better at describing plots and in doing so less likely to be influenced by irrelevant detail. He also begins to understand the motives of characters as the use of symbolism develops.

Stage of Formal Operations (11 years onwards)

This is easily appreciated by the adult since it shares the major features of adult thinking. The crude all or nothing perceptual mode is replaced by more subtle thinking which involves several shades of grey; so essentially the features which make child viewing distinct from adult viewing disappear during this stage and the adolescent is less immediately bound by the stimulus before him; he is capable of understanding interpersonal relationships in much the same way as an adult would.

Experimental Psychology

This is probably the dominant input into mass communication research from psychology. The reasons for this are that (1) like experimental psychology, mass communication research has tended to be empirical and has avoided over-devotion to theory, and (2) many issues in mass communication research concern learning and perception, which are central to experimental psychology. Research into learning was historically dominated by psychologists employing laboratory experiments. The strategies of research stemming from these are the greatest contribution of experimental psychology to mass communication research. Theory takes second place. The most widely used theory in mass communication research drawn from experimental psychology is *social learning theory*. This emphasizes learning through observation. Television and other mass media can only influence the viewer at a distance. So a theory which suggests that social behaviour can be learnt simply by observing others has great appeal to some communications researchers. Indeed, in some texts (e.g. Liebert, Neale and Davidson, 1973) social learning theory is practically the only theoretical approach guiding the discussion of mass communication. Social learning theory will be dealt with in more detail in the section on media violence.

Some aspects of theory in experimental psychology have been largely ignored despite at first sight seeming directly relevant to the mass media. For example, information theory (which concerns the processing of information) is little used because it concentrates too narrowly on one feature of the communications process, leaving the broader issue of *mass* communications research untouched. Although there have been a few studies of the visual processing of complete television programmes (e.g. Baggaley and Duck, 1976; Howitt, 1977) and films, these have ignored information theory. The topic of visual perception so thoroughly explored by experimental psychologists has again yielded little which commonly appears in the mass communication literature.

Some authors are adept at drawing ideas from experimental psychology to apply to mass communication interests. A good case of this is Eysenck and Nias (1978) who manage to cement much of Eysenck's personality theory into a discussion of sex and violence in the mass media. Unfortunately the importation of such experimental psychology theory also tends to involve the wholesale transfer of attitudes, methodologies, and standards of proof which may not be altogether appropriate without considerable caution. A methodological approach which deliberately destroys or reduces the social context of research to a shadow of social reality flounders in an area of research which accepts as one of its central tenets that the social context is all important. Experimental psychology made the important contribution of neglecting the social context of communications which later researchers had to restore in order to understand the mass communication process. The social context of the mass media is still ignored in much mass communications research stemming from laboratory experimentation.

Psychoanalysis and Depth Psychology

Predictably, with the tendency of experimental psychologists influenced by learning theory to dominate research into the effects of mass communication, those of a more psychodynamic orientation have taken a back seat. But for a brief period during the hiatus in mass communications research in the 1950s and early 1960s (Howitt, 1976), a number contributed from the depth psychology perspective. Much of this writing was concerned with the mass media and violence issue and was probably stimulated principally by the availability of projective measures of aggression. Before the 1960s measures of aggression which could be ethically used were restricted to self reports or the so-called projective measures such as the Rorschach test or the Thematic Apperception Test. It was not until the development of Buss's Aggression Machine (the famous electric shock machine of Milgram's [1974] experiments), which allowed a 'realistic' measure of aggression without falling foul of ethical principles, that violence research really took off and attracted the experimental psychologists. The big advantage of the projective measures of aggression were that no one had to be actually hurt. Showing someone a few inkblots or ambiguous pictures and researching their impressions for aggression did no harm. Of course, the more behaviourist psychologists tend to reject such measures as being 'inaccurate'—projective tests tend to be fairly unreliable, invalid, and subjective in interpretation. But some research was carried out using them, with no lasting impact on the field. The use of projective measures almost inevitably means that the researcher becomes more willing to use concepts from depth psychology in the interpretation of his data.

Some concepts which appear to have been transposed from depth psychology to mass communication research are done so less than perfectly. A classic case of this is the notion of *identification* which is used to denote that a viewer forms a close bond with some character or actor. This bond makes it more likely the viewer will copy the behaviour of the character or actor. The adage that it is wrong to have good characters doing bad things because this will encourage similar behaviour in the viewer reflects this. Stated blandly this seems reasonable. However, is this meaning of identification akin to the Freudian concept from which it appears to originate? For Freud, identification is the process by which a child comes to incorporate elements of the personality of one of his parents into his own. Liking is not an important feature of this—power is. The concept of identification in mass communication seems to be equal to *liking* a character. This revised definition helps to explain why no drastic consequences have been found such as accepting the undesirable behaviours of characters with whom one identifies (e.g. Howitt and Cumberbatch, 1971; Cumberbatch and Howitt, 1973). In order to accept that identification with good characters who do bad things is harmful, it is necessary to make the assumption that people are compartmentalized in their thinking. That is they believe that everything is black or white, good or bad. But the concept means different things to different researchers. Noble (1975) suggests it involves 'the viewer putting himself unselfconsciously into a character's shoes and consequently he believes that the events seen in the film are real' (p. 57). However, depth psychology made no great inroads, possibly because it was allowed to become a mere branch of 'effects' research. Consequently, it was quickly and easily replaced by the more experimentally based branches of psychology.

Social Psychology

Attitude formation and change dominated the early histories of mass communications research and social psychology. The most important theories of attitudes for psychology in general were not necessarily the most influential in mass communication. So common theoretical approaches to attitudes in social psychology such as cognitive dissonance and the other congruency and balance ideas made little impact on mass communication theory. Possibly the greatest overspill from attitude theory to mass communication was the functional theory of attitudes put forward by Katz (1960).

This suggests that attitudes serve purposes; we do not hold attitudes merely because we are persuaded to. The idea that attitudes are functional clearly has strong connections with the uses and gratifications perspective in mass communication research. However, as Katz is one of the major proponents of the uses and gratifications point of view as well, the reachover is less impressive than at first appears. Many theoretical developments in the psychology of attitudes came a little too late to influence the mass communication theorists since they had already decided that the mass media are relatively ineffective. There is no place for sophisticated theories of attitude change if the media simply do not change attitudes.

Social psychology was also moving away from attitude theory. The discipline diversified considerably in the 1960s. Many of the newer concerns had little or nothing to do with mass communication—risky shift, friendship formation, non-verbal communications, but many were much more social policy-oriented—education, racism, women, which bore much more closely on mass communications research. Social psychologists even turned from studies of aggression to studies of helping behaviour. From time to time the theory developed from these studies of altruism was applied to mass communications research. Many major theoretical concerns in social psychology, however, failed to permeate into mass communications research. Thus ethnomethodology, symbolic interactionism, cognitive social psychology, and others scarcely made any inroads at all.

This is not at all untypical of applied social psychology in general, which tends to leave laboratory-based theory in the laboratory. It does make the understanding of mass communication research a little more difficult for those with a thorough grounding in experimental social psychology. Mass communication research is a cross-roads between many intellectual disciplines. Different disciplines bring radically different standards, methods, objectives and ideologies to the study of mass media. Consequently psychologists operating in the field have to contend to some extent with all of these.

Some 'short-range' theories in social psychology receive some attention in the mass communication literature. Ideas about non-verbal communication are nowadays common in the social psychological literature. Patterns of eye contact between individuals, gestures of the hands, facial expression, styles of dress and other features can all have quite dramatic impact on perceptions of others. Some work in mass communication (e.g. Baggaley and Duck, 1976) has shown that, for example, style of camerawork may influence perceptions of programme presenters.

Conclusions

The study of the mass media has attracted people from sociology, economics, political science, and other disciplines. They have tended to import theory from their own specialisms and, more importantly, have brought to mass communication research a range of concerns which would not have been expected from psychologists working in the field. When exploring the mass media fully it is inevitable that concepts derived from these other disciplines become incorporated into the debate. Perhaps the word 'inevitable' should be replaced by 'desirable', since the influx of ideas seems to reveal the limitations of any one discipline. Such 'importations' will be discussed in this book where appropriate.

Psychology has contributed greatly to the discussion of the role of mass communications in society. Many branches of psychological research and theory have been plundered to enrich understanding of the mass media but none really dominates the field. During its early history behaviourist ideas and practices held sway and delayed the emergence of certain issues.

Part Two

THE MASS MEDIA AND CONFLICT IN SOCIETY

5

The Mass Media and Crises

DURING the Biafran War of 1967–70 normal channels of communication became disrupted. Newsprint was scarce and the major alternative medium of mass communications to the newspapers, radio, apparently lacked credibility. The distrust of the news media could be traced to a number of untruths that had been promulgated by them. For example, for propaganda purposes it was claimed that a radio station was broadcasting from Enugu, a town in fact occupied by enemy forces. Many people knew that Enugu had fallen. In the absence of trustworthy mass media, as often happens in crisis situations, rumour was rife. Mass poisoning of Biafrans was a common one (Nkpa, 1977). The International Red Cross had supposedly mixed a drug causing sexual impotence in men with table salt. Poisonous gas was thought to have been fed into disused oil pipelines killing ten battalions of Nigerian troops using them to get reinforcements through the Biafran lines. It was believed that disease was spread by Nigerian aircraft. A British offer of food, rejected partly because the British had been supplying arms to the Nigerian side, was also seen as part of a British plan to poison the Biafrans.

Journalistic folk-lore has it that one war at least was caused by a newspaper. The story is that William Randolph Hearst bought an ailing newspaper, the New York *Morning Journal*, and decided to make it a world beater. The 'World' in this case was a rival newspaper owned by Joseph Pullitzer. His opportunity came when a famous illustrator, Frederic Remington, was sent to cover a small-scale guerilla war in Cuba. A few patriots were rebelling against the Spanish so the illustrator cabled from Cuba: 'Everything is quiet. There is no trouble here. There will be no war. Wish to return.' However, he had not reckoned with the talents of Hearst, who expected that a war would increase newspaper circulation substantially. The absence of a war was easily dealt with. He cabled his illustrator the following message: 'Please remain. You furnish the pictures and I'll furnish the war.' The techniques used by Hearst to do this would embarrass most modern publishers. For example, his newspaper reported that three pretty Cuban girls had been stripped and searched by Spanish policemen on board an American ship. The story had had its impact by the time the ship docked in New York and the truth was revealed. The girls had merely been searched in private by matronly women. Hearst's men also claimed to have rescued a Cuban woman from prison and brought her to New York under a glare of publicity. In fact the so-called rescue was not too difficult as she was about to be released from prison by the Spanish anyway. Various other incidents were reported and when an American ship was blown up in Havana harbour, war was declared (Williams, 1969). It may be that the war was inevitable without Hearst's contribution since Spain had other powerful enemies in the USA. Perhaps Hearst's contribution was to ensure that the American public was favourably disposed towards the war.

The cases described above illustrate two major features of the role of the mass media in crisis situations:

1. The public have a heightened need for information which can be served by interpersonal means should the need arise.
2. The mass media can define reality for their audiences.

So far we have only offered anecdotal support for these. It is worthwhile considering more critical and research–based evidence in evaluating the above two points.

Information in Crises

The Yom Kippur war of 1973 provided Peled and Katz (1974) with an unexpected opportunity to study the Israeli people's need for mass communications during a time of national crisis. One of the curious findings of this research was that during the period of crisis, that is while the war was on, the majority of the Israeli people thought the radio and television news highly credible, whereas after cease-fire there was a substantial decline in the perceived credibility of the news. This can be partly understood in terms of a tendency of the population to rally around the government and to be generally much more supportive of the state during a grave emergency. At the peak, nearly 90% saw the radio and TV news as credible. In contrast, most people were inclined to disbelieve news transmitted by word of mouth (rumour). Perceptions of the worth of rumour varied in an almost complementary way to those of broadcast news. That is to say, rumour was increasingly seen as untrue until the ceasefire had occurred but afterwards became increasingly accepted. One reason for these changes was the return of soldiers to their communities. The word of those who had been involved in the fighting was highly trustworthy. Their contradictions of official government versions of events led to the decline in the credibility of the newsbroadcasts. Other data confirm this since shortly after the cease-fire about a third of Israelis said that contacts with those on active duty had lowered their confidence in the government's treatment of the situation. The researchers found that the people not only turned to the mass media for information during the crisis, but also for psychological reassurance during the early anxious days. The way in which the media and rumour interplay in this situation vividly illustrates the need to look at the social context of mass communication.

So communication needs change markedly during periods of conflict and tension. Support for this comes from sources other than rumour transmission studies. Tichenor *et al.* (1973) studied controversial community issues such as radiation emission standards for a nearby nuclear power station, the conflict between the need for costly improvements in pollution control in the mining and metal industries and the risk of financial problems causing job losses, and mercury contamination of water reserves. People in various communities were given newspaper articles about the local 'sensitive' issues. Recall of the content of these articles depended upon the degree to which each community saw the issue as causing conflict. Tichenor *et al.* do not believe that the most important role of the media was in causing conflict:

Issues ordinarily are created, not in the mass media, but either in professional groups or political institutions. Through one or more of these channels, issues become familiar in the community. The effect of mass media is ordinarily acceleration of the issue—acceleration of both awareness and of conflict dimensions. . . .

Once an issue is created, the process seems to be cumulative—so long as information inputs continue, either from the media or other channels. A general definition of an issue as controversial leads to more learning from media content about that issue, and that content itself is regarded as controversial. This process may continue either until resolution occurs, until the flow of information from various sources diminishes, or both (p. 77).

Howitt (1976) showed that there is a close relationship between the cultural setting and the need for or awareness of news. This emerged out of a study of the role of the media in the lives of pre-school children in England and the Republic of Ireland. Children were visited for 6 months for 2 hours at a time. The interviewers got to know the children and their families fairly well over this period. It was more than apparent from observation that the children had virtually no interest at all in television news. Attention levels dropped dramatically as soon as the news came on television. But nevertheless during one of the sessions the children were asked to tell the interviewer what sorts of things were on the news. As might be expected, there was a high proportion of children who did not or could not answer the question. Much more surprising was the fact that up to half the children were able to mention something that was on the news.

The key political event of interest was the political violence in Northern Ireland. This was perhaps the most enduring and dramatic of news stories at the time. About 40% of the English children mentioned news-related images. Royalty, crises, accidents, and generally unpleasant things were mentioned as well as some that were related to Northern Ireland. However, in the responses of the Irish children there were fewer references to events and items which were unrelated to the conflict in Northern Ireland. The English children collectively mentioned the following situation in Northern Ireland:

> Tanks, not good things, bombs, fighting, news about Ireland, bombs and people getting killed, fire things, bombs and things, place being blown up by bombs, guns shooting, fire engines, fires, broken houses, shooting and things, London fire—when Big Ben got caught by a bomb, and houses blown up by a bomb.

The Irish children said similar things, but more frequently and perhaps a little more fully:

> Army, soldiers (bad), shooting, bombs, bombs and cars, bombs and fires, Belfast, fire brigade in Belfast, bombs—I like seeing bombs in Belfast, I see pictures of men, fire brigade and ambulance fires, fires, things about Belfast, soldiers and cars, two dogs were killed—I saw it on the news (this was three days after the Dublin bombings), fires and soldiers in their soldier cars and shooting, fires and bee babs (i.e. fire brigade), Belfast, soldiers, dead people (shortly after Dublin bombings). Soldiers shooting, fire, some houses go on fire. Bombs and Gardai (police) . . . you can see the bombs and there was someone killed in it called Thompson and his daddy is dying—he lives in Springfield Road, talking about fires and bombs and dangerous things, some people are dead. Cowboys shot them, people in town were bombed up, a bomb, shooting, shooting at the men, a man talks, burning up things, bombs and daddies on the news and pictures and the man says bombs and fires.

There was a substantial difference in the numbers of children in the two cultures who mentioned images related to Northern Ireland. There are also certain similarities between the two samples in the sort of things mentioned. But for the Dublin children the Northern Ireland conflict situation is more central and they seem to be much more specific in their perceptions and descriptions of the events than the English children.

What can be said given these differences? First of all it is vital to remember that although England is a central party to the Northern Ireland situation, for historic and political reasons, the whole question of 'the North' is a much more salient issue to a citizen of the Irish Republic than it is for his English counterpart. As one commentator remarked, 'the North is Irish History'. It is difficult to be convinced, however, that the difference between the two cultures is due to differences in the news coverage of the media in the two countries. The reason for this is quite simply that although the Irish Television service is different from the BBC and ITV in its style of coverage, in Dublin, where all the services are available, the British channels are the most popular. In addition, the children's viewing of the news is so minimal that it is difficult to believe that it is having much direct effect alone.

The profound cultural difference is much more likely to have been responsible. Children learn norms, values, attitudes, patterns of behaviour, and the like as they are socialized through experience, interaction, and relationships with their families and others. Television may be seen as one part of this socialization process, both reflecting the society within which it has developed and operates, and helping to create in the child the informational base for these values and attitudes.

Creating a Crisis

There is little argument that many political and economic difficulties of the 1970s and 80s can be directly traced to problems in the availability and pricing of oil from the third world. The first major stage in this was the action of the petroleum exporting countries during late 1973. Price increased greatly; some oil assets were nationalized, some countries boycotted. Holland suffered particularly badly because supplies were refused by several producing countries. At first sight, this was a major crisis situation.

It is wrong to assume that supply problems hit all European countries equally. Kepplinger and Roth (1979) have outlined the way which the mass media in West Germany created an oil shortage crisis when there was no lack of supplies. Despite difficulties on a global level, West Germany had good oil supplies during late 1973, substantially up on the same period of the previous year. This was due to the availability of better quality crude oil, the rerouting of oil from other destinations, the ability of the Germans to buy and then sell oil at any price due to the lack of price controls in their country, and the length of time that it takes for oil to arrive at its destination.

In West Germany during the Autumn and Winter of 1973, the newspapers, despite differing political complexions, spoke with one voice on the oil crisis giving virtually identical interpretations of the situation. They predicted impending disaster. Sixty per cent of all newspaper comments implied that supplies were insufficient or that the situation would worsen. Kepplinger and Roth suggest that an interpretive framework for future events was laid down at this time. The tone of newspaper comment changed during the Autumn and Winter. During September, October and November pessimism abounded, but by December optimism prevailed. Many articles appeared in the early period of gloom but many fewer during the period of optimism. A series of opinion polls during November and December showed changes in the views of the car-owning public. During November roughly 70% thought that petrol would run short and cause serious supply difficulties. By December the numbers expressing similar fears had halved. These changes coincided with the changes in prognosis by the newspapers.

Sales of oil products began to rocket—that is people began to buy more than normally. Petrol and diesel sales increased 7%, heavy fuel oil increased 15%, and light fuel oil increased 31%. This is a lot of oil for an economy to absorb and there were serious consequences. The oil companies were not always able to supply fuel from stock. As a result, some home heating supplies were late and petrol stations out of stock. Sunday driving was prohibited for a while and speed limits lowered to conserve fuel. In fact fuel reserves had merely been shifted from the oil industry to the consumers for storage. There was no real change in consumption.

Other similar 'panics' have been created in recent years. In the United Kingdom supermarkets have at times been cleared of toilet rolls, salt, and sugar by over buying in of stocks. Of course, some of these so-called shortages have been precipitated by local rumours, which then feed into the mass communications system to exacerbate the situation.

Affecting Events

One question frequently raised about the role of mass media in situations of direct conflict is whether the mere presence of cameras and reporters in itself creates violence. Boorstin (1963) suggested that some events presented as news are really *pseudo* events lacking reality outside the mass media. It is impossible to know whether any one particular event is media-inspired or would have happened in the absence of cameras. A graphic example of media-'inspired' behaviour describes what happened when the light beam of a TV camera picked out a group of pickets: 'Instantly the marchers' heads snapped up, their eyes flashed. They threw up their arms in the clenched communist fist' (Burnham, 1968, p. 13). There is no difficulty in accepting that this was a response to the presence of cameras. Nevertheless, a distinction has to be made between normal behaviour which may not change in frequency or amplitude but may change in its timing to coincide with the presence of the news media, and behaviour which happens solely for the benefit of newsmen. There are examples of the direct influence of the presence of the media in conflict situations. Reporters for the British Independent Television News service were with a party of Nigerian troops who captured a prisoner during the latter part of the Biafran war. While the film cameras were rolling and with no apparent cause, the officer in charge of the troops shot and killed the prisoner. The film was shown shortly afterwards on British Television. Almost immediately the Nigerian authorities announced that the officer would be executed for this murder. Now there is no reason to believe that this was an isolated incident in the course of the war and it is difficult to accept that but for the presence of the film cameras the officer would not have been punished at all.

What was the importance of the news media's presence which produced this dramatic response? One feature of the situation was the British arms supplied to the Nigerian side. The Nigerian government clearly wished good public relations with their weapons suppliers. During the Biafran war, there was a lot of what is termed 'management' of the news. The Biafrans employed a Genevan public relations firm to publicize the effects of the war—the pain, misery, and suffering. Given this, the Nigerians could not ignore their own public relations. The execution was probably justice being seen to be done. As a rider, the execution was delayed while a photographer, sent to film the spectacle, changed his camera batteries. The execution, rather than a case of military justice, was an exhibition staged by the military for the news media, to deal with a situation directly caused by the presence of cameras in the first place.

The presence of the mass media may also inhibit violence. After all, the video surveillance cameras used by many shops and stores are designed to reduce theft, not to increase it. There is some evidence of the inhibitory nature of the presence of cameras at demonstrations. A film record of illegal or unacceptable activities provides legal proof which can result in sanctions. For example, during the London Vietnam War demonstrations in 1968, one demonstrator was filmed by the media aiding in an attack on a policeman. The film led to the identification of a student who was subsequently convicted (Halloran, Elliott and Murdock, 1970). Law enforcement agencies may also be similarly restrained by the presence of news media. It has been reported that during the Chicago riots of the 1960s, many police officers removed their badges to avoid identification and frequently smashed cameras to destroy evidence of their misconduct (Baker and Ball, 1969).

Of course, publicity in the mass media may swell the numbers participating in a demonstration. This may alter both the nature and size of the crowd attending the event (Lang and Lang, 1952). Sometimes increased publicity leading to larger crowds may create problems for maintaining civil order as the Kerner Commission noted (Report of the National Advisory Commission on Civil Disorders, 1968). There is evidence concerning the involvement of the mass media in recruiting demonstrators. In 1970 the Reverend McIntyre, a right wing fundamentalist preacher, held a march for 'total victory in Vietnam' in Washington. He presented a radio programme (Twentieth Century Reformation Hour) broadcast by 600 stations in addition to publishing a weekly newsletter. Lin (1974) interviewed participants in the demonstration and found that the most important initial source of information about the march came from McIntyre's radio programme. Only a small proportion heard about the march from friends and family. But actual attendance was influenced by quite different things. The majority claimed that personal convictions or curiosity persuaded them. The non-specialist channels of mass communication did little to inform and persuade. In other words, McIntyre's newsletters and broadcasts were much more effective than the mass media in shaping participation in the march.

Some have suggested that publicity given to marches and demonstrations encourages sightseers to attend in the anticipation of some violence (e.g. Halloran, Elliott and Murdock, 1970). On the other hand (Lang and Lang, 1952), it does not follow that the media's anticipations of a violent clash at a demonstration will always serve as a self-fulfilling prophecy to encourage violence. Such publicity may equally well bring out the 'cool heads' or increase the determination of participants to maintain a peaceful gathering. Furthermore, publicity given to demonstrations or riots may inform people that certain areas of a city have become dangerous and encourage their avoidance. It has been reported that the first death in a Detroit riot was a woman driving inadvertently through the area at a time when news of the riot had not been broadcast for hours at the request of Negro leaders (Warren, 1972).

Theories of News

Community conflict and crisis provide good contexts in which to consider theories of 'news'. In particular, ideas of why the news which is printed and broadcast is what it is become clearly highlighted. For simplicity's sake one major factor can be ignored—that is, the logistics of the news gathering process. By this we mean that 'news' cannot be made unless reporters or communication links to reporters are present, unless quick means of transmitting the pictures and information back to 'home base' are available, unless it is possible to get reporters and camera teams to the news, unless individuals or organisations are willing to give news to the press, and so forth. In short, the existence of news requires a technology and organisation by which to gather it. Naturally the characteristics, form, and content of the news will vary with the changes in the technology. But news is also a selective process—someone or some group of individuals has to decide what news to print or to broadcast of all that enters the system through the news gathering technology. These same individuals may also have decided how the technology should be deployed. How the news is selected can be conceived as a question of the psychology of journalism though normally it has been sociologists who have paid the subject most attention.

Three broad approaches to the selection of the news issues are relevant here:

News Values Approach

Journalists sort news on the basis of key features of its content. Certain sorts of content are more 'newsworthy' than others. Galtung and Rouge (1965), for example, drew up a list of aspects of news which make a news item more valuable than other news items. For example, a local murder is more likely to have more impact than one halfway around the world. The emphasis is on feature of the content of news and tends to suggest that there is something intrinsic to the story itself which determines what is news rather than the beliefs of those selecting the news.

Inferential Structure

This idea is clearly exemplified in the work of Lang and Lang (1952) followed by Halloran, Elliott, and Murdock (1970) in their studies of mass demonstrations. It suggests that journalists approach events with pre-set ways of structuring the world. In other words, they have a structure or system of ideas, beliefs, or knowledge which they use when trying to understand events they observe. So when covering the Vietnam War demonstration journalists had already a predetermined view that demonstrations were inevitably violent affairs. Consequently much of the discussion and debate in the press prior to the march was in terms of violent clashes. Because of this inferential structure built on conflict the news media tended to perceive the events of the march in this context and selected the events such that they fitted in with their expectations of violence. The old ideas in psychology of a perceptual set are not dissimilar.

Transactionist Viewpoint

This is based on the idea that there is an interaction between the news media and the audience which shapes the content of the media. That is, the news media tend to furnish materials which are in some way tailored to the need of the community. The transaction is not merely the press giving the public what it wants but the community actively giving the press news. There are interest groups in society which act as 'news producers'—supplying views, opinions, beliefs, and staging events for the press to consume.

These theories help us understand to some extent the ways in which news comes into being. In crisis situations and in conflict we can see each of these varying approaches operating to varying degrees. They are not mutually incompatible—they merely emphasise different features of the situation. Purely psychological theories of news, especially with reference to crises, are rare but the following is intriguing.

A Psychological Theory of News

Much news would appear to be useless to those hearing, reading or seeing it. Knowledge of air crashes in Tenerife, earthquakes in the Middle East, or a *coup d'état* in Africa seemingly offer little help to us in dealing with our daily lives. Yet people want news a lot. Judging by the manifest content of the daily press they tend also to prefer the dramatic story. There is then a sense in which the news serves the same functions as a good play—excitement, interest, and stimulation. It is larger than life and in some senses supplements life. Of course, some news is immediately pertinent and relevant to the consumer. News also serves in everyday social interaction as a topic of conversation. But in many ways our interest in news is paradoxical if we are hide bound by the idea that it is something other than predominantly entertainment.

However, research into the causes of pro-social behaviour threw up one line of argument about the social functions of news which was quite different. Harvey Hornstein, together with various colleagues (e.g. Blackman and Hornstein, 1977), proposed that news-consuming man uses the news to formulate actuarial statements about social reality. That is, man uses the news as a source of probabilistic ideas about the nature of his social universe. If newspapers report kindnesses shown by one person to another then the reader gets a favourable impression of his social universe. If, on the other hand, the news is full of con-men cheating frail old ladies out of their life-savings then quite the reverse impression of the social universe will be created. There is nothing particularly surprising in all this save the fact that Hornstein has demonstrated that these perceptions have consequences for the social behaviour of people. Let us take a simple example of this research —and one which is also a good example of the 'trickery' employed by social psychologists in their experimental work. Subjects for a piece of experimental work were asked to wait around before part of the research was due to begin. But in fact the real experiment had already begun and they could hear a radio playing music. This was interrupted by a news programme. Some subjects heard good news whereas other subjects heard bad news. These were adapted from real news stories. Examples of these are:

Prosocial News (i.e. Good News)

A middle-aged man will be saved thanks to a person he has never met. The man, who suffers from a fatal kidney disease, had only a short while to live without an emergency kidney transplant. WWBG had broadcast pleas for help. Late last night a respected clergyman came to the hospital and offered to help. The donor had refused the family's offer to pay his hospital costs. Even in this day and age, some people hear a call for help.

Antisocial News (i.e. Bad News)

A 72 year-old sculptress, beloved by neighbourhood children for her statues of Winnie the Pooh, was strangled in her apartment last night by what appears to be a self-styled executioner. The murderer, who has been identified as a respected clergyman, was a long-time neighbour of the victim. He had the keys to the apartment because he occasionally babysat for the victim's grandchildren and was in the habit of bringing up her mail and packages.

Various forms of pro-social behaviour were adversely influenced by the bad news—for example, cooperative behaviour such as returning lost wallets, beliefs that most people lead clean decent lives, and cooperation in a gaming situation (prisoner's dilemma) is reduced when subjects have heard some bad news. Interestingly Hornstein noted that these differences between pro-social and anti-social news did *not* emerge at the time Robert F. Kennedy was murdered by Sirhan Sirhan. Co-operative behaviour in the laboratory seemed adversely affected by this bad news; the good news provided in the laboratory seemed outweighed by the bad news in the outside world.

Hornstein tested several ideas relevant to understanding his general research findings:

1. He found that good and bad news caused by non-human agents did not have the same effects as had previously been found when caused by humans.
2. Changes in mood (happy, sad, etc.) do not seem to be necessary. Good and bad news have the same effects irrespective of mood change.

Conclusions

The Romans had officers called *delatores* to collect rumours from amongst the populace. Social psychologists (apart from Allport and Postman, 1947) have rarely made rumour an object of study. However, it is clear that the mass media and rumours both reflect the heightened need for information in wartime or crisis. But the mass media are not entirely to blame for events. Certainly they can exacerbate a crisis but they can also help nullify some dangers of the situation. The mass media seem able to help create crises—such as buying panics—but we should not forget the potential of the personal social network to do the same. Indeed, intensive study of these cases might well reveal that informal social communication accelerates whatever effects the mass media might have. Knopf makes the important points well:

Crisis situations increase the need for news. During most serious disturbances, news media are bombarded with calls from anxious citizens wanting information, clarification, verification of what they have heard. So important is the flow of news through established channels that its continued absence can help precipitate a crisis. In 1968 in Detroit the absence of newspapers during a protracted strike helped create a panic: there were rumours in the white community that blacks were planning to blow up freeways, kill suburban white children, and destroy public buildings: in the black community, that white vigilantes were coming into the area to attack the residents (Knopf, 1970, p. 17).

We should not forget either than the most dramatic claim about the power of the mass media (Cantril, 1940) concerned the panic created in the United States by the broadcasting of the play *The Invasion From Mars* as if it was a news story. The ways in which the audience tried to verify or dismiss what they heard makes fascinating reading.

Part Three

THE MASS MEDIA AND THE
TREATMENT OF MINORITY GROUPS

6

Race and the Mass Media

MASS communication often annoys and angers those whose position in society is sensitive. Critics of mass communication are frequently vitriolic, conflicting, and insistent. Such a response can be a good thing in that it is an almost inevitable consequence of exposing society to itself. Only the blandest programmes will offend no one. But sometimes the criticisms of the media seem particularly well founded. Should the media change to accommodate their critics? Should they remain aloof? It is not easy to decide how much licence the media should have to present issues in a partisan, biased, unfair, or even malevolent manner. This complex issue straddles questions of freedom of speech, freedom of the press, and freedom of action. These are political issues to which social science can make only limited contributions. There are constraints on what appears in the media. Broadcasters have a duty to be balanced and objective. Newspapers may be constrained also. For example, apart from the law, controls are imposed by press councils and advertising standards institutes which have considerable moral power.

Over the last two or three decades awareness of the needs of two so-called minority groups has grown. These are blacks and women. The black power movement and the women's liberation movement are probably the best examples of significant minority groups which see themselves as having a bad deal from the mass media. To describe women, about 51% of the world population, as a minority group may seem like a contradiction in terms but is justified because women lack access to power and privilege. Even if numerically conceived women are in the majority, their position is so similar to that of a minority group that they are usefully considered as one. From the point of view of the mass communication researcher, the literature relating these groups has common, overlapping themes and it is merely a matter of convenience that we separate them. The phrase 'A woman is the nigger of the world' says a lot. There is little point in reiterating at length the findings and assertions of thousands of books and articles showing the restricted opportunities for careers, career advancement, education, self-respect, and freedom that accrue to minorities. The reasons for all this are innumerable and subject to differences of opinion. However, few would deny that there is a lot to be done to provide better opportunities for both groups. No social scientist would claim that the mass media are the primary or major cause of this disadvantage. Minority groups have been persecuted, oppressed, and disadvantaged throughout time—long before the media of mass communication existed let alone gained a dominant role in our society. But this does not mean that the mass media are without fault. Do they reinforce racist attitudes? Even if the media do nothing to affect the lot of minority groups, the image of blacks and women presented in the media remains a thorn in the side, a constant reminder that society treats minority groups badly.

There are several questions which have been asked about the mass media and minority groups which might usefully be listed:

1. Do minority group members have equal opportunities to gain employment in the media? Although at one level this is merely a question of job opportunity, clearly the more minority group members employed by the mass media, the greater the chance that they can influence the content of the mass media and ensure a 'fairer' treatment of the minority group.

2. What is the nature of the mass media's treatment of the minority group? This can be considered at several different levels—do the media actively propagandize in favour or against the minority group? Do the mass media ignore or under-represent the minority group? Do the mass media present the minority group in a highly stereotyped, limited social role? Do the mass media subtly reinforce existing beliefs about the minority group?

3. Do the mass media promote racist attitudes?

4. Do the mass media contribute to the poor self-images that characterize the attitudes of minority groups towards themselves? Do the mass media help persuade minority groups that their position in society is fair?

5. Can the mass media work to the advantage of the minority group, reduce prejudice against them, and create a more positive self-conception amongst minority group members?

Although there is not sufficient evidence to evaluate all of these issues for both women and blacks, these questions will underlie the following discussion of the media's treatment of blacks. Women and the media are discussed in the next chapter.

Ethnic Identity and the Media

The increase in the consciousness of a minority group possibly determines its response to and criticism of the mass media. Although no evidence for this deals specifically with blacks, there is ample evidence from other ethnic minority groups. Jeffres and Hur (1979) sampled ethnic minorities in Cleveland, U.S.A. They included Czechs, Greeks, Hungarians, Irish, Italians, Lebanese, Lithuanians, Polish, Puerto Ricans, Romanians, Slovacks, Slovenians, and Ukranians. Some thought that their media image was favourable (Hungarians, Lithuanians, Czechs, and Slovenes), others neutral, and others unfavourable (Lebanese, Polish, Puerto Ricans, and Italians). Relatively few thought the mass media succeeded well in covering their communities. Higher awareness of ethnic consciousness (as indicated by cooking ethnic food, celebrating ethnic events, and not being an American citizen) led to a belief that the media covered their ethnic group badly. Possibly the increase of self-awareness of blacks and women as cultural groups has led or will lead to an increase in complaints about media stereotypes of these groups.

Public Opinion

Assessing historical trends in public opinion is difficult because of the *ad hoc* nature of most public opinion polls. Only rarely have the same survey questions been used repeatedly over a period of years. There seems little doubt that attitudes towards Negroes have become at least superficially more liberal. Erskine (1968) overviewed various polls from which the following trends are gleaned. Americans were asked in 1944: 'Do you think Negroes should have as good a chance as white people to get any kind of job, or do you think white people should have the first chance at any kind of job?' Only 42% were opposed to any job discrimination while the majority were in favour of such discrimination. The same question asked in 1963 suggested that 82% were against job discrimination: a major shift in opinion. But we should not assume that this means quite what it appears to mean. For example, in the North the majority of whites in 1958 stated that they would prefer a white to a black dentist, doctor, and minister but in the south they preferred a white dentist, doctor, minister, schoolteacher, lawyer, judge, hospital nurse, insurance man, salesgirl in a department store, policeman and taxi-driver. Simon (1974) reviewed trends in American public opinion. Amongst her comparative data were figures that suggested the percentage disapproving of segregation on buses for negroes increased from about 45% in 1942 to about 80% in 1963. But more important are her suggestions about what underlies public opinion:

'Most white Americans do not accept the conclusion that the United States is a racist society, that blacks are treated unfairly, and that separateness and inequality in social matters are basic dimensions of American life. Instead, they focus on the institutional changes that have occurred in such areas as public transportation, housing, education, and employment opportunities. . . . Most whites do not believe that Negroes are treated unfairly. In the absence of that feeling, there is not much basis for optimism that in the foreseeable future blacks will become first-class citizens in American society in contexts and behaviour that go beyond "formal" equality and institutionalised integration' (p. 75).

If this is so then it would appear to be in itself condemnation of the mass media which clearly must have failed in some way to educate the public about realities in Western society. There is no way of knowing whether such failures are due to omission, the audience's blinkered perceptions, the media advocating that blacks are fairly treated, or any one of a number of other possibilities. It does however show the need for great caution when considering the meaning of public opinion. Accepting public opinion as a true picture of society is dangerous as it paints too rosy a picture.

Content of the Media

Zimet (1976) claims that the images and pictures presented in children's books and school texts mirror the prejudices of society back to the child. She suggests that the following processes are at work in this sort of material:

1. *Selection*—blacks tend to be portrayed as 'baddies' more than whites.
2. *Distortion*—American Indians are presented as articulate and attractive but use a 'composite image' from the past to do so.
3. *White is Rightism*—whites portrayed as superiors to blacks.

There is not enough space to go into much detail of the ways in which minorities are presented in the mass media. The treatment of blacks and women have great parallels and it is not unusual for a researcher to simultaneously research the portrayal of blacks and women. But there are obvious differences. Blacks rarely appear in advertisements directed at a white audience whereas women do so frequently, if decorously. The parallels are not so much in terms of the rates of appearance but in the way that the advertisements bind women and blacks into menial and subservient roles. Culley and Bennett (1976) suggest that trends in the presentation of blacks differ according to the medium in question. Magazines increasingly use blacks in advertisements though largely in a background role. Newspapers, on the other hand, very rarely portray blacks at all in advertisements. In O'Kelley and Bloomquist's study (1976) blacks, orientals, and Indians made up only 5% of characters in advertisements. Black media differ too. Chapko (1976) carried out an analysis of the models used in advertisements in *Ebony* (a black oriented publication) over the period 1964–74. He suggests that the black consumer has steadily but increasingly rejected whites as a model to emulate over the period. The numbers of white models declined and darker skin tones in the black models became more evident. Chapko sees basic economics as the cause of the advertisers' change in practice. Blacks are increasingly using black products. The role of economics in determining the content of advertisements should not be underestimated. Kerin (1979) investigated the audience's response to the physical characteristics of models in advertisements. The advertisement was the same—for body oil—but the features of the model in the advertisement varied systematically. Facial features were either negroid or caucasian, the hair style was either afro or wavy, and the skin tone was either dark, medium or light. Combinations of these yielded 12 different variations on the basic advertisements. Ratings of the quality of the product involved were related both to these features and the reader's characteristics. Three main trends emerged: blacks tended to rate the product more highly when the model had black facial features, whites when the model had white facial features; blacks associated quality with the combination afro hair style, darker skin tones, and black facial features in particular; and the appearance of the model accounted for about 17% of variation in ratings of the product.

But often the processes involved in the media's presentation of race are rather subtle. UNESCO (1973) published the results of a content analysis of headlines dealing with racial matters in the British press. Words to do with conflict occurred in association with race 18% of the time and violent words were associated with race 15% of the time. Examples of this are: RACE HATE, RACE CLASH IN TEXAS, RACE RUMPUS OVER WILSON, and TENANTS' THREAT ON COLOUR. Such combinations present race in the context of trouble, perhaps creating an image of race as a problem.

Examples of the presentation of race and possibly even racism in the mass media are familiar to most of us. Instances of crude racist propaganda are uncommon. Researchers tend to stress the covert way in which the mass media surreptitiously create distorted or defamatory images. If race relations are usually reported in terms of problems and crises this may well affect perceptions of racial issues which might be conflict-free otherwise. A covert message that blacks are subservient may even be more effective than crude and blatant propaganda against blacks. The infrequent appearances of blacks in the media may make it more difficult for blacks to improve their self-perceptions.

Effects of the Media's Treatment of Blacks

It is tempting to assume that because the mass media show blacks infrequently but in menial jobs, this defines what black people are and can achieve. Admittedly if people took the contents of the mass media as a true reflection of blacks, inevitably their ideas would be crude and unfavourable. But there is no reason to believe that people assimilate ideas in such a mechanical way. People simply do not respond in this simplistic way to what they see and read. It is, at the very least, clumsy and ill-conceived to take statistics about the content of the mass media as a sign of how the viewer will respond. The audience may not see the mass media's content in the same way as the content analyst's statistics. Consequently it is vital to seek stronger evidence of the effects of the media's treatment of race. One can argue convincingly on the basis of content analysis that the media could scrutinize their products for ways to promote the cause of blacks. This would be so no matter the inferences drawn by the audience from the media.

If the media, purposefully or inadvertently, derogate black people two main undesirable consequences might follow. The first is that the *whites* accept this negative view. The second is that the *blacks* accept it. Racism is not merely attitudes and behaviours of whites towards blacks, it is a means by which the blacks come to accept their inferiority. A magic wand might rid society of all prejudice against blacks, but a history of low incomes, poor educational facilities, poor housing, a rootless culture, and taking the least out of society could still leave minorities with a poor self-concept, insecure over their abilities and potential.

Effects of the Media on Blacks' Self-Concepts

Do the mass media contribute to the blacks' own conception of themselves? If so, given the nature of the mass media's treatment of blacks, does this serve to reduce the pride of the blacks in themselves or, at least, maintain it at a low level? These are big questions to tackle. The forces producing poor self-images in blacks spread throughout culture. It is not easy to distinguish the effects of the mass media from those of, say, education or employment. Any research on this is bound to be tentative.

Tan and Tan (1979) studied the relationship between television consumption and self-esteem amongst blacks and whites. The methodology used was very simple. Media consumption was correlated with measures of self-esteem. Self-esteem is essentially self-liking, self-admiration, and self-respect. For whites in the study self-esteem was measured by means of the Janis-Field Feelings of Inadequacy scale. Items from this scale include: 'In general, how confident do you feel about your abilities?'; 'How confident are you that your success in your future job or career is assured?'; and 'How often do you have the feeling that you can do everything well?' For blacks (and this may be a methodological failing), a somewhat different measure of self-esteem was used. Perhaps it was not self-esteem but esteem for one's own race that was measured. The black subjects answered questions like: 'Who do you think are more dependable? Blacks/Same/Whites'; 'Who do you think are smarter? Blacks/Same/Whites'; and 'Who tries . . . to get ahead more? Blacks/Same/Whites'. The blacks saw blacks as nicer, more dependable, smarter, and better behaved than the whites. Blacks were seen as inferior because they did not try to get ahead enough. Despite this, some blacks saw themselves as generally inferior to whites.

Both blacks and whites were asked to say what kinds of television programmes they watched and how much they viewed. Whites tended to watch movies, national news, local news, news special presentations and documentaries the most. Blacks preferred crime and adventure and situation comedies. Self-esteem scores were correlated with extent of viewing for TV public affairs (news) programmes and TV entertainment programmes separately. For whites watching entertainment programmes did not relate to their self-concept. For blacks, however, there was a relationship. The more TV entertainment programmes watched the lower the blacks' self-esteem. This would make sense in that such programmes portray blacks relatively infrequently and largely in negative caricature. The black watching such programmes would see his race unflatteringly presented. More difficult to understand is why a positive self-concept correlated with watching news and public affairs programmes in whites but not in blacks. After all, blacks are portrayed relatively unfavourably in these programmes also.

Effects of the Media's Treatment of Blacks on Whites

One of the most thorough studies of the relationship between the content of the mass media and the attitudes, perceptions, and beliefs about minority groups was carried out in Britain at the beginning of the 1970s (Hartmann and Husband, 1972, 1975). The researchers concentrated on adolescents (and their parents) because at this age they would have some knowledge about coloured people. In addition, adolescents' media consumption, although distinct from that of adults, includes news as well as entertainment programmes. It was reasoned that sources of knowledge and belief about immigrant groups could theoretically, if less easily in practice, be divided into: a) situational sources (primarily direct personal experience), and b) media sources. If the children do find out about immigrants from the mass media there are two possible implications: (1) Mass communication contributes ideas, images, and beliefs which are distinct in kind from those obtained from other sources, and (2) Mass communication serves as a microcosm of society and merely mirrors back ideas, images, and beliefs already common amongst the audience. They suspected that the influence of the media would be different for adolescents with direct contact with immigrants compared to those living in areas with no immigrants. The sampling included areas of *high* and *low* immigrant densities. They also looked at children in schools with many immigrant pupils and those with few. The evidence supported their expectations. High density regions (even more than the numbers of immigrant children attending the school) had the greatest hostility towards immigrant groups.

Hartmann and Husband asked the children: 'Can you tell me what you know about coloured people living in Britain today?' Following this the children explained where they had got their ideas from. No specific questions were put concerning the mass media as a source of ideas. Nevertheless many claimed that the media provided them with their ideas. Personal experience was the commonest source mentioned followed by the mass media in one form or another. As predicted by the researchers, and as might be expected, children in the areas allowing little or no personal contact with racial minority groups mentioned the mass media most frequently. Conversely, personal experience was mentioned most often in areas with many immigrants. There is some merit in the argument that the children were essentially ignorant about where their information about coloured people comes from and merely named as a course of the most plausible one. To circumvent it Hartmann and Husband provide evidence to strengthen their data. They compared the media consumption patterns of those claiming the media as sources with the others. It emerged that the media source children were heavy consumers of the media. This gives added credibility to the argument that the children really did know from where they got their ideas. Whether this is definitive proof of the value of these sources attributions is debatable since their argument disintegrates if we assume that low media consumers are unlikely to rationalize their guesses about the source of their ideas by blaming the mass media. But this is a difficult area of research and perhaps we should not expect the same rigorous standards of proof to prevail as in less complex situations.

Accepting for the moment the validity of the source attributions, the question remains whether the images of race provided by the media are derogatory or hostile towards immigrants. Hartmann and Husband classified ideas about coloured people into categories like:

1. Objects of prejudice: people discriminate against them or are in some way hostile (e.g. 'people are prejudiced against them', 'people discriminate against them').
2. They are disadvantaged (e.g. 'they are poor, they can't find jobs').
3. Poor housing (e.g. 'they live in slums, they sleep ten to a room').
4. They are a source of trouble (e.g. 'they cause riots').
5. Numbers (e.g. 'there are too many of them coming in', 'there'll soon be more blacks than whites in this country').
6. Taking jobs (e.g. 'they take white people's jobs').
7. Taking houses (e.g. 'they cause a housing shortage').

Not all of these are prejudicial towards blacks. To know that they are objects of prejudice, that they are disadvantaged, or that they live in poor housing suggests much that is potentially sympathetic. Indeed, it transpires that none of these (apart from the Objects of Prejudice category) is related to prejudiced attitudes towards blacks.

In contrast, the sorts of things which the children attributed to personal experience are almost all of an affective or evaluative nature. These are much more like statements of attitude.

> some are good, some are bad, just like whites;
> they are dirty;
> they are hardworking;
> they are clean;
> they should have the same rights as anyone else;
> their cooking stinks;
> they won't work but live on National Assistance;
> I can't stand them.

Whereas personal experience seems to worsen attitudes towards black overall, the mass media, although contributing ideas, do not seem to be making much, if any, difference to attitudes concerning blacks in Great Britain. The authors themselves conclude from this data:

> . . . the media did not seem to have any direct influence on attitudes as such. It would appear that the media serve to define for people what the dimensions of the situation are. How they feel about the situation, thus defined, would seem to depend on other factors, particularly on where they live (p. 108).

The implication is that the media contribute definitions of social reality which interact with contact to produce prejudice or tolerance. This goes a little beyond the data. It is important that the evidence shows the media create their own images and do not simply reflect back society's images of black people. The mass media were cited as sources of ideas about the *problems* caused by coloured people more frequently than as sources of *knowledge about good things* about the black immigrant.

Hartmann and Husband also produced evidence concerning a quite distinct process leading to racism. This is *media induced 'relative deprivation'*. Psychological research has shown that comparisons between individuals may be as important, if not more important, than absolutes in determining satisfaction with life. What is earned as an absolute figure may be a poorer predictor of pay satisfaction than what is earned relative to those one feels should earn more or less than oneself. If you earn relatively more than someone whose work is seen as less valuable then you are more likely to feel satisfied. One thing that the mass media might do is to bring to people images of affluence in society. They might even create impressions of greater wealth than actually exists. Advertising partly underscores this by suggesting the sumptuous and desirable life-styles associated with certain consumer goods. The mass media bring to the poor images of the rich which previously may have eluded them. In itself this would not lead directly to prejudice. After all, blacks are hardly more fortunate than most whites in this respect. Another link in the argument is needed. This is that the state of relative deprivation is a source of frustration which becomes converted into aggressive feelings. Instead of being expressed against the original source of frustration, the aggression becomes directed towards blacks. There is a connection between relative deprivation and hostility towards racial groups. Can it be shown that the *mass media* can induce such a state of relative deprivation and that this created racial prejudice?

Hartmann and Husband used two questions from their survey to investigate television-induced relative deprivation. One concerned whether affluence depicted in programmes made the viewer wish for such a life style. The other asked whether seeing the wealthy and successful on television made viewers dissatisfied with their own position. About two-fifths of viewers registered no feelings of deprivation. There was a significant (but small) tendency for those who experienced 'television-induced relative deprivation' to be hostile towards blacks. Although Hartmann and Husband regard this as at best only tentative support, it is consistent with their expectations. The findings, if substantiated by other research, provide a mechanism by which the mass media, without promoting racism directly, develop the conditions in which it is worsened. However, other research suggests that people are unaffected by images of affluence in the mass media (Fox and Philliber, 1978).

Eliminating Racism

So far we have considered the effects on racial attitudes and ethnic self-consciousness generated by outpourings of the mass media. But the mass media sometimes actively propagandise against racism. The most familiar examples of these were the British programme *Till Death Do Us Part* and its American development *All In The Family*. In both these programmes, the central character, Alf Garnett or Archie Bunker, personifies the bigot—racialist, jingoist, right wing, pugnacious to the extreme. They are surrounded by other characters who provide a much more tolerant and reasonable view of society. These programmes are intended to make the audience laugh at bigotry by poking fun at intolerance. By doing so the shows undermine the ideas and beliefs which underpin the racist ideas of the viewer. Both programmes were criticized by those who felt it dangerous to expose racist and similar views in the mass media since there is no guarantee at all that the viewer will recognize that the bigot is a buffoon, a figure of fun, whose views need to be rejected for what they are. Instead the viewer may have considerable sympathies with the character. He may be seen as honestly and steadfastly holding on to sound moral and social values despite the endless carping antagonism of his family. A basic explanatory principle in mass communication research, selective perception, would suggest that where feelings run so strongly (as in racism) the tendency to interpret race-related ideas in ways congruent with one's own point of view would be aroused. Possibly, despite the good intentions of the writers and producers, conditions favouring an increase in racism are created.

Vidmar and Rokeach (1974) carried out a study of U.S. adolescents and Canadian adults to find out whether responses to the programme differed according to whether the viewer was prejudiced or not. In the U.S. sample the measure of prejudice was a question referring to attitudes towards negroes (e.g. Do you think Negroes are as intelligent as white people—that is, can they learn things as well if they are given the same education and training?). For the Canadian sample, in order to make the research culturally relevant, prejudice was measured in terms of Canadian ethnic groups (e.g. In your opinion do you think Canadian Indians are so unreliable that they can never be trusted to take care of themselves, or that they are perfectly capable of managing their own affairs?). Both samples saw the programme as funny and enjoyable. Of the main characters, Archie Bunker was the most admired by members of the audience. Surprisingly he is seen as 'a winner' by a large proportion of the audience though the majority thought it was wrong to refer to various minority groups using derogatory words like Coons and Chinks. Twenty per cent of the audience claimed that the programme made them become aware of their unknown prejudices. Many sympathized with the bigoted Archie Bunker to quite a marked degree. Response to the programme was mediated by pre-existing values and beliefs. Admiration of Archie Bunker, seeing Archie as a winner, seeing Archie as not being made fun of, and seeing the ethnic slurs as being alright were all more common amongst the prejudiced viewers, though the bigot and the non-bigoted viewers enjoyed and laughed at the programme equally. Selective perception was working to reduce the programme's effects on bigotry.

Brigham and Giesbrecht (1976) carried out a similar study, though they included the opinions of both the blacks and whites. For whites, there were significant correlations between expressed racial prejudice and liking and agreeing with Archie Bunker and seeing his racial views as valid. For blacks, racial attitudes (including a favourable response to the black power movement) were unrelated to attitudes towards the content of the programme. However, the more it was enjoyed the more the programme was seen as beneficial. A Dutch study by Wilhoit and de Bock (1976) employed rather a different methodology. A group of subjects was interviewed several times during the period of broadcasting of the series so that responses to individual episodes could be assessed. Intolerant people were less likely to watch the programme. As might be expected, evaluation of individual events was linked to intolerance and ethnocentrism. For example, intolerant and ethnocentric individuals thought Archie Bunker's racist arguments more reasonable than did racially tolerant viewers. Recall of items from one of the shows at a later date was not related to prejudice, suggesting that selective retention (recall of items congruent with one's own point of view) does not operate in this context. Finally, those high on intolerance and authoritarianism were more likely to say that the programme had caused them to be uncertain about their own beliefs.

Surlin and Tate (1976) studied the response of high and low authoritarians to the humour of *All In The Family* by presenting subjects with a number of 'jokes' from the series. For example:

Archie: Look, I know you'se kids go by what you call this new morality —skirts up to here, hot pants up to even further, see-through blouses, movies with people in bed, sometimes three, four o' them.

Mike: But, Archie, people's bodies—the fact that they go to bed—they make love—it's part of life!

Archie: So's throwing up! But I ain't paying three bucks to see it.

Response to the humour in the series was determined in a complex way by culture, sex and authoritarianism as well as the particular object of the joke.

But there is no simple statement about the audience's response to the humour that can be made. How far the humour can help reduce bigotry is difficult to know as a consequence. *All In The Family* failed to live up to the intentions of its makers as witnessed by its failure to change the audience drastically. Despite 'preaching' against racialism, circumstances contrived to reduce the impact of these efforts—the bigoted individual tends to see in the programme support for his own bigotry, the non-bigoted also tend to find some support for their view. But this in itself does not mean that such programmes do not have the net effect of reducing racism. The Dutch study suggests that racists tended to be made uncomfortable by the programmes.

Conclusions

The research described in this chapter demonstrates the great difficulty of using the mass media to manipulate the attitudes and opinions of members of the audience. This does not mean that attitudes and opinions are not affected by the mass media, but merely that precise statements of the likely effects of the media may elude us. There can be little argument that the media have a responsibility to present minorities as real members of society capable of a wide variety of roles within that society. Minority groups gain little from being ignored and perhaps sympathetic treatment might enhance the self-esteem of minority group members. Certainly it is possible to find much that is distasteful about the treatment of minority groups by the media, but there is not much psychological evidence that racist images in the mass media dramatically increase racism in the audience. There is also little evidence of any substantial decline in racism as a result of programmes which ridicule bigotry.

7

Sexism and the Mass Media

HOMO MASS MEDIA, the being totally reared by television, radio, and the newspapers, might respond to the sexually stereotyped, even sexist contents of the mass media by adopting these lock, stock, and barrel as the framework for his own view of the world. *Homo Sapiens,* however, is dependent on a vast array of social and cultural institutions and practices which make it far less certain that the mass media will serve similar functions for him. Therein lies the difficulty. The issue of sexism in the mass media may not be an entirely recent one but the rise of the women's consciousness movement of the 60s probably made it inevitable that the media's treatment of women would become focused upon. After all, virtually no dramatic social problem goes by without an accusatory finger being pointed at the media. In a way sexism has all the characteristics of an issue likely to produce 'scapegoating' of the mass media. This does not mean that the media are blameless, but merely that they attract more criticism than they warrant. The reasons for this are simple. Sexism, at least according to the rhetoric, is everywhere. It is so fundamental to most cultures that no simple piece of social surgery could eradicate it. If sexism is endemic in the family, the school, religion, industry, commerce, personal relations, and almost everywhere else, then where does one begin reconstructive surgery?

Because the mass media deal in symbols they form an immediate source of concern. The symbolism of the media, more than anything, provides a constant reminder, graphic and immediate, of the position of women in society. Not only are the media major traffickers in cultural symbols but symbolic in other ways. For instance, the media are mass organizations which are intimately intertwined with the broader socio-political and economic system. Thus if women's subjugation is seen to be due to economic and political factors, then the media's role can easily be conceived in the same light. If big business both owns the media and needs to repress women, what better object of criticism than the big business *media* organisations? Furthermore, the mass media like many other organizations fail to give equal job opportunities to women. That is they employ them in lowly, non-executive positions. But, inevitably, the presumption of the power of the media to control the minds of the audience makes them a prime target. This together with the relative simplicity of changing the media compared with the church (how do you change something when you have no access to its power structure?) or the family (how do you begin to deal with so many individual units?) probably accounts as much as anything for the icy glare the women's movement gives mass communication.

There are many ways of looking at sexism and the mass media. These include:

1. The mass media as inequitable employers of women.
2. The mass media as transmitters of sexist material and imagery.
3. The mass media's effects on sexism.

The list could be much refined but most research has concentrated on section 2—the sexist content of the media. It seems self-evident to the authors of content analyses that sexist content inevitably leads to sexism in the audience. Consequently despite innumerable content analyses of sexist images, it requires a thorough search to find evidence of the effects of sexist material in the media. Some might argue that sexism is so pervasive in all social institutions it is unlikely that the mass media's effects could be separated out effectively from these. Some brave souls have attempted to tackle the effects questions as will be seen.

What the Polls Say

It might be useful to look at some data from public opinion polls concerning women and their changing roles in society. They provide a relatively 'objective' background for a discussion of the effects of mass communication on public opinion. De Boer (1977) surveyed a number of public opinion polls dealing with attitudes to women at work. It is difficult to generalise on all feelings about all women since they vary with circumstances. Mothers with young children are treated in a much less laissez-faire manner, for example. The broad features of the data are, however, relevant. A U.S. poll asked, 'All in all, do you favor or oppose most of the efforts to strengthen and change women's status in society?' In 1970 around 42% were in favour but by 1975 the figure had increased to 63%, which indicates rapidly changing opinion in this area. In 1936 the following question was asked: 'Do you approve of a married woman earning money in business or industry if she has a husband capable of supporting her?', and 18% said yes. But by 1969 the figure had risen to 55% and to 68% in 1976. In 1970, 71% of women agreed that 'Taking care of a home and raising children is more rewarding for a woman than having a job', but this declined to 51% by 1975. Similar trends were found for men's answers to the same question. In 1976, 85% of American women agreed that to some extent women are better off than five years previously.

International comparisons show similar 'liberated' trends. A poll of 1977 found that the following percentages thought the role played by women in their country is changing a great deal or a fair amount:

U.S.A.	91%
Scandinavia	80%
Canada	87%
France	79%
Australia	82%
United Kingdom	83%
Japan	71%
West Germany	60%
India	30%

In the Western nations there seems to be little variation in these percentages. Similarly, data on equality of educational opportunities in the Western nations suggest that 80–90% of the population feel that women have the same educational opportunities as men. Relatively few—around 30–55%—of the populations thought that women and men have equal job opportunities. Erskine (1971) also looked at the surveys of public opinion about the role of women in society. Lest inadvertently we confuse ourselves by assuming that the march of progress in this area has been enormous, it is worthwhile noting some of her figures. Since 1937 the American Gallup Poll has asked whether the respondent would vote for a woman president. In 1937 only 27% of men would, whereas by 1969 this figure had increased to about 58%. This seems steady and remarkable progress. But female respondents have not changed quite so dramatically. In 1937 40% of women would vote for a woman president, a figure which had levelled at around 50% in the late 1960s—hardly a meteoric rise in opinion and certainly less than the corresponding figure for men. Women's consciousness of their sex seems less elevated than men's consciousness of women. In the stereotype of women some characteristics are highly valued. For example, in 1952 most people thought that there would be less graft and corruption in government if more women were in power.

Certain attitudes which, through modern eyes, could be seen as unfavourable to women have changed for the better. In 1937 three-quarters of respondents were against women working but by the late 1960s this figure had declined to around 40%. But there has always been a tendency for people to agree that women deserve equal pay if they do men's work. Perhaps this reflects more of an attitude to 'fair play' than an attitude to women as such. Finally, there seems to be a general tendency over the years to decry the abilities of women. Thus most people in 1946 thought women less creative and intelligent than men. In 1970 nearly 50% of respondents thought a woman could not run a business as well as a man. According to De Boer (1977), only 52% of Germans in 1971 were definitely against a law prohibiting mothers with children under 10 years from working. In 1976, a U.S. poll showed that 53% preferred a male doctor and 7% a female one, 45% preferred a male lawyer and 5% a female one. 59% preferred to deal with a male police officer and 2% a female one. But, of course, there was a strong preference for female nurses, female shop assistants, and female hairdressers. However, since these are considered predominantly female occupations (or effeminate as in the case of hairdressing) a rather negative attitude underlies these preferences. Embarrassment was not a major factor in these choices. For example, while more females than males prefer women doctors, the greatest number of females prefer a male doctor. Males overwhelmingly prefer a female nurse. Whatever the explanation, these figures seem out of line with a superficial acceptance of liberated attitudes to women apparent in the replies to other survey questions.

The Sexist Content of the Media

Content analyses of the media and sexist imagery therein would probably make a book length review in their own right. Of necessity, only a taste of this research can be given in these pages. Books like *Print and Prejudice* (Zimet, 1976) and articles such as that by Busby (1975) give a more complete coverage. Goffman (1979) presents many visual examples of the treatment of women in the book *Gender Advertisements*. It is difficult to summarize the many findings but easy to provide a short epithet like the *media are sexist*. The following examples, taken from various aspects of the media, provide some indication of the types of content analysis which have been carried out. They are all American examples but often reflect trends discernable in other countries.

Advertising

Courtney and Whipple (1974) reviewed four studies of women in television commercials. According to them, TV commercials do nothing to show that the structure of the family is changing or that women are capable of responsibility outside the domestic scene. This applied equally to voices over (unseen commentators) where male voices predominate. The voice-over is the one that tries to persuade. It is confident and authoritative. The lack of women in this role reveals social attitudes. In television advertising the female is typically a young housewife framed by the domestic environ- ment. No suggestion is given that the housewifely and professional roles can coexist without severe problems of adjustment.

Maracek *et al.* (1978) looked at the changes that might have occurred in television during the period 1972–4. The issue of the authority of the voice- over expert was again to the fore. There was no evidence of a real change in the way that the voices of unseen males contribute 'authority' to the message being transmitted. Nor were women any more likely to be seen as an on-screen 'expert'. What had happened was that female experts were added to advertisements which still retained the male authority. So females did not replace authoritative males but simply supplemented them. Without the reassurance of an authoritative male nothing could be allowed to change in the slightest. Even when females appeared they tended to be associated with 'female' products. The authors see all this as allowing the advertisers 'to have their cake and eat it'. It placates the critical women's organizations without any substantial alteration to standard practices based on traditional social ideologies.

Denise Warren (1978) takes up a similar issue concerning apparent change without real change. She asked whether the integration of new ways of looking at women in advertising has fundamentally changed the dis- advantaged place of women in the social and economic order. She suggests that the advertising industry merely adopted the rhetoric and superficial attitudes of the so-called sexual revolution to its own needs. The new image of women gives them a body to be used for pleasure but requires that they respond to a threat—'fear (of) sexual inadequacy unless they buy separate products to control each part of their reeking bodies which are dissected across America's television screens and magazine pages' (p. 172). Structur- ally there is very little to choose between the women being sold soap flakes as a route to love or deodorant to achieve the same ends.

Magazine Fiction

Franzwa (1974) claims that the females in the women's magazine fiction are portrayed in one of only four ways:

(a) Single and looking for a husband
(b) Housewife/mother
(c) Spinster
(d) Widowed or divorced but soon to marry

Except for the spinster (which is defined by the absence of a man), each of these roles are described in man-dependent terms. In a content analysis of women's magazine fiction between 1940 and 1970, clear and familiar trends emerged. In the 40s and 50s as many as a quarter of female characters did not work before they got married and once married relatively few of them worked. Even when the female characters worked they were often portrayed as having tremendous conflicts between their work and housewifely roles.

Lazer and Dier (1978), in a somewhat more sophisticated study than most in this area, compared the characteristics of the real work force with that of magazine fiction. Since 1940 the proportion of women in the U.S. labour force has increased 60% and married working women threefold. This was not the case in the magazines they studied (*Atlantic Monthly* and *Saturday Evening Post*). There was an imbalance of the sexes, half of the characters at least being men whereas at most a third of the characters were women. Characters not identified as either sex account for the rest. Over the period 1940–70 there was no important change in the percentage of women in these stories. Furthermore, there was no increase (a decrease in point of fact) in the numbers of women in employment in magazine fiction despite a 50% increase in the real labour force.

In the real work force the numbers and proportions of men and women in various types of employment have become more equal recently. In the fictional work force there has been no such trend towards similarity. Both men and women tend to be professionals in the fictional work force, whereas, of course, most people in the real work force have rather unglamorous jobs. In many ways, the degree of 'misrepresentation' of the jobs of men and women is equal. Lazar and Dier argue that 'although many of those men and women in fiction who do work are engaged in activities different from and often more glamorous than those of real men and women, the number of working women is so small that the undesirability of work for women is the louder message' (p. 181).

Children's Programmes

White Streicher (1974) analysed cartoons broadcast at the times when children are most likely to be viewing. Although many of the cartoons consisted solely of male characters, none had exclusively female characters:

> 'Cartoon females were less numerous than males, made fewer appearances, had fewer lines, played fewer lead roles, were less active, occupied many fewer positions of responsibility, were less noisy, and were more preponderantly juvenile than males. Mothers worked only in the house; males did not participate in housework. In many activities in which girls showed some form of skill (e.g. cheerleading), their

performance was duplicated by a dog or another pet. Other stereotypes appeared. The female who really had a *lot* of lines was Maid Marian, Robin Hoodnick's girl, who was constantly nagging, complaining, wanting, talking, until someone put a bag over her head' (p. 127).

But White Streicher points out that in cartoons males too are often portrayed in stereotyped ways.

Dohrmann (1975) took a random selection of educational programmes from the *Sesame Street, Electric Company, Misteroger's Neighborhood,* and *Captain Kangaroo* series. In particular, she was interested in the distribution of the following two characteristics between the sexes.

1. *Active mastery*—physical aggression, verbal suggestion, leadership, heroism, achievement, ingenuity, etc.
2. *Passive dependency*—victim of physical aggression, follower, asks for advice or protection, is rescued, is incompetent, etc.

Males were much more likely to demonstrate active mastery than passive dependency. Females were equally likely to exhibit either trait. The male child showed ingenuity, achievement, and heroism, whereas the female child tended to be led, to be an object of insult, and to be helpless. Female adults were even more passive. The pattern of male dominance and female passivity also persisted in interactions between the two sexes. Dohrmann writes that these programmes provide symbolic messages of comparative gender worth. This 'disservice' is compounded by the acclaim given to these 'quality', educational programmes, which only underlines the validity of their sexist messages.

Women's Daytime Television Serials

Mildred Downing (1974) studied the daytime serial on television. She comments on the absolute uniformity of the settings of these soap operas. Ninety per cent of characters in the sample she studied were middle class and the actors and actresses predominantly trim and good looking. But instead of clerical workers dominating as they would in the population, the characters tended to be drawn more from the ranks of the professionals. The blue collar worker is ignored. The over-representation of professionals applies only to men since there is only a slight trend for women. Eighty-four per cent of the programme episodes dealt with romantic love, 98% dealt with interpersonal relationships, 98% dealt with personal problems, but only 15% dealt with social problems and 6% with community or world affairs. Downing describes the way in which the programmes are produced

—essentially with a low budget but high profitability, scripts written around a storyline and characterization received by scriptwriters from the head writer; the serial may be taped live with very few retakes and very limited rehearsal. She argues:

'Emerging from this complexity of institutionalized procedures, economic pressures, and domination by male production staffs is an image of women which is far from unacceptable. . . . She is liked and respected by the male acquaintances, not merely sought as a sexual object as she is in prime time television drama. She does not act solely as an adjunct to male activities and interests. She is a responsible member of a family structure, exercising judgement and offering support to parents and children alike. Her opinions are solicited and acted upon. She enjoys the friendship of other women' (p. 137).

This comment is interesting for many reasons but primarily since it takes a step beyond the routine 'look how badly women are presented in the media' argument. It recognizes that the criteria for judging the presentation of women in the media might extend more widely than their work roles. But at the same time it highlights the problem of defining just how women should be portrayed. Is it really to the long-term advantage of women that they be represented in this goody-goody way, any more than it would be if they were presented as mere accessories for men, fleshy in car hi-fi systems? It is comparatively easy to say what is wrong with television's treatment of women, yet very difficult to specify in detail what it should be.

Prime-Time Television

Tedesco (1974) took a sample of prime-time dramatic programmes excluding cartoons. Characters were rated in terms of personality descriptions as well as their major demographic features. Thirty-six per cent of males but 60% of females were not employed. Males who killed were more frequent than males who were killed; females who killed were less frequent than females who were killed. Personality descriptions like powerful, smart, rational, and stable fitted the males more closely than the females. Females, though, were more attractive, fair, sociable, warm, happy, peaceful, and youthful. However, both males and females in prime-time drama were towards the 'favourable' ends of all these personality dimensions. Females tended not to be found in adventurous situations, but are younger and more are married. Tedesco describes prime-time woman as 'lacking independence'.

Lemon (1977) studied dominance patterns in two-person interactions between the sexes. She coded the partners in the interactions as dominator, dominated, or equal. Programmes were classified as situation comedies or crime drama. It turned out that inter-sex interactions were affected by the type of programme considered. So in situation comedies males dominated females 23% of the time, females dominated males 13% of the time, and 64% of the time males and females were equals. However, males were much more dominant in crime drama. In these males dominated females 47% of the time. The interactions tended to be more equal in family or domestic situations. Where occupational status was relevant to the interaction, it was much more important than sex in determining the nature of the interaction. Lemon suggests:

'. . . if women . . . are given more roles of higher occupational rank and, most important, shown working in the context of their job, inter-sex . . . dominance patterns would most likely change' (p. 78).

In this she seems to imply that the sexism of the media is not a cause of sexism in society but merely a reflection of social reality. The way she proposed to remedy the imbalance in dominance patterns presumably involves positive discrimination in favour of presenting working women.

Turrow (1974) studied patterns of giving and receiving advice, as well as the giving of orders in TV dramatic characters. Areas of expertise could be divided into traditionally male ones (e.g. business, law, government) and traditionally feminine ones (love, the family, personal problems). Men give directives and orders much more frequently than females. This was surprising given that much of the drama took place within the domestic rather than work environment. The daytime programmes gave greatest dominance to women than the evening ones but the same trends were evident in these also.

Covering Women's Rights News

So far the manner in which the media portray women in fiction has been described. A similar but more problematic analysis could be applied to the way in which women are treated in the news. But it is probably somewhat more intriguing to consider the way the news media have covered issues of women's rights. Everyone is familiar with the often condescending and mocking treatment that the press gives to 'women's libbers' and 'bra burners'. This may be unfortunate but is only one aspect of the issue. What of the way in which treatment of women's rights has changed historically? Butler and Paisley (1978) describe a study of American magazines over the period 1922–76 directed at the changes in the treatment of women's rights.

1922 marked the first appearance of an article on women's rights in American magazines. Curiously, the early period was a peak in the production of such articles. In the period 1922–6, 252 pages of American magazines dealt with the theme. This was the highest total until the late 1960s and early 1970s. The feminist movement of the 1960s was, of course, the main cause of such a resurgence of attention. It emerged that the media, despite the sexism of fiction, were by and large strong advocates of equal rights amendments in the 1970s.

Farley (1978) chose to search women's magazines, in particular, to see if they supported or opposed legislation on sex equality. Magazines like *McCall's, Playgirl,* and *Ms* gave a lot of attention to the issue whereas others, like *True Romance, True Experiences, Secrets* and *Modern Romances* did not. But this does not correspond precisely with advocacy of equal rights legislation. So, for example, *True Love* and *True Romance* were strongly favourable towards such legislation despite giving relatively little coverage to it. There was some evidence that editors' perceptions of their readers' attitudes to equal rights legislation had some influence on whether it was given lengthy treatment. Those believing that their readers would be against equal rights legislation gave the subject the most attention. Farley writes:

'Although these editors were able to agree on the importance of informal debate on the Equal Rights Amendment, they and their magazines are as diverse as the groups they serve. This analysis suggests that short coverage is not always linked with low commitment or long treatment with advocacy. Some editors, believing their readers to be . . . supporters already, gave the amendment little coverage . . . even as others were bucking editorial policy, protest letters, and their own beliefs about what their readers wanted to hear to advocate passage. Perhaps the first American woman to edit a women's magazine was mistaken when she said that women's magazines would not change the *status quo.* The evidence . . . suggests that women's magazine editors are trying to do just that' (p. 192).

Such data and arguments as these put into context the otherwise beguiling idea that the mass media paint women in a bad light, contributing to keeping women, unidimensionally, in the role of mother and housewife. The situation is much more complex than that. This is not to say that the media can be absolved from responsibility to improve their coverage of women. It merely points out that rushing headlong from the results of a few limited content analyses of women in the media to a universal condemnation of the media is too simplistic. For example, there are great discrepancies between the way that women are dealt with in fiction and in the news pages and editorials. It is also important because of a tendency to confuse the limited exposure of women in news stories with a deliberate policy on the part of the news media to misrepresent women. But this gets us into untold depths of complexity concerning the functions of the mass media in society.

The Effects of Sexism in the Mass Media

Evidence that the sexist content of the mass media contributes to the maintenance of the *status quo* is hard to find. Little research evidence has been collected and consequently most of those contributing content analysis in this area tend to rely on arguments which suggest that if the contents of the media are so sexist, then they cannot possibly be doing anything to advance women in society. This is, of course, quite a compulsive argument but unacceptable in so far as it is based on assumption rather than fact. The argument may be flawed, for example, because the content analyses concentrate on uninfluential programmes, ignoring those which present women in a better light. In addition, many of the content analyses show that the situation is very complex indeed, with women in some contexts being shown favourably. Furthermore, we are forced to assume that the reader or viewer fails to recognize the stereotyped nature of the media's treatment of women. If they do recognize it their response may be very different.

Miller and Reeves (1976) claim that the sex role portrayals in the mass media had been so heavily stereotyped in the past that it is very difficult indeed to work out their causal influence on the already highly stereotyped sex role perceptions of young people. They suggest that chinks are showing in the sexist curtain and that women are being shown increasingly in non-traditional work roles. It is hypothesized that those children who are the most aware of female characters in non-traditional work roles such as police officers, park ranger, and high school principals will be more likely to accept such non-traditional roles as appropriate for females. Of course, it is possible that those who are tradition-minded will avoid watching pro-grammes which portray such 'modern' conceptions of women. Neverthe-less, the data largely supported their suggestion despite this alternative and competing hypothesis. Tentatively, it appears that the media's portrayals of women in non-stereotyped work roles may effectively change the gender stereotypes of children.

More convincing is a study by Davidson, Yasuna, and Tower (1979) which looked at the response of 5- and 6-year-old girls to various cartoons taken from prime-time television. The cartoons were designated by the researchers as sexually stereotyped, neutral, or negatively stereotyped—a negatively stereotyped cartoon being one which promotes a favourable view of the potential of girls. The sexually stereotyped cartoon was from a series called *Jeannie*. In this the female lead was a servant to the male lead character. An exciting trip is rejected by some female characters and Jeannie, herself, rather unsuccessfully tried to assist two males. In the negatively stereotyped cartoon boys try to build a clubhouse but fail miserably and eventually allow two girls to help them. The clubhouse gets built but the boys will not allow the girls to join. Eventually the girls gain admittance by taking over the building. Finally, the girls show their stuff by proving their athletic and sporting prowess against boys and everyone eventually agrees that it is good that they allowed girls to join. The neutral film cartoon was an episode from the series *Scooby-Do, Where Are You?*

The data showed that the reverse stereotype cartoon in which girls were shown to be at least as competent as the boys produced a significant effect. In comparison to both the neutral and highly stereotyped cartoons, the children who viewed this programme gave fewer stereotyped responses about the female role. There were no differences between the highly stereotyped and the neutral cartoon (which in retrospect may not have been as neutral as the authors originally thought since the two girls portrayed corresponded to an assertive plain Jane and a dumb blond). The programmes seemed to have left the stereotype of the male role unaffected.

A fairly similar study of children in the 5–10 age range was carried out by O'Bryant and Corder–Bolz (1978). The researchers showed four specially made commercials for a fruit drink which varied in their sex role content. Some of them showed women in their usual *traditional work roles* (telephonist, model, manicurist) whereas in some women were portrayed in *reversed role* situations as pharmacists, welders, butchers, and manual labourers. These particular work roles were selected because they were rather less familiar to young children than, say, teaching or bus driving. The children were asked to say which tools were used by the different sorts of workers from drawings (the occupational *knowledge* test), to indicate whether certain jobs were for a man, a woman, or both (the occupational *stereotyping* test), and to say which jobs they personally would like to do (the occupational *preferences* test). Knowledge, stereotyping, and preferences were measured both before and after seeing the advertisements. Some children only saw the traditional role advertisements whereas the others saw the reversed role advertisements. Both boys and girls learnt about occupations from the advertisements. There was more stereotyping of jobs as being for females only in the traditional work role condition. The girls in the reversed role condition increased their preference for traditionally male jobs. Girls shown the traditional role advertisements became more traditional in their attitudes. But these trends applied to girls only. Boys tended to reject both male and female jobs more after seeing the advertisements. This might be because they saw only females doing the jobs and so rejected them as being for girls.

Another study, again involving commercials, was carried out by Pingree (1978). She took a sample of children from the ages of about 9 years to 14 years. Two types of advertisements were taken from television—some featured women in non-traditional roles such as women doctors and professional drivers, a woman accountant working on an Alaskan pipeline, a woman baling hay and driving a tractor, and a woman professional golfer. The other type of commercial featured much more traditional feminine roles—all very familiar involving an obsession with domesticity. Some of the children were told that the commercial they were going to see featured people acting while the other children were told not that they were actors but real people doing the jobs for real. Some children were told nothing. In general it emerged that children who viewed the non-traditional adverts were more non-traditional in their attitudes towards women afterwards. Furthermore, there was a sex difference: girls overall had less traditional attitudes to women than boys did. Unfortunately, the data on the perceived reality of the people in the commercials tended to be a little difficult to understand. For example, irrespective of the content of the commercials, those told that they featured actresses were less traditional in their attitudes about women than those who were told they were real women.

The evidence gives no strong indication that broadcasting traditional sexist stereotypes has much effect on the audience. However, attempts to present a more positive image of the capabilities of women did produce improvements. Perhaps this is consistent with the view that sexism is so endemic that the media could contribute relatively little which could not be obtained from many other sources. The studies also tend to concentrate on girls, which may be a little mistaken given that where both sexes are studied rather different results are obtained for boys. A programme which changes girls' attitudes favourably may produce the reverse effect on boys.

The findings of these limited and artificial experiments may not match closely the 'true' changes in society. Bush *et al.* (1977–8) compared adolescent perception of sex roles between 1968 and 1975. In fact they concentrated on self-esteem and other features that might reflect the influence of the feminist movement. But, there was little change in the proportions wishing not to get married, little change in evaluations of being female, no change in self-esteem over the period of girls relative to boys, and so forth. The authors suggest that in general the adolescent girls show less changes in attitude to themselves and their sex roles than might have been expected under the onslaught of publicity given the women's movement during the period. They also suggest that we may have to wait until the new ideology filters through to new generations of parents and teachers, for example, before any substantial revisions can be expected. On the other hand, Richmond and McCroskey (1975) claim to have evidence that women's opinions are becoming more and more accepted in society. Since this is a self-evident truth historically (e.g. the suffrage of women) the study's importance is only relative. They suggest that the distinction between topics on which men are experts and those on which women are experts is becoming increasingly blurred. The exception to this is politics, where most prefer a male's opinions to a female's. However, whether this is an effect of the mass media is not considered.

Conclusions

The conclusions to all this are bound to be predictable. Busby (1975) may as well provide such a summary:

'Though research is beginning to develop in these areas, content is the only one that has been heavily examined so far. Since the same cultural forces have influenced writers, producers, directors, and publishers, it is not surprising to find a similarity of sex-role imagery across media. Also, since the mass media have been dominated primarily by one group—white, American males—it is not surprising to find a similarity of imagery in all the media. The media sex-role studies that have been completed in the 1960s and early 1970s can be used as historical documents to measure future social changes' (p. 127).

While in this chapter some more recent evidence has been provided than Busby reviewed, it is difficult to claim much progress. The impression is that the recent content analyses are a little more open-minded in the sense of painting a more open, less black and white picture than earlier research did. At the same time it must be asked what should be the paths of research into sexism and the mass media in the future? Clearly some sort of monitoring exercise to feed back to the media a statistical account of their treatment of women is appealing and analogous to Gerbner's studies of television violence (e.g. Gerbner *et al.*, 1976, 1978, 1979) but this would require some consensus on the sorts of analyses which would be profitable to programme makers. Again, clearly long-term studies of changes in sex role stereotypes in society would provide a useful monitoring service. But the major problems arise with the question of whether there should be an increase in the number of effects studies testing whether the media cause sexism. Quite whether we should engage in hot pursuit of the same sort of will o' the wisp that television violence appears to be is problematic. If that issue remains hotly debated, how could we expect an early resolution of the sexism issue? Certainly some of the concerns of the women's movements about the employment of women in some media organizations (e.g. Mills, 1974), if fully implemented in the form of the greater penetration of women through the media, might lead to some more drastic improvements.

Part Four

SEX, VIOLENCE, CRIME, AND JUSTICE

8

Violence and the Mass Media

CONFESSION is good for the soul. In this case it might also allow the reader to form a realistic assessment of the arguments in this chapter more easily. Several years ago we published a book (Howitt and Cumberbatch, 1975) outlining our position on the issue: Does mass media violence cause violence in society? This was a critical account of research on the effects of the mass media. At the same time it was a rebuttal of the view commonly promulgated that the level of violence in society is significantly altered by mass media violence. Our view was not shared by many in the scientific community. The mass media violence research 'industry' has constantly churned out in recent years the very view that we rejected. Consequently, the reader is warned that what is to be presented is the gospel according to Howitt and Cumberbatch. The gospels, of course, have many different interpreters.

Origins of Mass Media and Violence Research

Theoretical Concerns

Late in the 1950s a small number of prominent social psychologists began to drift into mass media research almost unintentionally. The common link amongst them was an interest in aggression and its causes. An outline of the story will highlight the features of one of the most controversial branches of mass communication research. The casual way in which this branch of research becomes incorporated in the mass media and violence argument reveals a lot.

Feshbach (1955, 1961) was impressed by the Aristotelian argument that watching plays allows the viewer to discharge emotional energy vicariously. Thus by witnessing aggression, we release aggressive tensions which could otherwise be directed against others. This is known as the *catharsis theory*.

Notice that it assumes that aggression is caused by a build-up of tension. In the history of psychological theory, the idea that an individual could become charged with aggression was common in many schools of thought including such opposites as Freudians and Behaviourists. Feshbach reported an experiment which, on the face of it, supported the catharsis theory. He compared the aggressiveness of individuals who had seen a clip of violent film with those who had not. Those who saw the violent film were the least aggressive afterwards. Leonard Berkowitz, another social psychologist interested in the theoretical basis of aggression, smelled a conceptual rat. He pointed out that there is more than one reason why an individual seeing a violent film should aggress less afterwards. His argument was that many people, especially middle class Americans of the sort who become university students and subjects in experiments, have an ingrained dislike of aggression. To act aggressively would cause them much anxiety. For such individuals violence is only acceptable in limited and prescribed conditions which justify its use. Berkowitz thought Feshbach's aggressive film reduced aggression because it heightened anxiety about being aggressive and thereby inhibited its use—not because of some process of discharging aggressive energy.

Berkowitz *et al.* (1963a, b) carried out a similar but by no means identical study and deliberately varied the degree of anxiety about aggression the film aroused. Verbal statements preceding the film either justified the aggression shown in the film or established that the aggression was morally unwarranted. Berkowitz found support for his ideas. The justification of aggression in the film allowed an increase in the aggressiveness of the viewer. But this was true only in very restricted situations. An increase in aggression was found only (a) in subjects who had already been angered before seeing the film and, (b) were allowed to aggress against the source of this anger, (c) when the aggression was measured within a short period of seeing the film, and (d) when the filmed violence, as already indicated, was justified. These are highly unusual circumstances, rarely reproduced in real life. Thus the results of the experiment do not readily lead to the view that mass media violence increases violence in society. There are other reasons for caution: the film used was a very short clip from a feature film, the research took place within a psychology laboratory, and there were absolutely no undesirable consequences of aggression (e.g. being arrested or getting one's nose punched in return). These limit the generality of the research further.

About the same time, another field of research stumbled into the debate. This was research on imitation or modelling which led to what is now known as social learning theory. Basically social learning theory stands in contradistinction from some rather more traditional approaches in psychology. In psychology the view that much of what the individual is, does, and believes is *learned* from the vast society milieu around him is not controversial at all. But just how this learning takes place is disputed.

Traditional learning theory, working with concepts developed by studying cats, rats and mice, had concentrated on the gradual building up of complex behaviours from simpler ones through processes of trial and error, reward and punishment, repeated 'training' trials, and so forth. Some learning can be established by such methods. However there must be alternatives since a child could not learn so much so rapidly if there were no speedier methods of learning. The problem is made more difficult since much learning does not come from deliberate training.

The incompleteness of the traditional learning approach is simply and dramatically demonstrated by showing that quité complex behaviours may be imitated by a viewer without repeated training sessions. A child who sees an adult playing aggressively with a toy may well aggress against it using exactly the same sort of mannerisms and expressions. This is virtually impossible to explain in terms of traditional learning theory. It is learning without repetition, instant learning, which is quite distinct from the slow building up of learning implied by earlier theories. In this sense social learning theory is inevitably very important. The problems arise when one is trying to explain when and why people imitate. It is not at all surprising to find that people can imitate complex things fairly readily, but that does not mean that they necessarily will.

Learning through observation is clearly pertinent to mass communication theory. It becomes very complicated when applied to newspapers, radio, and books. Being influenced through modelling by written language and the symbols it contains presents new problems. Immediately we consider the non-visual media in this context, it has to be assumed that people actively construct behavioural images (a presumably highly abstract and intellectually demanding task). Once this assumption is made then it becomes difficult to accept any simple causal link between the modelled behaviour and the behaviour as reproduced. But some psychologists have tended to accept that there is such a simple causal link since Albert Bandura (Bandura 1962, 1965) reported his first work on imitation. In one condition of Bandura's original experiments a pre-school child watched an adult modelling aggression against a blow-up plastic toy clown on a television-like console. This form of presentation was as effective as a 'live' model in encouraging the imitation of this aggression. So here was a clear example of children being able to reproduce televised aggression. It is problematic though whether the so-called aggressive acts against a plastic toy designed to be abused are the same as the interpersonal violence and violent crime which are at the root of worries over violence in the media. Nevertheless, this type of study was taken, along with those of Berkowitz, as proof that at the theoretical level at least the media, particularly television, could cause aggression in the viewer.

But we know that already. It is not contentious to assert that it is *possible* to learn aggression from the mass media or to be influenced by the mass media to be aggressive. To say otherwise would be tantamount to asserting that people cannot learn. What is contentious is the assumption that because theoretically the mass media could influence the viewer's aggressiveness, they do so in practice. Perhaps the only voices against this are those which promote the idea of catharsis. Even so, there is nothing in the notion of catharsis which intrinsically excludes the possibility that the mass media also stimulate people to greater aggression. *Why* should people be influenced by the violence they see on television is a more profound question than could they be or even are they influenced. More profound because it encourages consideration of the psychological mechanisms of media effects and generates wider hypotheses. For example, people may be influenced because they learn what is expected of them from television; because they learn about injustices done to their ethnic group; because they learn that violence can be an effective means to various personal and political ends; because they learn that other people are violent; because they become more used to the consequences of aggression and accept it more easily; because they learn that manliness and aggressiveness are synonymous, and so on. It is equally profound to ask why people may be *uninfluenced*. Reasons for this might include that the mass media teaches nothing new about violence which has not been learned from other sources; that the mass media essentially say that the use of violence is wrong or counterproductive; that the mass media show the consequences of aggression; that knowledge about how to aggress is already possessed; and so forth. Considering the issue in this way immediately demonstrates that the simple link between media violence and the level of violence in society is just one of many possibilities. Knowing that the mass media could influence the viewer to be more aggressive becomes merely one of the multitude of alternatives which could enrich our understanding of mass communication.

So during the early 1960s, laboratory-style experimental psychology of this sort was making a contribution to the arguments about the effects of media violence. These contributions tended to be less than consistent. For example, Walters *et al.* (1962, 1963) essentially replicated the research of Berkowitz and found that aggression could be aroused in some of those conditions in which Berkowitz found no differences. So, for example, Walters found increases in aggression in unangered subjects, whereas Berkowitz only found this when the subjects were angered. Furthermore, aggression did not have to be justified in Walters' studies. Although at one level these studies agree, they disagree when relatively precise comparisons are made. Likewise some researchers found aggression increases when cues to aggression are present in a film (i.e. expressions of pain on the actors' faces), whereas others found that aggression decreases in similar circumstances (Goranson, 1970; Hartmann, 1969a and b).

As already seen, it is easy to dismiss laboratory experiments into the effects of filmed violence as too far removed from reality to be of much use in evaluating media violence effects. A list of complaints about such studies springs easily to mind: laboratory studies ignore the milieu of individuals, organizations, groups, social, economic, historical, and cultural factors which might be expected to mediate between the mass media and the response of the audience. Laboratory studies almost always merely show a snippet of film or video lasting a few minutes which in some way is supposed to be analogous to the array of different programmes, different media, conflicting contents, and different patterns of media consumption which constitute people's actual use of the media. Laboratory studies take place in a limited 'social' environment which encourages people to perform aggressive acts. Is this in any way equivalent to the 'real' world which punishes much aggression? Whether one should rush to discard such research is a different matter. The question is not whether the laboratory researchers have chosen research methods which are too far removed from real life to be convincing, but whether we can use their findings in any way to ameliorate the social problem of violence in society. Our answer is, probably not. The theory is just not strong enough, nor is the empirical evidence.

Field Studies

During much of the same period, field studies of the effects of media violence got under way. These investigate any relationship between exposure to television violence and the aggressiveness of the viewer. As ever, a correlation would not necessarily prove cause. However, the general feeling would be that to find a correlation between the amount of TV watched and the amount of aggression exhibited would be circumstantial evidence of a cause for concern. In fact this correlational evidence proved to be rather less consistent than the inconsistent experimental evidence. Some researchers found evidence of a correlation (Lefkowitz *et al.*, 1971) whereas others found no such evidence (Pfuhl, 1960), and some found a slight negative relationship in some circumstances (Eron, 1963). As convincing support for the anti-TV violence lobby this fell far wide of the mark.

Political Initiatives on Media Violence

There were various initiatives of a political nature into the effects of media violence in the 1960s. This initially produced little research directly relevant to the issues raised. In Great Britain, the Home Office 'inspired' Television Research Committee, despite having funds available for considerable quantities of research, chose to explore other 'socially more meaningful' questions. In the short term the Committee produced nothing which tackled the question of the effects of the media on violence. In America, the National Commission on the Causes and Prevention of Violence was set up to investigate the roots of the unrest which typified the United States in the 1960s. As part of this a special task force on the mass media was created. One tangible outcome was a book of papers on TV violence edited by Baker and Ball (1969) and made up of speculative material. It contained virtually no material which was new, empirical, and investigated the effects of the media on violence. One reason for this was lack of time and other resources. Much more important from the research point of view was the later Surgeon General's Committee on Television and Social Behaviour, which had funds to finance research and a modicum of time in which to contact and organize social scientists. In all, nearly two million dollars were spent on the enterprise which produced twenty-three independent research projects and forty technical papers from researchers widely spread geographically. The immediate stimulus for the Committee was a letter sent in early 1969 by Senator John Pastore to the American Surgeon General. In this he essentially requested that a research committee be formed to produce definitive evidence on the effects of media violence. Amidst complex political chicanery, researchers produced their research fairly hastily. (For a lengthy discussion of the politics of this Committee see Canter and Strickland, 1975.)

It is virtually impossible to summarize the findings of the Committee, the intrigues surrounding the selection of its members, the 'blackballing' of certain distinguished academics, and the many contributions of the research teams in a short space. Many volumes have done so already. These deserve careful scrutiny by those wishing to understand the issues fully. The Committee felt justified in claiming the following:

> '. . . the two sets of findings (experimental and survey) converge in three respects: a preliminary and tentative indication of a causal relation between viewing violence on television and aggressive behaviour; an indication that any such causal relation operates only on some children (who are predisposed to be aggressive); and an indication that it operates only in some environmental contexts. Such

tentative and limited conclusions are not very satisfying. They represent substantially more knowledge than we had two years ago, but they leave many questions unanswered' (Surgeon General's Scientific Advisory Committee on Television and Social Behaviour, 1972, pp. 18–19).

This was the verdict of essentially warring factions on the Committee. As such it is probably much more circumspect than it would have been otherwise. Paradoxically, the only place where television is known for certain to cause aggression is in committees on media violence. Television violence research is a political activity. The conclusions of the Committee were also rather more tentative than many of the conclusions of authors of individual reports to it. However, in fairness, the body of literature available to the Committee was not as comprehensive or equivocal as would normally be demanded by social scientists. The Committee provided new evidence from various laboratory, field, and correlational studies which apparently tends to point in much the same direction. This was an important achievement in itself. On the other hand, there were some studies, notably the Feshbach and Singer (1971) field experiment, which suggested rather different conclusions. This is criticised in detail in the report of the Committee. There are very obvious difficulties in using the Committee's conclusions to formulate social policy on broadcasting. Are the conclusions sufficiently strong to justify a reduction in media violence? The suggestion that only those *predisposed* to violence are affected tends to move the focus of concern from the television to the child (Liebert, 1975). Lacking information about what sorts of violence in what sorts of contexts produces what sorts of effects, it is difficult to be precise about what is required. For example, do we treat news and fictional programmes as one, when we advocate the reduction of violence in the media?

But this is, of course, to assume that the conclusions of the Committee and the authors of the individual reports are correct. Some psychologists, perhaps only a handful, would argue that the Committee was wrong. Howitt and Cumberbatch (1975) produced the longest of the criticisms of the Committee's findings. They point out some of the obvious things hinted at already—that it is not easy to extrapolate from laboratory based studies to real life contexts, that the studies often conflict in important detail, that many of the studies are methodologically flawed, and that it is relatively easy to argue rather different conclusions from the literature than the Committee did. Furthermore, they propose a theoretically integrated synopsis of the literature. A little later in this chapter we shall take a look at some of the more recent studies which are claimed to support much the same sort of conclusion that the Committee reached. These will be examined using the self-same methods used previously to see whether they share the same failings as the earlier research.

The similar but independent conclusions of Kaplan and Singer (1976) deserve attention. They reviewed the literature of the effects of fantasy aggression on the viewer's aggressiveness. Although detailing the evidence for each of the major positions on the effects of television violence (catharsis, imitation, no effects, etc.), they show that there are problems with each of them. Brunswick's conception of probabilistic functionism forms a guiding principle in their argument. This requires that an estimate be made of what contribution a variable (in this case media violence) makes to aggression in society *relative* to all the other determinants of aggression. Laboratory experiments cannot be relied on to provide this information since experimental designs deliberately reduce competing sources of variance to a minimum. These competing sources of variance would be those factors contributing to violence in society which are not mass media. The question becomes under this system 'what percentage of variation in aggression (measured in natural contexts) is attributable to television viewing?' (Kaplan and Singer, 1976, p. 37). This is very different from asking whether it has been proven under laboratory conditions that subjects shown an aggressive film are made more aggressive than those not. Kaplan and Singer, after a lengthy discussion of the studies in this area, conclude:

> Often reviewers have drawn strong inferences from studies they believe to show an activation effect. On the basis of these studies, some people have condemned the broadcasters and have suggested remedial action. Some of the studies cited by these reviewers, however, show only minimal effects and some studies showing no effects have been ignored. Our review of the literature strongly suggests that the activating effects of television fantasy violence are marginal at most. The scientific data do not consistently link violent television fantasy programming to violent behaviour. Any change in social policy concerning the showing of TV fantasy violence is hard to justify on the basis of the current available data. New studies may change this picture and of course there are other grounds on which people can argue for programming changes (pp. 62–63).

This conclusion is very much in line with the Howitt and Cumberbatch position. It is perhaps a little more equivocal but still very much out of step with dominant opinion in this area.

In 1977 the Home Office in Britain published a review of research relevant to screen violence and film censorship (Brody, 1977), in which the same kinds of evidence were again reappraised. Faced with the somewhat more difficult task of making an evaluation of the research from the point of view of the censorship debate it was necessary to probe more deeply than whether media violence makes the audience violent. Questions of the emotional impact of violence on the viewer had to be dealt with, for example. Certain comments on the research field, especially coming from a non-researcher in the field, deserve mentioning. The most important is expressed in the following passage:

> . . . anyone who reads the results of research into the effects of films is likely to be disappointed, and it is hardly surprising that critical observers from outside the social sciences, if not from within, are becoming increasingly disillusioned with research, suspicious that it cannot answer the questions put by those who wish to express the case for or against censorship on the proved effects of exposure to obscenity, media violence, scurrilous political literature or when great pains are taken to collect detailed data about patterns of exposure and anti-social attitudes and behaviour, researchers have still tended to point to any modest correlations they have found as evidence of a causal relationship (p. 126).

It is difficult for those of us indoctrinated by training in the social sciences to appreciate fully the incredulity with which some of our methods and procedures must be viewed from outside. Sometimes, as we have seen, this poor view of social science has been worsened by taking research from a purely theoretical context and forcing it to fit the 'common sense' questions of politicians and bureaucrats. As Brody points out, only part of the inadequacy comes from the methods and practices of social scientists; some of the confusion arises from the complexity of the issues, processes, and subject matter being studied. But clearly social scientists who study the same research findings are drawing conclusions which are more varied than can be accounted for by mere differences in emphasis.

Most reviews of the TV violence issue since the Surgeon General's Committee Report accept that there is a causal link. By and large they stick fairly closely to the type of research discussed by the Surgeon General's Committee. One example of this, important to mention largely because of the distinction of the senior author, is *Sex, Violence and the Media* by Eysenck and Nias (1978). This book looks for a theoretical basis to understanding the effects of the media. It is a little complacent about the difficulties of generalizing from experimental to naturalistic situations. None of the correlational studies reported are particularly recent (with the possible exception of Belson's) and many of them show *no* relationship between violence viewing and aggressiveness. Most of the experimental field studies listed are flawed methodologically (according to Howitt and Cumberbatch and Kaplan and Singer) and most of the laboratory experiments have been mentioned already as unimpressive evidence for media effects. No new data and few new arguments on TV violence are given. Nevertheless, the authors follow the Surgeon General Committee's line but with a little more force:

> 'The evidence is fairly unanimous that aggressive acts new to the subject's repertoire of responses, as well as acts already well established, can be evoked by the viewing of violent scenes portrayed on film, TV or in the theatre' (p. 252).

Eysenck and Nias admit that many studies 'have major or minor methodological faults' but claim that these 'tend to cancel out' (p. 252). No evidence is provided that such a cancelling out process actually occurs. Conceptually it is difficult to appreciate quite what it could mean. It might be attractive in a simplistic sense for two 'wrongs' to make a right but quite illogical. Misdial a telephone number two thousand different times and you still get two thousand wrong numbers, though you might make a lot of new friends. The Eysenck and Nias review tends to substitute weight of numbers for critical analysis and consequently merely reiterate what had been said before.

The More Recent Research

The pattern of research into the effects of the mass media was established during the 1960s. Since the Surgeon General's Advisory Committee initiated its mammoth research programme there have been a number of studies which reproduce, with varying degrees of originality, the basic paradigm established early on (e.g. Drabman and Thomas, 1977). By reproducing the basic laboratory research strategies, the researcher inevitably continues to suffer the same endemic difficulties. This makes it almost inevitable that the new research fails to clarify the issues and usually merely adds to the research mountain. Much of the more recent research on media violence makes no attempt to answer the effects question and merely reports endless complex content analyses of violence on television. By and large these only affirm that there is a lot of violence on television and that the amount holds relatively steady over time, there being no strong upward or downward trend in the number of violent acts apparent (Gerbner *et al.*, 1978, 1979). The authors of such studies often seem to conceive them as part of a monitoring process, seeking to plot trends in the amount of violence in the media. The most important of the newer studies attempt to fill a gap that persists in the literature. This is the need for research which deals with real people in the real world. At the same time it is necessary to effect as good control on extraneous variables as is achieved in the laboratory experiment. Ultimately these are very high aspirations but there have been a number of interesting attempts to incorporate them into research. Some of these deserve our attention since they have not received much critical scrutiny to date.

Belson's London Study

Most research in social psychology is produced for the consumption of social psychologists alone. However, the TV violence issue is so 'newsworthy' that from time to time research findings are carried in newspapers and discussed in programmes. Sometimes the desire to make research findings available to a wide public encourages the researcher to use the media in much the same way as a public relations firm uses the media to promote the interests of its clients. For example, the researcher might produce a 'press release' for distribution to newspapers in the hope of stimulating interest in his research. In some ways this is good and, especially if research is of public interest, perhaps the public has a right to be informed. The difficulty comes when deliberately or inadvertently this publicity short-cuts the usual channels of scientific scrutiny, especially so if assertions (based apparently on scientific findings) are made which have serious implications for social policy. William Belson's study of over 1500 adolescent London boys, financed by the American Columbia Broadcasting System, using his Stable Correlate method, brought this issue to the fore. Shortly after Belson first reported his findings, the following appeared in a Sunday newspaper:

'Academics at the symposium wanting to examine the details of his full report were told they would have to wait until it was published.

'Belson says he is perfectly open with his findings and says scholars can study his research methods, although this must be done at his London offices.'

The problem is that Belson made fairly strong claims about the need to reduce the levels of violence in television programmes. These were apparently justified by the research he had carried out, but access to them was very restricted. For example, an American researcher might have to travel over 3000 miles at great expense merely to read through the reports under less than adequate circumstances, that is, hurriedly. This seems to be out of line with parts of the following passage taken from the ethical principles of the British Psychological Society.

'The psychologist has a general obligation to make the results of his research available to other psychologists, to related scientists, and allied professions' (British Psychological Society Scientific Affairs Board, 1978, p. 48).

Just what had Belson found and just what implications for television programming policy were being drawn? According to the press release issued by Belson at the time (Belson, 1977), *serious violence* is increased by long term exposure to:

'plays or films in which close personal relationships are a major theme and which feature verbal or physical violence;

'programmes in which the violence seems just thrown in for its own sake or is not necessary to the plot;

'programmes featuring fictional violence of a realistic kind;

'programmes in which the violence is presented as being in a good cause;

'Westerns of the violent kind.'

His recommendations included the following:

'Steps should be taken as soon as possible for a major cut back in the total amount of violence being presented on television.'

Scrutiny of the evidence in the book eventually published (Belson, 1978) reveals that the picture is much more confused than the clear statements of the press release would imply. The Stable Correlate method has appeared in various research reports published by Belson (e.g. Belson, 1967, 1969, 1973) and has occasionally been criticised (Parker, 1963; Belson, 1963). Essentially what it does is to try and control for the various competing explanations of a relationship between two variables. For example, if we find that heavy TV viewers tend to commit more serious acts of violence than light viewers of TV, we may find it difficult to prove that this is the result of watching a lot of television. There are many competing alternative explanations. For example, perhaps working-class youths watch more television and also tend to be more aggressive than middle-class youths. Thus, the relationship between viewing and aggression is due to social class, not a direct causal effect of viewing on aggression. In order to take into account this competing explanation of the original relationship, we need in some way to control for the differences in social class. Belson's method involves taking the high and low TV viewing groups and dividing each of these into separate subgroups—one working class, one middle class. Further competing explanations can be taken into account by subdividing these four groups more. The procedure continues until nothing can be gained by further divisions. Perhaps all of the competing explanations have been taken into account or the subgroups are becoming too small to allow further analysis. The final stage involves working out the aggressiveness of heavy viewers. Then for the light viewers we *weight the numbers in each of the final subgroups in such a way that there is essentially the same number in each of the subgroups as in the equivalent subgroup of the heavy TV viewers, and then work out the mean aggression score for this weighted sample of light viewers.* These two means are the levels of aggression allowing for the initial differences between the heavy and light viewers.

It is called the *stable* correlate method since it ignores variables which could not be affected by those in the original relationship. So, in our example, there is no realistic possibility that watching a lot of television or being aggressive are causing viewers to be working class. Social class is a stable correlate of aggression and TV viewing because it cannot be affected by them but it can affect them. Of course, Belson has a difficult task deciding what 'stable correlates' to include. He takes a long list of possibilities (may be as many as two hundred or more) and eliminates those which are uncorrelated with the original variables. Unless the stable correlate variable is in fact correlated with both of the original variables (in this example, viewing and aggression), it is impossible for it to explain the original 'presumed' causal relationship. There is no guarantee that all 'control' variables have been included, of course, but Belson is very thorough.

The research itself consisted of extensive interviews with London adolescents. Information was gathered about the boys' mass media use, their aggressiveness, and other important features of their lives. Of course, despite elaborate questioning procedures designed to increase the validity of these self-reports, it is uncertain whether boys report their aggression honestly. Other questions are equally suspect. For example, Belson asked the boys to indicate what programmes they watched. The list included some that had ceased to be broadcast in 1960. Given that the research was carried out in 1972–3 and that the boys were aged 13–16 years, boys were being asked to make meaningful statements about television programmes they could not have seen since they were 3 years old! Exactly what influence such rather silly features of the research had on the total pattern of results is unclear. Even ignoring these criticisms the results are not as clear-cut as at first would appear.

One impressive finding of Belson's study is that boys with high levels of exposure to television violence commit 49% more acts of *serious* violence than those seeing little. It is so impressive as to be almost unbelievable. Social scientists have never seriously contended that media violence is that harmful. Typically only relatively small 'effects' have been claimed at worst. Obviously, the sheer magnitude of Belson's findings arouses suspicion. Bearing in mind that Belson writes 'this finding, for serious violence is probably one of the most important results of the enquiry' (p. 390) it is worthwhile listing the main reasons for mistrusting such findings:

1. *There is equally strong evidence that TV viewing in general and exposure to non-violent TV have as much effect as violent TV.* In order to establish with conviction that there is a causal relationship between watching violent TV and aggression it is necessary to show that the relationship is specific to violent programmes. If exposure to non-violent programmes also correlates with aggressiveness in the viewer, then it is difficult to argue that violence on TV is having an effect. Belson's data clearly show that exposure to violent TV, non-violent TV, and all sorts of TV are equally correlated with aggression in the viewer. So Belson needs to explain why non-violent TV seems to be as dangerous as violent TV.

2. *The relationship between TV exposure and aggressiveness is not a simple one despite the claims made about TV violence.* Belson's method of analysing his data tends to give the impression that there are two groups of subjects—those who watch a lot of violent TV who tend to be aggressive, and those who watch very little violent TV and tend not to be aggressive. That is, the more violent TV, the more violent the viewer. This simple relationship makes it possible for Belson to imply that cutting down on media violence would reduce violence in society. Close inspection of the data reveals this to be shortsighted. In fact (according to graphs in Belson, 1978, pp. 380–2) the relationship between violence and viewing is curvilinear and not the straight line implied by Belson's policy recommendations. Thus, although aggressiveness increases with increased violence viewing for the first part of the graph, there is a peak after which the aggressiveness of the viewer declines with increased exposure to violent TV. That is, heavy and light viewers of TV violence alike are less aggressive than middle range viewers. Whether there is a positive or negative relation between viewing and aggression depends on where the split is made between heavy and light viewers. If it is made before the peak of the graph the relationship is positive, if after negative! In addition, it is equally logical to argue that we can reduce aggression in society by

increasing the amounts of violence watched as by decreasing it. For some reason, Belson seems purblind to this possibility, which objectively is just as logical although not appealing to Belson's emotions.

Belson's report is vast and deals with many facets of the TV violence issue. We have merely dismissed the evidence Belson claims to be the most crucial. Other evidence he presents (e.g. that linking less serious acts of violence to TV violence) fails to meet his own criteria in various ways. For example, he cannot eliminate the possibility that aggressive boys like to watch violent programmes rather than violent programmes cause them to be aggressive. As one of the 'strongest' correlational studies of the effects of media violence in recent years, it dramatically reveals the sorts of oversights made in evaluating this sort of data.

An Experimental Field Study

Given the limitations of correlational field studies and reservations about over-zealous generalization from laboratory experiments, alternatives are needed. The obvious one is to carry out laboratory-style experiments in the real world. These are the so-called field experiments in which experimental manipulations of key variables are carried out in natural settings. These have been rare in mass communication research. Credible field experiments on such complex topics are not easily arranged and carried out. Neither have they been well received. One of the earliest attempts to do such research (Feshbach and Singer, 1971) was subject to a barrage of criticism (e.g. Liebert *et al.*, 1972) which may have discouraged others thinking along the same lines. Much of the criticism of the Feshbach and Singer experiment was probably motivated by scepticism about the claim to have found catharsis. But, it is important to add that a replication (Wells, 1973) failed to reproduce the findings. Nevertheless, a series of experimental field studies was carried out a few years later by a group of psychologists based around the University of Wisconsin. These included Leonard Berkowitz whom we have already mentioned (Parke *et al.*, 1977). Not only this but a cross-cultural replication was carried out by Leyens (Leyens and Camino, 1974) in Belgium.

Superficially the methodology employed and the relative consistency of the findings in these studies are impressive. However, they tend to hide rather more intriguing conclusions that might be drawn. The research took place in institutional settings and involved late adolescents who were being held for delinquency offences. Each research site was a penal institution structured around a cottage system. A cottage was the basic housing unit and was self-sufficient and self-contained. Each accommodated about thirty boys randomly assigned to that cottage by the institution. Researchers observed the activities of the boys over a 3-week period to obtain baseline measures of aggression and other activities. Then, on a random basis, members of the cottages were shown over a period of several days either a number of aggressive films or non-aggressive films. During this phase the behaviour of the boys continued to be monitored. Finally, after the film shows had ceased, the boys were observed for yet another 3-week period. the films were full-length, uncut, cinema films.

The results can be stated clearly. Those delinquents who saw the aggressive films were more aggressive than those who saw the non-aggressive films. This was particularly so during the period when the films were being shown, though it seemed to persist in the post-film weeks. These findings emerged when comparing pre-film and film period measures and when comparing the experimental with the control group. The Howitt and Cumberbatch (1975) no-effects position is obviously incorrect. Or is it?

Criticisms of this research may revise this. First of all, most of the evidence comes from the ratings of observers sited in the cottages. These were undergraduate students. There is no reason to think that they were oblivious to which experimental condition the subjects were in—that is, unaware of whether the boys saw the aggressive film or not. There was also no reason to think them unaware of the beliefs of the researchers. After all they were students of professors who had argued for many years that media violence was harmful. One should not be too surprised if they were inadvertently influenced by this to make their ratings accordingly. Naturally there is no proof of this since we are dependent on the writings of Berkowitz *et al.* for our information about the research. The authors give quite impressive figures for the inter-rater reliabilities of the observations. As these are based on an initial, pre-experimental period of observation and no reliability checks were made later on, it cannot be assumed that the raters remained as reliable throughout the research.

More important are the rates of aggression in the pre-film and the film periods. In the pre-film period the boys were allowed to watch the things on television they normally did. No restrictions were placed on what the boys viewed. However, during the film period, the boys were not allowed television at all. Their entertainment consisted solely of the films they were being shown. In a real sense the pre-film aggression levels represent the aggression caused by television *and all other sources* put together. Many of the boys showed very little aggression at all during this time. During the film period, *when TV was prohibited*, aggression rates in the boys increased substantially. Indeed, for certain groups of boys who were initially unaggressive, the effect of one violent film (or a series of violent films) was to increase their aggressiveness something like forty- or fifty-fold (judging from the graphical data presented). Now this is remarkably powerful evidence of the lack of effects of television on aggressiveness. A single violent cinema film had many times the effect that the usual television diet had! This is, of course, making the generous assumption that television was solely or mainly responsible for the pre-film levels of aggression. The data is thus much more in line with Howitt and Cumberbatch's (1975) argument than apparent at first. This is crucial since Parke *et al.* (1977) cite Howitt and Cumberbatch as an example of those who seriously question the generalizability of laboratory findings. Parke *et al.* appear to think that their field experiments make such a position untenable. Patently they do not. Indeed, at face value the data vindicate planners of television programmes. But, in truth, the contrast between the effects of the television diet and the cinema films is so great that it is more likely that the methodology has 'grey' areas hiding inadequacies.

Conclusions

This discussion of the effects of mass media violence has emphasized the 'no effects' point of view. No apologies are offered for presenting this minority view since most discussions blandly accept the harmful effects thesis. One of the most surprising things has been how readily textbooks in psychology and social psychology have adopted this viewpoint. Even more surprising is that some of the worst of the studies are heralded as methodological 'wonders', held up to textbook writers for admiration. The best example of these is a study by Lefkowitz, Eron and Walder (1971). Essentially what they did was to follow up a sample of children 10 years after an earlier study (Eron, 1963). This had found a modest correlation between assertiveness and liking violent TV programmes. In the follow-up 10 years later it was found that those initially high on liking TV were more assertive. However, this only applied to ratings of liking TV violence at the age of about 7; it did not apply to ratings 10 years later. Thus there is apparently some sort of delayed influence. What the textbook writers tend to ignore is that the ratings made at the age of 17 were retrospective and presumably applied to the child at the age of about 11 or so. The statistical analysis may be impressive, but the data on which it is built is crude. Refined statistics applied to crude and unsatisfactory data are worthless. Nevertheless this study receives by far the most attention in the texts (e.g. Baron, Byrne, and Griffitt, 1974; Neale and Liebert, 1980).

In many ways mass media violence research has been a profound embarrassment to the researchers themselves as well as mass communication research in general. Despite being the most intensively researched aspect of the media, it remains hotly debated and inconclusive. Excuses about the lack of research just do not apply, though it might be argued that the wrong sort of research has been repeated *ad nauseam*. If researchers cannot give satisfactory answers to questions on which they have spent much time and money, what chance is there that they can come up with anything worthwhile in less researched areas? A partial excuse is that much difficulty comes from insisting on proof of a causal relationship between viewing and violence. Many research questions do not impose this requirement. The problems created by the threat to ideologies concerning freedom and censorship by evidence of the harmful effects of the media should not be underestimated. The best weapon in the armoury of those favouring the censorship and control of the mass media is proof that TV harms those least able to decide for themselves what is fit to view. The price of proving one way or other the effects of the media is an undermining of either the pro- or anti-censorship lobbies. While finding that TV promotes a favourable attitude to foreign holidays raises no hackles, it is unlikely that research threatening deep-seated ideologies will pass unqueried, unchallenged, and unscorned.

9

Sex, Eroticism, and Pornography

STANDARDS of what is obscene and pornographic have changed substantially. So, in succession, during the last 50 years worries have been expressed about the effects of Rudolph Valentino in the *Sheik* on the sexual behaviour of young girls; the effects of showing a married couple asleep in the same bed; the effects of portrayals of full frontal nudity; the effects of scenes of sexual intercourse real or simulated, and so forth. The march of progress or the slippery path into moral decline is not smooth. Taking the long-term view, standards concerning what a consenting adult should be allowed to see, hear, or read have changed considerably. This has taken place essentially as a series of hiccups. So in the 1930s the cinema became less liberal as a result of the activities of the Hays Office. This, among other arbitrary edicts, limited the length of a screen kiss to a few seconds. A single legal decision (for example, the *Lady Chatterley's Lover* case) opened permissive floodgates. The abandonment of the Lord Chamberlain's duties in the theatre effectively threw out pre-censorship of plays in Great Britain by the establishment in the 1960s. The events which led to these changes in standards cannot be detailed here nor can the contribution of individuals be fully explained. There are signs that certain men in their role of censors have contributed more to the changes in standards in the mass media than most. For example, John Trevelyan, the British film censor of the 1960s, saw his role as walking the tightrope between the forces of change and reaction, subtly moving the boundaries without too much concern over his own point of view. He was almost more of an arbitrator than a censor. The role of the police in this process cannot be overstated either, since they are major interpreters of the law. Consequently they can vary considerably the standards accepted in the community. Individual citizens have also from time to time used the courts to change the standards of what is decent.

Is Pornography a Problem for Mass Communication Research?

Pornography is not a major issue in connection with the truly *mass* media. Nudity and depictions of sexual intercourse in television programmes may cause some concern but there is a substantial gap between these and what is shown in pornographic magazines. On the other hand, there is no evidence or definitive argument to prove that crudely pornographic material is more harmful than the relatively mild erotica shown on television. There is no dividing line that can be drawn. This is especially so given constantly changing standards. Anyway, as an extreme case, the study of pornography may tell us something of the effects of milder 'erotic' depictions in the media. Sometimes the mass media are subject to accusations much like those laid at the door of out and out pornographers.

There have been occasions when the media have overstepped the mark. The 'topless radio' programmes in the United States are an instance (Carlin, 1976). These are daytime programmes, usually aimed at women listeners, in which listeners phone in to the station for an 'on-air' discussion. These debates were on vital national issues such as varieties of oral sex. The above fell somewhat foul of the public attitude that although what consenting adults see, read, or listen to in private may be alright, it is wrong that young people should be involuntarily exposed to the same material. A lunchtime programme broadcast on radio could be heard by youngsters. Action by the broadcasting licensing authority stopped the broadcasts which had attracted large audiences and had been copied by several stations.

Scott and Franklin (1972) investigated the changing standards concerning sexual matters in the mass circulation magazines. They were *Readers Digest, McCall's, Life, Look, Saturday Evening Post, Time* and *Newsweek*. Equivalent sets of issues from 1950, 1960, and 1970 were used to enable comparisons over time. Each reference to sex was tabulated by type and classified as liberal, neutral, or conservative. Over successive years there was an increase in the number of sex-related items and the proportion of space devoted to them. Surprisingly, attitudes did not become markedly more liberal although there was a decline in the number of conservative attitudes expressed between 1950 and 1960. Fornication, adultery, prostitution, promiscuity, venereal disease, abortion, birth control, pregnancy and illegitimacy became treated slightly more liberally. Sex education, censorship, and women's sexuality tended to become more neutrally (rather than more liberally or more conservatively) evaluated. This might reflect the greater complexity of the issues involved. The mass media seem at least to respond to changes in social values. Whether, in fact, they lead public opinion is more difficult to judge. A content analysis of sexual intimacy in

American prime-time television (Fernandex-Collado and Greenberg, 1978) revealed some striking trends. Sexual intimacy was taken to include verbal references as well as visual depictions. Most sex on TV takes place between unmarried partners (47%), prostitution accounted for another 28%, and homosexual acts, rape, and intercourse between married partners were all relatively infrequent at around 6%. This would create an interesting worldview in those who believed what they saw on television. Visual or verbal references to sex occurred at a frequency approaching twice per hour.

For what it's worth, pornography tends to be thematically (apart from in the obvious ways) different from the content of the rest of the mass media. Bearing in mind the earlier discussion of sexism in the mass media, pornography provides a better balance between the sexes while retaining the crudest of sexist attitudes. Smith (1976) chose to study the motifs of pornographic paperback fiction. He typifies the structure of these books as a string of sexual episodes tied together with transitional non-sexual activity. Over the publication dates covered (1967–74), the amount of sexual content increased substantially. Quite unlike any other sort of media, women were very well represented numerically. Thirty-eight per cent of all female characters were housewives, a good many more were students, and most of the rest were clerical or secretarial workers. Overwhelmingly they were young and white. It is a male-dominated world in terms of attitudes and instigations to action. It is also surprisingly free from weird individuals either sexually or socially defined. The males have their sexual organs in good working order and sexual problems are rare.

So although it is recognized that pornography as such is of relatively minimal concern to the mass communications researcher, nudity, eroticism, and sexuality feature in more run-of-the-mill communication. Since there is no evidence of argument which proves that bare breasts in a daily newspaper are less 'harmful' than close-ups of genitals engaged in sexual intercourse, an investigation of pornography might be helpful in understanding the mass media a little better. This is not to say that there are no major differences in standards between the two. In terms of public acceptability there is an obvious and deep division. However, the point that everything in this area is relative should not be forgotten. Bare breasts in newspapers previously might have warranted prosecutions for obscenity.

Pornography, Erotica, and Public Standards

One of the common themes in the literature on pornography is the question of offence to the public's standards of decency. This provides the only powerful alternative to the usual complaint that pornography causes rape, illegitimacy, and other related social problems and so should be banned. If it cannot be proven that pornography causes such harms, then it is useful to fall back on the argument that 'normal' people just do not want pornography around. Despite the fact that research shows that 'normal' people often do voluntarily expose themselves to pornography (e.g. Burns, 1972), there are fairly large-scale anti-pornography pressure groups which are clearly outraged by it. In this section two studies which suggest how problematic the question of public taste can be will be considered.

The differences in male and female responses to erotica are almost certainly less real than apparent (e.g. Byrne and Lamberth, 1971). Although women are more likely to express a lack of interest in such material, their sexual responses to it measured physiologically are more like men's than their attitudes. Stauffer and Frost (1976) studied the differences in interest of males and females in sexually-oriented magazines of the type freely available in shops. Of course, the bulk of such magazines are aimed at a male readership so it would not be at all surprising that women should be disinterested in these. But *Playgirl* and *Playboy* cater for the two sexes and are produced by the same organization to similar standards. Having established that males and females were equally interested in the feature articles found in a non-sexual magazine (*Saturday Evening Post*), the authors went on to compare interest in sexually-oriented magazines appropriate to each sex. The findings were clear. For example, 90% of men judged the nudity in *Playboy* as of an appropriate degree of explicitness, whereas only 60% of women judged the nudity in *Playgirl* to be so. The men and women were asked to list a number of adjectives which described how they felt as a consequence of reading the magazine. Significantly, as many as a third of women said they felt dirty, cheap, guilty, rotten or bad. The authors suggest that the women's ambivalence about male nudity is a reaction to the social meaning of a woman enjoying such sexuality rather than the content itself. What is interesting is the fairly large differences between individuals and the sexes in response to such magazines. Our next example shows the problem of a censor trying to negotiate his way through public standards.

The Andy Warhol film *Trash* was refused a certificate for public exhibition by the British Board of Film Censors in the early 1970s. Howitt (1972) showed the film, in its original uncut form, to a varied group of individuals which included clerical staff, postgraduate trainee teachers, students, middle-class housewives, and others—not a scientific cross-section of society but a reasonable selection of different points of view. The film itself has caused the censors problems because it linked drugs and sex in one plot. The film included total male and female nudity, oral sex, attempted rape, masturbation with a beer bottle, intercourse with a very pregnant woman, drug injections, and heroin addiction amongst its wares.

There was no advocacy of the use of drugs as a way of life and the film had a somewhat moralistic tone despite the activities portrayed. The response of this audience to the film is intriguing and a little unexpected. They were asked to list those incidents, episodes, or scenes from the film by which they personally felt upset, disgusted, or offended. About a quarter had not found anything of this sort at all but the remainder had. The most common nominations were the scenes in which the 'hero' injected himself with heroin. Not because of a moral position, but as one wrote, 'the needle scene made me feel bloody ill . . . just can't look at needles'. Sixty-two per cent of the audience were upset by this 'mainlining'. The next most frequently mentioned scene was one in which the 'heroine' masturbated with the aid of a beer bottle, although only 19% of the audience mentioned it. This cannot be understood easily in terms of moral condemnation of the act since rather fewer complained about the scene of attempted rape. While considering the issue of moral objections, more intriguing although numerically less impressive was the 8% of respondents who complained about the scene in which the hero attempts intercourse, at her invitation, with a very pregnant girl. Although the woman's breasts were bare and her bulge manifest, the nudity in the scene was less frank than other scenes involving intercourse. Some of the audience worried about the consequences for the unborn baby, although in the film the woman reassures the man on this matter. A 39-year-old married man with one child wrote: 'Slight upset at the idea of Joe having intercourse with the pregnant woman—but this is my *own* problem and the sense of upset died away as the sequence went on.'

Squeamishness rather than moral outrage seemed to pervade responses to the film. There was certainly a number of people who objected in some way to the bad language or the nudity but this amounted to only a tiny percentage. The audience had a variety of interpretations of what they saw the 'message' of the film to be though none considered that it was actively promoting drugs. This contrasts markedly with the fears of the British censors. Eventually, with some cuts, the film received a certificate.

Standards of offence to public taste are like shifting sand and change continually, perhaps to accommodate to new standards of explicitness or new shocks. They do not easily provide a ready answer to coping with pornography and erotica.

Major Reviews of the Effects of Pornography

The social scientific literature on the effects of pornography cannot be adequately reviewed in a short space. The data is not sufficiently clear nor the researchers sufficiently of one mind to allow such a summary.

Consequently probably the best way of introducing the reader to this area is to present an overview of some of the major attempts to reach firm conclusions in this area. Obviously summaries of summaries have limitations and additional evidence is cited when necessary.

The Presidential Commission on Obscenity and Pornography

The most important of the initiatives into the area of obscenity and pornography was the Commission on Obscenity and Pornography which, in 1970, reported its findings to Richard Nixon, the President of the United States. It had been instigated in 1967 by President Lyndon Johnson through Public Law 90–100 enacted by Congress. The duties of the Commission were:

1. With the aid of constitutional law authorities, to analyse the laws pertaining to the control of obscenity and pornography; and to evaluate and recommend definitions of obscenity and pornography;
2. To ascertain the methods employed in the distribution of obscene and pornographic materials and to explore the nature and volume of traffic in such materials.
3. To study the effects of obscenity and pornography upon the public, and particularly minors, and its relationship to crime and other antisocial behaviour; and
4. To recommend such legislative, administrative, or other advisable and appropriate action as the Commission deems necessary to regulate effectively the flow of such traffic, without in any way interfering with constitutional rights.

The Commission made a number of recommendations as requested. The major ones were:

> The Commission recommends that federal, state, and local legislation prohibiting the sale, exhibition, or distribution of sexual materials to consenting adults should be repealed (p. 51).

> The Commission recommends . . . prohibiting the commercial distribution or display for sale of certain sexual materials to young persons (p. 56).

> The Commission recommends . . . prohibiting public displays of sexually explicit pictorial material, and approves—(prohibiting) . . . the mailing of unsolicited advertisements of a sexually explicit nature. (p. 60).

These recommendations seem to be based on the view that research evidence shows no significant effects of pornography on crime, delinquency, sexual or nonsexual deviancy and severe emotional disturbances; that there is a good deal of evidence to suggest that exposure to such material is a part of growing up in many normal individuals; that a large proportion of people object strongly to and would be offended by receiving unsolicited sexually explicit material; and that there is no research evidence on the effects of pornography on young children so they should continue to be protected from it. Obscenity and pornography may promote sexual arousal but this does not mean that they lead to deviant and socially condemned practices.

In many ways these recommendations are relatively bland. Indeed if implemented they would probably have only changed substantially the prosecution rate for those who engage in the sale of sexually explicit materials. Adults who want such publications, as the technical reports of the commission shows, do not have too much trouble obtaining them. Seen in the context of the late 1960s and early 1970s, little of major consequence would have changed. Had the same recommendations appeared 30, 40, or 50 years earlier then the changes would have been much more profound. But the recommendations of the committee found little favour with the establishment. Senate did not like the recommendations and Richard Nixon, who left office in disgrace over Watergate and came nearer than any other United States President to being impeached, whose Vice-president Agnew was forced to resign in rather sordid circumstances, whose closest assistants in the White House served prison sentences, responded to the claims of no danger in pornography with the following grand words:

> If that be true it must also be true that great books, great paintings, and great plays have no enobling effect on man's conduct. Centuries of civilisation and ten minutes of common sense will tell us otherwise.

This sort of rejection could have been anticipated from the Commission's own data. For example, their researchers found that about 50% of people thought that erotic material lead to a breakdown of morals and lead people to commit rape (Abelson *et al.*, 1970). But the Commission was not unanimous about these conclusions and there were several dissentions and minority reports. The main reason, and the lynchpin in the argument, for the dissent lay in the interpretation of the effects research commissioned or collated by the technical staff. The report of the effects sub panel states that:

> Research to date . . . provides no substantial basis for the belief that erotic materials constitute a primary or significant cause of the

development of character deficits or that they operate as a significant determinative factor in causing crime and delinquency.

This conclusion is stated with due and perhaps excessive caution, since it is obviously not possible and never would be possible, to state that never on any occasion, under any conditions, did any erotic material ever contribute in any way to the likelihood of any individual committing a sex crime. Indeed, no such statement could be made about any kind of nonerotic material. On the basis of the available data, however, it is not possible to conclude that erotic material is a significant cause of sex crime (p. 243).

The evidence in favour of this position was seen by some to be merely a biased selection of the available research evidence. In a minority report by Hill and Link, which dissents from the major conclusions of the commission, majority view is described as 'a Magna Carta for the pornographer' (p. 385). These Commission members draw on a critical review of the research evidence by Victor Cline, a psychologist, in order to challenge the conclusions of the Commission. Cline goes through much of the Commission's evidence and shows how rather different conclusions might be drawn, that is if the selection of evidence is less biased in favour of the no-effects viewpoint. There are points at which arguably the Commission ignored conflicting evidence. Cline's viewpoint is not quite so overwhelmingly conclusive as it at first appears. Certainly he fails to make criticisms of all the Commission's findings.

An important feature of the research is those studies linking exposure to pornography with various 'deviant' sexual activities. There is some evidence that the more *sexually active* individual is more likely to be exposed to pornography (Abelson *et al.*, 1970; Zetterberg, 1970). However, sexual activity is not the same as sexual crime. In a study by Walker (1970) sex offenders often said pornography had something to do with them committing their crimes. This conflicts with other evidence (e.g. Gebhard *et al.*, 1965). Such claims are difficult to evaluate since there is the possibility that the sex offenders use pornography as an excuse for their crimes. The offenders might believe there is something to be gained by admitting to being led astray by undesirable material. One additional problem is that this sort of evidence can only paint a black picture since it would not make sense for non-offenders to be asked such a question.

But the major focus of Cline's attention had to be the so-called Danish experiment in which virtually all legal control on pornography was abandoned in the mid-1960s. Sexually explicit materials had been relatively freely available for several years before these changes. Ben-Veniste (1970) described the changes in sex crimes reported to the police over the period 1958 to 1969. The theory is that if pornography causes sex crimes then there should be a surge in rates of sex crimes once pornography became freely available. This did not seem to happen. During the period in question there was a reduction in sex crimes reported to Copenhagen police. The trends included a 48% decline in rape, a 61% decline in exhibitionism, a 77% decline in peeping, and a 78% decline in homosexual offences. What do these changes in reporting rates mean? Had there been a substantial change in the number of offences actually occurring? Had offences stayed unchanged but reporting become less frequent? No radical change occurred after the change in the law. Ben-Veniste (1971) and Kutchinsky (1971) examined whether other factors such as changes in public attitudes, changes in police practice, and changes in the law could account for these big reductions. Apparently they could not. These other changes were just too small. Cline (1971) takes issue with these claims, pointing out that Kutchinsky (1971) found that changes in the reporting rates of *certain* sex crimes could be explained wholly by changes in public attitude to the crime and reporting it to the police. (This was so for the crimes of exhibitionism and indecency towards women.) Nothing in this undermines the view that freeing pornography from legal controls does not worsen the crime rate. It does work against the view that a sexually less repressive society would allow individuals to express their sexuality without committing sex crimes. But given the massive under-reporting of sexual offences, the data is probably so inadequate that one could not wish to make judgements of this sort in any case without casting all caution to the wind.

There is other data on sex crime rates in Copenhagen during this period. Bachy (1976) questions the figures put forward by Kutchinsky. He refers to evidence covering a relatively greater period than that of Kutchinsky. This data, collected from police sources in Copenhagen, is substantially different. For example, Kutchinsky suggests that rape and attempted rape remain just about constant after the freeing of pornography, and that intercourse with minors and indecent exposure decline. In contrast, Bachy's data suggests rape, attempted rape, and intercourse with minors increased but agrees that indecent exposure has declined. Bachy is willing to conclude that:

> we cannot conclude anything, or that the situation with respect to crime has not changed much since the legalization of pornography, or that it has become worse (p. 42).

The reason for the uncertainty is that standards had changed in many ways. For example, legal public nudity had increased, which probably reduced the number of complaints about indecent exposure. The one conclusion that Bachy is unwilling to go along with is that things had improved following changes in the law. The rationale behind this is unclear given that he willingly admits the total invalidity of such statistics. But Bachy's attitude is better understood by looking at his impressionistic account of the under-lying context of pornography. This he sees as:

> closely bound to violence and prostitution, to drugs and exploitation, to shady business and politics. These connections make it one of the cancers corroding Western society (p. 43).

Although, for obvious reasons, criminal statistics from the so-called Danish Experiment have received considerable attention in discussions of the effects of pornography, less consideration has been given to the figures from other countries. These may have had similar changes in the availability of sexually explicit materials without the dramatic changes in the law that occurred in Denmark. For example, in Great Britain over the last few years there has been much more 'pornographic' material freely available. It would be expected that the cumulative effects of such material on the moral standards in society and on crimes like rape, unlawful sexual intercourse, and indecent assault should be reflected in crime statistics, if the material was having any effect at all. But in fact, examination of the criminal statistics leave a rather undramatic picture of changes in the last few years. For example, if we take recent figures (Command Papers, 1978) the changes in the numbers of indictable sexual offences recorded by the police in England and Wales can be examined. (That is, the figures for sexual crimes *known* to the police rather than *individuals prosecuted* or persons convicted.) Although these figures change from year to year, it is difficult to discern consistent upward trends in *total sexual offences*.

Year	Total Sexual Offences	Rape	Indecent Assault on Female	Unlawful Sexual Intercourse
1969	23,526	869	12,181	5,158
1970	24,163	884	12,609	5,216
1971	23,621	784	12,400	5,282
1972	23,505	893	11,977	5,385
1973	25,736	998	13,294	5,503
1974	24,698	1052	12,417	5,050
1975	23,731	1040	11,809	4,860
1976	22,203	1094	10,901	4,608
1977	21,313	1015	11,048	3,924
1978	22,367	1243	11,814	3,705

For some of the specific crimes there seem to be clearer trends. Indecent assault on females has tended to decline slightly, unlawful sexual intercourse seems to have declined markedly, and only in the case of rape has there been an upward shift. Taken at their face value, it is difficult to see a pattern in these statistics which enables statements like 'sex crimes are on the increase' to be made. The change in the numbers of rapes known to the police may be due to changes in attitude towards reporting such crimes. During the 1970s the public became more aware of the double victimization of women who have been raped. The first victimization is the sexual assault and the second is the profound psychological shock of publicly being interrogated about one's sex life during the course of the trial. The feeling was that women were not reporting rapes because of this, which allowed rapists to go free. Perhaps the publicity given to this injustice encouraged more determined women to come forward. Furthermore, the Sexual Offences Amendment Act of 1976 made it possible for rape victims to remain anonymous in court, which may account for the big increase in the reported rape figure in 1978. But of course this is to play guessing games with the crime figures, the validity of which as a measure of true rates of crime (or even as indicators of changes in the true rates of crime) is suspect. It is important to know what the official statistics say since these enable us to discount some of the wilder claims which are made about sex crimes. Misconceptions about crime statistics fuel the pornography debate.

But just as claims that the Presidential Commission failed to adequately report data the same charge could be laid against him. For example, he quotes the findings of a study by Mosher and Katz (1971):

> The data clearly support the proposition that aggression against women increases when that aggression is instrumental to securing sexual stimulation (through seeing pornography) (p. 393)

which is an accurate transcription from the original report. However, it conceals the fact that 'aggression against women' is shorthand for saying the subject was required as part of the experimental procedures to verbally aggress against a female experimenter. Seeing pornography as such definitely did not increase aggression. Telling subjects that they could take part in a further piece of research if their aggression levels against the female experimenter were high enough did. The subjects were perhaps merely keen to take part further in the research. General conclusions about the effects of pornography on aggression against women are meaningless when the truth is revealed.

Longford Committee

In Britain, the Longford Committee Investigating Pornography, was announced in 1971 and reported in 1972. Its outstanding features were that it had no formal basis in government or any other institution, and the ribald, mocking, and intense press coverage that the activities of the chairman of the committee, the slightly bumbling 'do gooder' Lord Longford, received. The Committee comprised a remarkable collection of notables, dignitaries, churchmen, pop singers, disc jockeys, authors, and others. In the course of its information gathering the committee received evidence and advice from an even wider variety of individuals and organizations. Furthermore, much to the delight of the press, the committee chairman took it on himself to enter into a fact-finding mission to foreign parts to view the lewdest of displays first hand. Given a clear initial anti-pornography stand on the part of Lord Longford, this and other similar episodes were much relished by the media.

The report itself inevitably was anti-pornography. The evidence adduced was substantially below the calibre normally required by social scientists. Naturally, the American Pornography and Obscenity Committee was alluded to since it had published its weighty volumes the year before. The Longford Committee considered anecdotal evidence very favourably. This almost invariably supported the anti-pornography viewpoint. The anecdotes used would:

> show to any fair minded person that pornography is *capable* of causing serious damage (Longford, 1972, p. 102).

It is impossible to pick out a representative anecdote since no common theme seems to emerge. One in particular is probably worth mentioning. This came from the headmaster of a boarding school. Sexual assaults on younger boys, including buggery, were occurring at his school. A scrap book full of different types of pornography featured in the activities of the culprits. The report goes on to describe the statements of a psychiatrist called in to investigate the boys:

> One boy, aged 14, 'was led by the pornography to seek female satisfaction in the villages around'. Three other boys, all aged 15, had 'sought further stimulus by attempting arson, burglary and by collecting offensive weapons and ammunition'. Five other boys had sought further stimulus in witchcraft and drugs. In the case of one of them it had precipitated epileptic type attacks and amnesia, and another boy suffered severe depression and required treatment at a mental hospital.

In contrast, five of those involved had become so disgusted by the whole process that they decided to give it all up and turn to Christianity for help (p. 110).

Despite the assertions of the expert investigator (the psychiatrist); the causal connection between exposure to pornography and real-life sodomy, sexual assault, and even turning to Christianity is a little tenuous. That is not to say that it is not real, merely that we are forced to *suppose* that reading pornography is not a consequence of the disturbed personalities of these boys but a cause. It would seem to be going a little far, after all, to suggest that an epileptic type fit, arson, and other seemingly unrelated activities are induced by pornography. In any case anecdotes of this type may overemphasize the negative consequences rather than help us come to a balanced assessment of the overall effects of pornography.

The remaining evidence used by the Longford Committee consisted largely of a partisan criticism of the American Obscenity and Pornography Commission's data and interpretation. Longford essentially follows the line of the American dissenters who asserted that the majority report signatures had failed to evaluate the data as fairly and objectively as it deserved. The methodological criticisms of psychologist Victor Cline are stressed in some detail together with a similar, if derivative, evaluation by Maurice Yaffé, a British psychologist. Yaffé, in his conclusions about the data available at that time, manages to produce yet another version of the usual researcher's plea 'more research needed':

Only time and continued research effort will provide the answers (p. 498).

The Committee failed to find in the opinion of those pillars of society, expert psychologists, a unitary and undisputed statement that pornography has undesirable consequences. Perhaps this encouraged the Committee to view with disfavour the English legal definition that obscenity is that which tends to deprave and corrupt. They wished to substitute the following:

An article or a performance of a play is obscene if its effect, taken as a whole, is to outrage contemporary standards of decency or humanity accepted by the public at large (p. 33).

The Committee felt itself supported by many 'decent' sectors of society. These provided encouragement which probably served to promote the belief that the public at large (whatever that means) would be outraged (whatever that means) by pornography. This is probably true for some of the more extreme forms of pornography but debatable for much of the material which the Committee's report condemns. So while the public at large (by almost any definition) would be outraged by pictures of an adult having sexual intercourse with a 7-year-old girl, less unanimity would be found in responses to the type of nudity carried by the typical men's magazines.

Eysenck's Book

It is worth mentioning the book *Sex, Violence and the Media* by Professor Hans Eysenck (Eysenck and Nias, 1978).

Since he has written at some length over the years about sexual behaviour, Eysenck's opinions might be expected to be better founded than most. The book intertwines the research on the effects of erotic material with the separate literature of mass media violence. This only detracts from the clarity of the presentation rather than adding depth or illumination. Despite Eysenck's chosen structure, the issues involved are not quite the same and the implications of the data in the two areas somewhat different. One reason for this is, of course, that the heightening of normal sexuality (not sex crimes) seems to carry no universal reprobation and might be positively valued by some. Increasing aggression might be generally less acceptable.

Having complained that researchers tend to be seen as a little tentative in their conclusions giving the layman the impression that little or nothing is known, Eysenck redresses the balance by making strong recommendations based on the evidence which caused others to equivocate. Not that his recommendations are particularly objectionable but merely they are not very relevant to the research evidence he cites. For example, he recommends censorship of portrayals of perverted sexual behaviour—sadism, incest, rape, and 'other demonstrably harmful types of behaviour' (p. 256). Presumably this is based on some limited evidence that *one* rapist tended to find images of forcible sexual intercourse with unwilling partners erotic (Abel *et al.*, 1975) and the research (Gebhard *et al.*, 1965) which found that sex offenders were more likely to report being aroused by sadistic themes than controls. However, Eysenck himself writes of the latter that:

> the limitations of the study make any conclusions very uncertain (p. 116)

and since the former is based on a single rapist, it seems to be very weak evidence for the sort of censorship which Eysenck advocates.

Eysenck's second recommendation is that:

the content of a presentation should be judged in relation to the prevailing tone of the presentation (p. 257).

By this he means largely that censorship should be applied to sexual material:

only when it is joined with undesirable secondary matter, such as violence, anti-female sentiments, or the celebration of male *machismo* (p. 260).

He feels that protecting women in this way is as much their right as it is that of racial minorities to be protected from racist propaganda. Whatever sympathies one has with Eysenck's dislike of the treatment of women in pornography, he confounds the issue of sexual explicit material with that of the censorship of unwelcome ideas. The denigration of women does not become acceptable simply because they are allowed to keep their clothes on. Essentially Eysenck falls into the trap that he later recommends others avoid. He writes:

We suggest that the many absurd and often ludicrous suggestions for censorship of what is obviously acceptable material should cease, as they only bring the whole notion of censorship into disrepute (p. 268).

The reference is to those who object to the racist content of, for example, Robinson Crusoe, or protest against the Robinson's Golly on pots of jam. But because Eysenck is not offended by these in no way means that those worried about such crypto-racism are more ludicrous than he in seeking censorship. Some might baulk at allowing freedom to pornographers to denigrate women but the problem of where to draw the line on free speech is not solved by reference to the standards of an atypical psychologist.

All of this is capped by the curious suggestion (intimated to be half serious but as thoroughly argued as any other point in the book) that censorship should be applied irrespective of 'artistic worth' or the 'intent' of the artist. This appears to clash with Eysenck's earlier suggestion that censorship should be applied if there are undesirable secondary themes associated with the erotic material, but he feels that an objective index of sexual activity could be developed. This would free the law from the subjectivity which plagues it at the moment. The logic is that sex oriented material tends to be described as obscene or pornographic when it contains activities which are towards the top of a scale of sexual activity. Thus mutual oral sex to orgasm is high on his scale and is associated with feeling that a passage is obscene or pornographic. Eysenck would appear to see no difference between the so-called 'split-beaver' photograph (female genitals fully exposed) and a Picasso which featured similar detail of the female anatomy—at least in terms of the need for censorship. It is likely that a substantial proportion of the general public would agree (surveys have shown that some familiar works of art are rated as more obscene or pornographic than *Playboy* covers by some sections of the general public). However, as a serious development in censorship it seems to be a retrograde move.

The Williams Committee

The Williams report was published in November 1979 (Report of the Committee on Obscenity and Film Censorship, 1979). Its objectives were, of course, rather wider than the scope of the present discussion, but it did overlap in some part. The report makes independent but informed judgements about the claims of psychologists concerning the effects of obscenity and pornography. The Committee was particularly scathing towards those who fail to recognize the social context in which both research and erotic material exist. For example:

> Eysenck and Nias do not so much dismiss these objections, as ignore them. They leave the unsuspecting reader ignorant that substantial reservations have been widely voiced about the implications of these experimental studies, and this, in our view, diminishes the value of their work as a contribution to the scientific literature. Their book is indeed aimed more at the popular market, drawing partly on press reports to illustrate the alleged effects of media violence (including the now celebrated *Clockwork Orange* murder, but again omitting the information that the young murderer had not actually seen the film); but we thought it a pity that the lay reader should be presented so incautiously with one side of the story (p. 68).

The Williams Committee attempted to see what case could be made from official statistics in England and Wales that there is a link between pornography and the number of sexual offences. They list four major arguments:

1. That no records exist of the availability of pornography over time or even firm evidence of when pornography became increasingly available.
2. The increase in rates of sexual offences began long before pornography has been alleged to have become generally available.
3. The increase in rates of sexual offences has been less than the increase in the rates of crimes in general.

4. In the period 1973–7, which was a time of stability in the rates of rapes and sexual assaults, it is claimed by some to be a period in which pornography was most freely available.

These criticisms make it difficult to argue on the basis of present statistics that pornography acts as a stimulus to the commission of sexual offences. The Committee makes a number of proposals which make partial reference to the effects of literature on pornography:

> The law should rest partly on the basis of harms caused by or involved in the existence of the material: these alone can justify prohibitions; and partly on the basis of the public's legitimate interest in not being offended by the display and availability of the material: this can justify no more than the imposition of restrictions designed to protect the ordinary citizen from reasonable offence.

> The principal object of the law should be to prevent certain kinds of material causing offence to reasonable people or being made available to young people.

> Only a small class of material should be forbidden to those who want it, because an objective assessment of likely harm does not support a wider prohibition.

> The printed word should be neither restricted nor prohibited since its nature makes it neither immediately offensive nor capable of involving the harms we identify, and because of its importance in conveying ideas (p. 159).

These proposals are very liberal indeed. The typical assumption that pornography should not be thrust upon unsuspecting individuals is a major provision to protect those disliking pornography but assumes that the objection is to seeing it rather than its existence. The only pornography to which the Committee objects is that in which an illegal or violent act actually takes place rather than is simulated. Consequently models should not be younger than 16 nor should excessive real violence be depicted. The Committee does appear to shift ground a little. In the main body of the text it feels it unwarranted to draw conclusions about the effects of pornography without being able to prove that there are no effects and in the above passages seems to take the lack of effects for granted. However, nothing in the above proposals seems unreasonable on the basis of research evidence, especially if the interpretations given of sex crime statistics by the Committee are accepted.

Conclusions

While there is no doubt that sexual depictions are sexually arousing to many (Davis and Braucht, 1971; Mosher, 1971) this is in itself not at all surprising and would not be seen as reprehensible by the vast majority of people. There is sufficient evidence to warrant such effects of pornography and erotic materials proven. But this is not at all the same thing as saying that pornography and other erotic material causes sexual crimes or encourages 'perverted' sexual activity. In this overview some of the evidence on the effects of pornography on sexual deviance and sexual crime has been detailed. By and large there has been little in our review to suggest such a link is proven. It is a little simplistic to assume that sexual deviance and sexual crimes are caused by a high degree of sexual arousal (whether caused by pornography or not). There is much more to it than this. For example, how does one explain on this basis the desire to humiliate the victims which manifests itself in many sexual attacks?

Policy recommendations do not altogether flow freely from the evidence reviewed. Some authorities see no justification in censorship and prohibition given the failure to find evidence of clear-cut undesirable consequences of pornography. Whether this means that alternatives to present arrangements are desirable is a different matter. After all the evidence either way is not particularly convincing. The 'safety' measures for protecting the young from pornography at points of sale may not be effective at all in preventing the material from eventually reaching them.

10

Crime and the Mass Media

THE unholy trinity sex, violence and crime have not concerned communications researchers equally. Violence research is *the* dominant theme in mass communications research. Obscenity and pornography because of inherent methodological and ethical difficulties receive less attention. The final member of the trinity, crime, although often blamed on the media has surprisingly been relatively ignored. The likely reason is that crime is so frequently mentioned in the same breath as violence that they are assumed to be synonyms. While public concern about crime is dominated by violent assaults, most crime is not violent. Juvenile delinquency, partly because of its links with popular culture, is blamed on the media. Many see mass communications as the embodiment of Fagin, schooling youngsters in crime. Such worries are understandable. The concept of a teenager is relatively modern. Juvenile delinquency is also a relatively recent concept. Both gained at the same time that television emerged. The temptation to assume a causal link between parallel events is powerful.

What Missing Your Newspaper Really Means!

Probably the most dramatic of all research on crime and the media is that of Payne and Payne (1970). They compared crime rates during newspaper strikes with normal levels. Various theoretical ways in which newspapers could contribute to crime rates are offered. Some are obvious, such as newspapers providing (1) a cathartic release of tensions which would otherwise lead to crime and (2) information about who commits crimes and how. But two imaginative suggestions are made. The first is that newspapers by reporting crime encourage those who use their criminal activities to seek publicity. The second is that fear of publicity and stigma inhibits a potential criminal from committing crime—quite opposite mechanisms depending on different motives.

In Detroit in the 1960s there were several newspaper strikes lasting for periods of up to several months. Comparisons were made between strike and non-strike periods using crime figures by the police department. Two different types of crime were considered—expressive crimes (such as rape, murder and assault) and non-expressive crimes (such as burglary or motor car thefts). The distinction is not very clear although Payne and Payne see it as being between crime which is *an end in itself* and crime which is a *means to achieve other ends*. They hypothesized that expressive crimes would not be affected by newspaper strikes whereas non-expressive crimes would. Car thefts, robbery, and burglary (the non-expressive crimes) were down in the region of 10–20% during the strikes. For the so-called expressive crimes, there were no consistent trends either way. Payne and Payne claim tentative support of their hypotheses from this data.

But how much faith can be placed in these findings? The most important limitation on such data is that crime statistics may not be very reliable. As we have discussed earlier, simply because they are produced by official agencies does not guarantee their validity. In essence the crime figures are social constructions. They are not simple, direct, and clearcut measures of the amount of crime in society but subject to inaccuracies in reporting. One implication of this is that the more serious crimes would be relatively accurately reflected in the crime statistics—it is very difficult to ignore a murder. The less serious crimes such as shoplifting are more likely to be inaccurately recorded in crime statistics. However, the fact that crime rates are subject to such social factors is not, in itself, an explanation of Payne and Payne's findings. One further dimension needs adding in order to draw out the implications fully. The police and the public may be influenced by the press's treatment of crime! The public may be led to believe by the press that certain sorts of crime are on the increase or that there is too much crime. This would encourage them to report offences which otherwise might have gone unreported. The police may be 'encouraged' by the publicity given to crime to show they are doing a good job in detecting crime and arresting criminals. In the absence of the press publicity the police may not need to look at their public image so much. That is, the police may define fewer events as crimes than might otherwise have been the case. Payne and Payne could be confusing expressive crimes with the more serious crimes which the police cannot overlook. Serious crimes would not be expected to vary with strike/non-strike periods which is very much in line with the actual data.

Payne and Payne's research has been reviewed rather critically because it flies in the face of other studies. Given that reinterpretation of their findings was relatively easy, it is tempting to disregard their conclusions. This view is encouraged by other research. Davis (1952) adopted the strategy of relating the amount of crime coverage in newspapers to the amount of crime reported in the Uniform Crime Reports of the FBI during the period 1948–50. It was concluded that for the four Colorado newspapers studied there was substantial variation in the amount of crime they reported at any one time. There was no relationship between the newspaper reports and the amount of crime actually being committed as indicated by criminal statistics. Clark and Blankenburg (1971) related the amount of violence in television programmes each year between 1953 and 1969 to the amount of violent crime recorded. There was no correlation between the two.

Two conclusions follow from all this. The first is that there is no simple causal link between the mass media and crime. The second is that the media do not reflect in any simple and consistent way the levels of crime in the community. Crime is reported on bases other than its frequency in the community.

In England, Halloran, Brown and Chaney (1970) took a somewhat different approach. They compared the television viewing habits delinquents reported to probation officers with those of a matched sample of controls equated in terms of age, social class, sex, intelligence and school attainment. Sheer exposure to television did not discriminate between delinquents and non-delinquents. There was some suggestion in the data that delinquents tended to prefer 'exciting' programmes. In America, Pfuhl (1960, 1970) studied data on about eight hundred boys and girls who completed an anonymous questionnaire on their delinquency (e.g. wanton destruction of property). There was no evidence, according to Pfuhl, that amount of exposure to television and radio actually differentiated between delinquent and non-delinquent youth. However, there does appear to be some association between the use of some mass media and delinquency. This is particularly the case with the cinema. Delinquent youth is more likely to go to the cinema than non-delinquents. The interpretation of this, according to Howitt and Dembo (1974) and Howitt and Cumberbatch (1975) in a sub-cultural account of these relationships, is that certain media serve as a focus for the social activities of delinquent youth. Delinquency is itself a social activity (most delinquent acts being committed by groups of young people rather than isolated youths) so it is not surprising that delinquents, a sociable group, choose the cinema as a base for their recreation. They probably also frequent coffee bars, pubs, street corners, etc., for much the same reasons.

William Belson (1975) studied a large sample of approximately 1500 London boys in the age range 13–16 years in order to elucidate the factors which contribute to juvenile theft. The types of theft involved were many and varied including buying stolen goods, avoiding payment of fares, stealing money, stealing cars, cheating someone out of money, stealing milk, stealing from family or relations, and stealing from shops. The research, although based on essentially simple methods, was thorough to an extreme and very exacting. The researcher took great pains to ensure that the self-reports of thefts were honest and that the many potential causal factors in juvenile stealing were as adequately measured as possible.

The methodology employed was very much like that in Belson's study of aggression (reported in Chapter 8). Since it was a correlational study, some control for a wide range of competing explanations for any relationships found was necessary. For example, if young people who steal watch more television this may not be a causal relationship. There might be a tendency of working-class youths to steal more *and* watch more television. That is not due to television influencing young people to steal. This can be controlled for by equating groups so that the heavy and light viewers are identical in terms of their social class distributions. When this has been done, it becomes unlikely that any differences in theft rates between high and low viewers is explicable in terms of social class. In fact, Belson's technique (called the Stable Correlate Method) weights the distribution of the group of light viewers such that it follows the distribution of the heavy viewers in terms of the most likely extraneous variables which could be causing the correlation between viewing and crime.

The data gave no hint that television is a school for crime. In the early analysis, the greater the amount of stealing the lower the *interest* in watching television and the less actual viewing. This was the case before the extraneous variables were controlled. The differences in viewing behaviour between thieves and the rest disappeared following the use of the stable correlate method. Thus television had no causal influence on theft. Activities such as going to the cinema, getting the latest fashions, dancing, riding a motor bike or scooter, going around with mates, getting into fights with other boys, and having a bit of a wild time were associated with thieving. On the other hand, gardening, welfare work, reading, and going to church or chapel were uncommon in thieves. This fits in with Howitt and Dembo's (1974) subcultural account of apparent media influences, mentioned earlier. It shows a syndrome of street culture activities which are associated with crime. Street culture means those activities that adolescents engage in when the focus of their behaviour is outside their home and the established social order.

Milgram and Stotland (1973) carried out a series of experiments which are worth examining carefully. These included some in which the content of regular television transmissions was systematically varied. Consequently they are very naturalistic experiments into the effects of the media on crime. In one of these experiments a special version of a programme called *Medical Center* was produced. A character in this made an abusive telephone call to a medical charity. Milgram and Stotland wished to know whether this caused 'anti-social behaviour' in the form of similar telephone calls to an authentic medical charity. This authentic charity had some public service advertising during the programme. The experiment compared abusive telephone calls directed to the charity following a 'neutral' episode of the programme (i.e. one which did not show the fictional abusive phone calls) with those received following the critical programme. One important finding was that the number of abusive phone calls following the critical programme was tiny. Furthermore, abusive phone calls were no more frequent following the critical programme than the neutral programme—less so if anything. The lack of effects, given the large audience reached by these programmes in the most naturalistic of all possible experimental research settings, is highly significant. These findings were similar to a variety of studies directed by Milgram and Stotland. All of these left little or nothing to implicate the media in crime.

Crime Coverage and the Shaping of Public Opinion

It has been speculated that media coverage of crime defines for the public the level of crime in their community. That is the public estimates the amount of crime in the press, notes its fluctuations, and reaches conclusions about crime rates. They would need to make allowance for the selectivity of the press and ignore other sources of crime news in the community. Not surprisingly, given such a complex task, attempts to link news with perceptions of crime rates have produced rather negative results:

Three studies are pertinent to this:

1. Davis (1952) found little consistency in changes in crime rates over time, public perceptions of changes in crime rates over time, and the changes in the crime coverage of newspapers over the same period of time. Although it was possible to point to some changes consistent with the hypothesis that crime reporting influences perceptions of crime rates, it was equally possible to point to opposite examples where crime reporting and the public perception of crime were completely at variance.
2. Roshier (1971, 1973) related the type of newspaper read by his subjects to various perceptions of crime and crime rates. Little association was found. The only exception was the suggestion that the public tended to believe that more crimes were solved than really are. The news media tend to overemphasize solved crimes since they attain much of their crime news from court proceedings.
3. Croll (1974) studied several English local newspapers. He found a

negative correlation between estimates of crime rates given by the readers and the news space given to different types of crime. While it is very difficult to explain this negative relationship, it gives absolutely no support to the hypothesis linking public perceptions of crime rates to rates of crime coverage in the news media.

The failure of these studies to find relationships appears to be as much to do with the way in which the question was conceptualized as the lack of influence of the media on the audience. Essentially the news user in the model acts as a highly competent statistician forming accurate estimates of how much crime there is reported in the newspapers he reads. However, the public's perceptions of the amounts of crime reported in the press are highly inaccurate in the first place. So it is not surprising that the hypothesis fails (e.g. Roshier, 1969).

The assumption seems to be that it is the frequency of news stories in the press which influence beliefs about crime rates. One feature of news reports that might have an influence is not so actuarial in nature. For example, opinion polls consistently suggest that the public perceives crime to be on the 'up and up'. This is precisely the message the news media offer. Newspapers frequently contain stories of the trends in criminal statistics. It may be that these are accepted by the public and form the basis of views about crime rates. In this way it would be only specific types of reports—statistical ones—which influence the public's perceptions. That is, the public do not act as their own statisticians but rely on experts.

The mass media mirror crime rates very poorly indeed (Cumberbatch and Beardsworth, 1977). This, together with the failure of the studies reported above to establish any major effects of news media content on the audience encourages sympathy with the conclusions of Cumberbatch and Beardsworth:

> All in all, there seems little evidence to support the view that the mass media are an important 'window on the world' of crime. Since primary experience of crime is so infrequent this poses the baffling problem of where the public obtains its knowledge and beliefs. The problem of the etiology of beliefs and attitude becomes even more puzzling if it is true—as has been reported—that even experience of vicitimization does not influence an individual's attitude toward crime (Ennis, 1967). (p. 86).

Certainly we can reject the simple statistical actuary model of the news user that seems to underpin virtually all of the research discussed above.

The Creation of Moral Panics

Some writers on the mass media have turned away from what they see as the relatively simplistic 'stimulus/response' model of media effects. They stress much more subtle and elusive processes by which the mass media may have an influence on crime. Cohen and Young (1973) give these the titles *amplification* and *sensitization*. As will become very clear, these require rather different orientations and standards of proof from those described earlier.

Stanley Cohen (1973, 1972) focuses on the British mods and rockers phenomenon of the 1960s. These apparently warring factions of young people, each with highly distinctive fashion styles, would descend on seaside towns and cause havoc, according to the press. The initial source of information about where to go during these periods seems to have been word of mouth. Only a tiny proportion of mods and rockers interviewed claimed to have gone to the seaside town directly as a consequence of what they heard in the media. The contribution of the mass media, according to Cohen, was the creation of a definition of events. By this definition the mods and rockers were cast into the role of social deviants. In time they began to live up to their image more and more. By defining those attired in the fashion of mods and rockers as hooligans, the press contributed to the interpretation of everything these youngsters did as hooliganism. Thus, the press and public (and perhaps the mods and rockers themselves) came to be *sensitized* to seeing mods and rockers through hooligan coloured spectacles. Events which were trivial and normally unnewsworthy would be used as part of an inventory of charges to be laid against the mods and rockers. This fed into court and the legal system to produce increased sentences for mods and rockers. This harsh response in its turn fed back to the community and press, heightening concerns about the threats to the established social and moral order posed by the mods and rockers. Through these means, moral panics or overstressed concerns about moral standards in society are created. Cohen summarizes his position as follows:

'. . . the societal reaction in general and the mass media in particular could plausibly be thought to have had the following sorts of effects. . . .

1. Reinforcing and magnifying a predisposition to expect trouble: "something's going to happen".
2. Providing the content for rumours and the milling process, thereby structuring the "something" into potential or actual deviance; such rumours and images facilitated deviance by solidifying the crowd and validating its moods and actions.

3. Creating a set of culturally identifiable symbols which further structured the situation and legitimized action.
4. Spreading hostile beliefs and mobilizing the participants for action.
5. Providing the content for deviant role playing by transmitting the stereotypical expectations of how persons in particular deviant roles should act.
6. Magnifying the Mods-Rockers dichotomy and giving the groups a tighter structure and common ethos than they originally possessed.
7. Polarizing the deviants further against the community and—through the actions of the police and courts—setting a spiral of deviancy amplification.'

Of course, the sensitization model would force one to assume that the 'real' picture of violence, vandalism, and trouble was much milder than the picture painted by the press. Cohen (1973) implies this in some of his writing. For example, the estimates of costs of malicious damage during the seaside clashes seem to be rather low. Damage to property during the clashes does not even seem very far in excess of 'normal levels'. In other cases the press seems to blame the mods and rockers for things which are explicable on other bases. Thus one newspaper blamed the clashes for loss of trade in the town due to cancellations of visits by people afraid of the violence. Deck chair hires and admissions to the swimming pool declined compared to the equivalent periods of previous years. Cohen points out that most of this was due to abnormally low temperatures rather than people being deterred from their trip to the holiday resort by violence. This theme is returned to in Chapter 13 in the discussion of deviancy amplification.

Conclusions

1. There is no simple relationship between the sheer amount of exposure to crime in the media and criminal behaviour.
2. There is no simple link between the coverage of crime in the news media and the audience's perceptions of the amount of crime in society.
3. Some have argued that the news media through a process of labelling influence criminality.

11

The Courts and the News Media

EMBEDDED in any discussion of the control of mass media is an inescapable dichotomy. This is between the benefits of a free (unfettered) communications system and the costs of an unbridled freedom for the news media to report, print or broadcast, anything. Few, if any, would argue that there are not costs and advantages of either extreme. There might be considerable argument though about where the point of fair balance between costs and benefits lies. This fundamentally irreconcilable conflict between freedom and control of the mass media is dramatically illustrated by the free-press/fair trial debate. While not all countries have a constitution like that of the United States which provides for both freedom of speech and the right to a fair trial, most would publicly subscribe to the underlying sentiments at some level. A newspaper, unfettered, may be free to publish truths, hearsay, half-truths, and lies which would certainly not be allowed during the court proceedings itself. If certain sorts of evidence are unacceptable in courts of law, then it is hardly reasonable to allow them to be published contemporaneously in the news media. For example, why disallow evidence of previous convictions in the courts, if the jury can read information of previous convictions in the press? Simple instances like these are elementary examples of what is, in fact, a set of very complex issues.

The basic question is can the news media in some way change the course of justice? In other words, what is the influence of news reports prior to, during, and (even) after a trial on the verdict of the court? The issues are closely related to the law on contempt of court, though, of course, contempt is a wider issue. In Britain (which lacks a constitution guaranteeing both a free press and fair trial, and without, for various reasons, a history of major confrontations between the news media and the courts) the issue of the relationship between the news media and the courts has not been such a pressing one as in some other countries. Even in Britain, though, there have been a number of notable episodes in which the interests of justice and the activities of the press clash. The main reason for the relatively small number of instances of direct confrontation between the news media and the courts is the tendency of the press to behave very circumspectly and to 'play it safe' in relation to the courts. The law on contempt in Britain is notoriously imprecise and precedents have only a very limited degree of applicability. News media lack firm and realistic guidelines within which to work. Given this and the facts that (a) the Law on Contempt allows summary (i.e. without trial) sentences of *unlimited* fines and imprisonment in Superior Courts and that (b) until 1960 not even the possibility of an appeal, it is not surprising that the news media have tended to be cautious. Furthermore, it is noteworthy that there has been no trial before a *jury* for contempt of court this *century*. So it could be said that the issue has not even been referred to public opinion (albeit in the form of a jury) but left in the hands of the judiciary alone.

So the law on contempt, as far as it applies to the news media, has been little tested by and large. The essential principle underlying the application of contempt to the news media seems to be that certain sorts of news stories may prejudice the outcome of a trial. For reasons of conciseness, we might refer to this as prejudicial publicity. The reasons why the news media are assumed to have the power to influence the outcome of a trial are not too explicit but a few quotations, apparently of disarming frankness, help reveal a lot:

> It would, we think, be going much too far to say that professional judges are never influenced by what they may read or hear, but they are by their training and experience capable of putting extraneous matter out of their minds. A judge, therefore, does not need the law of contempt to protect him from prejudicial matter, although wholly unrestricted comment immediately before and during a hearing could be embarrassing, and might constrain him to demonstrate in some manner that he had not been influenced by it (p. 22).

> Much of the law of criminal evidence is based on the assumption that juries are more open to prejudice than professional lawyers in taking account only of strictly relevant matters (p. 23).

> . . . I would not have any contempt. . . . Certainly never in a judge-alone case (Lord Salmon) (p. 98).

> (Report of Committee on Contempt of Court, 1975.)

It appears that we need to control the news media largely for reason of the frailty of the jury. But the general sentiment underlying the quotations is fascinating since it is similar to practically every fear of the adverse effects of the mass media on the audience—whether it be the effects of television violence on children, advertising, election broadcasting, or pornography. The view is commonly expressed that there are two classes of people: (a) individuals incapable of withstanding the onslaught of the media and (b) persons resistant to the corruptive influence of what the media choose to publish or transmit. There seems no objective evidence at all for the view that the judiciary are robust in contrast with the juror's frailty but clearly there are some legal procedures, such as the appeals procedures, which are built, in part, on this assumption.

There are several problems with the law on contempt. One of the most intractable is the time dimension within which it operates. For example, if a newspaper publishes, after the suspect has been charged, evidence about that crime which is yet to go to trial, that newspaper risks contempt proceedings against it. It seems clearly accepted in England and Wales that a criminal charge is the marker in the judicial process which separates the period in which the press is relatively free to report the crime and events related to it and the period after which comment and reporting are severely curtailed until the verdict has been reached. In Scotland (which does not have the same legal system as England and Wales) the position is less clear. At one time this marker between the pre-trial and trial phases seems to have been shifted to an earlier stage by a statement arising out of events of 1960. The Lord Justice General said:

> Once a crime has been suspected, and once the criminal authorities are investigating it, they and they alone have the duty of carrying out the investigation. If a newspaper arranges an interview with any person in any way involved with the suspected crime and then publishes the results of the interview, or an article based upon it, the newspaper is doing something which in all probability will interfere with the course of justice and hinder a fair trial (Report of Committee on Contempt of Court, 1975, p. 11).

Even this tough definition would appear to exclude prejudicial publicity before a crime is known to the police. But it would be naive to believe that possible prejudice does not exist before this. For example, it is common in the news media to give accounts of ongoing frauds. There are many pieces of investigative journalism which expose crime well before there is any police involvement. These reports include tape recorded evidence, pictures, hearsay evidence, and other forms of proof not necessarily acceptable in courts of law. Witnesses and victims are photographed or interviewed, sometimes even the offender. The offender may add injury to injury by manhandling the reporter. Such reporting almost certainly creates an impression of guilt, and almost certainly a later trial is prejudiced in the sense that the word is used in law. However, no one has really questioned the media's right to do this except in cases like the South African Government's initial legalistic response to the Moldergate scandal.

Clearly it has to be accepted that the news media may have some role in the legal and judicial process. The matter seems to be one of balance but the point of balance has not been too clearly defined. It is difficult, if we accept that the press has a positive role to play in justice, to see that this necessarily has to end at the point where the judicial process is beginning.

Another element in the temporal dimension of the law on contempt is that although it is not acceptable to publish material which relates to previous convictions, sometimes, by accident, circumstances contrive to make it impossible to avoid doing so. For example, the Kray brothers had been tried and convicted on one set of very serious charges which the news media duly reported, but shortly afterwards they were tried on a totally separate set of charges. It is unlikely that any of the jurors in the second trial were unaware of the results of the first one. As clearly as in any other case, the Krays were prejudiced by the publicity given at the first trial. However, the news media were not in contempt of court. Nor was the second trial abandoned because of the risk of prejudice. It seems that the need for a free flow of information becomes paramount to risks of prejudice in these circumstances. Nevertheless, had the reporting of the first trial been delayed until the start of the second, then this would be contempt. Reports of court proceedings cannot be held back for printing at the time of a later trial since 'prejudice' would ensue.

During the course of the trial, following charging, the only information which may without question be published is what we might term a 'fair and accurate' account of the court proceedings. However, to anyone with a knowledge of the workings of the mass media such a phrase and such a situation rings a familiar warning bell. This is because underlying it is the assumption that the way in which the media influence the course of justice is by printing damaging information which has not, could not, or will not, be presented in court. But the mass media are capable of rather different sorts of process which might have some considerable influence on the jury.

As we have seen in other contexts, the mass media by their very nature are *selective* in what they report but similarly they are also *constructivist* in the sense that they create reality. It is literally impossible for the news media to present all the court news, still less all the news that there is. In any case, what is news is largely defined by the mass media themselves, which further reinforces the description of constructivist. With this sort of notion in mind, it is possible to see independent contributions to the course of justice which do not necessarily in any way contravene the law on contempt. The news we hear is the product of the means of selection, editing and even recruitment of materials. The press treatment of a court case is bound to be, at best, a pale imitation of what actually goes on in court. The news values of journalists will tend towards the selection of the most sensational and personifiable aspects of a hearing. It could be that the selection of vital aspects of the proceedings might feed back to the jurors. For example, in the Jeremy Thorpe case (the British Liberal party leader charged with conspiracy to murder), if it is reported out of many things that have been said in court only that his counsel admits that Thorpe has homosexual tendencies, despite Thorpe's previously denying it, then the choice of this one news item out of many that could have been selected may elevate it to a greater importance than it might otherwise have warranted in the minds of the jury. There is no direct evidence which suggests that the selectivity of the press influences the jury, but it does have broad parallels in what is called the 'agenda setting function' of the mass media for which there is more support (e.g. McCombs and Shaw, 1972). The phrase 'agenda setting function' refers to the tendency of people to accept what the mass media present as the major issues of the day whether or not they accept the media's viewpoint on them. It could be that the media define as a key issue the fact that Thorpe's homosexual tendencies are not admitted whereas they had previously been denied. This in turn might lead to the view that the testimony of those claiming amongst other things that Thorpe was homosexual was in general much more credible.

One of the most revealing cases of the role of the news media in relation to the courts is that of Peter Hain, the Young Liberal, who was accused of bank robbery. Before going into any detail on this, it should be said that in many ways the criticisms of the press in this sphere assume that the process of law is one of unfettered fairness. To the extent that it is not there exists the possibility, if not the likelihood, that the press might have some role to play in correcting the balance. Fairness is a relative concept and there is some reason to believe that, for example, the police have a much more manipulative role in pre-trial publicity than some might suspect. Mass communication researchers use the concept 'news management', which is a powerful and descriptive phrase for a fairly complex social process (e.g. Chibnall, 1977). News, as we have constantly reiterated, does not just happen. Sometimes it is sought by the news media but sometimes it is given. Like the army in Northern Ireland, or Vietnam, government ministers, and many others, the police are in a position to give valuable information to the news media. Sometimes it is given because it suits their purposes, sometimes as part of a process of controlling the press. Sometimes, of course, the police will not give information when it suits their purposes to remain quiet. All of these are aspects of the process of news management—that is, control over the reporting activities of the news media by manipulating the availability of information. The Peter Hain case provides a concrete example of this process.

> We had agreed with Wandsworth police not to release news of my detention and charge until the identity parade on Monday. It is unusual for someone to be charged before an ID parade, and even more unusual for it to be held three days afterwards. In view of the fact that I was publicly known, both the police and my solicitor were anxious that there should be no publicity before the parade. Otherwise it might be invalid.

> But could the police be trusted to keep this agreement? Indeed, the *Daily Mirror* acting on a police tip-off, had rung my parents several times while I was still in detention and before I was charged. Only my parents' steadfast refusal to confirm the story prevented the paper carrying it. Even with the police officially refusing to release or confirm the charge, it was highly likely that a police officer, somewhere would *unofficially* release it to a Fleet Street contact, and perhaps make himself some pocket money in the process (Hain, 1976, p. 19).

In the end, according to Hain, it was Scotland Yard that released the information to the press before the identification parade. Of course, this resulted in a welter of publicity, some of which was partly due to the efforts of Hain himself. Parts of the publicity Hain describes as treading a very thin line between the *sub judice* rules. It allowed for appeals to witnesses and also for Hain to publicly deny involvement.

The response of the news media broadly favoured Hain and was one way that the balance was partially redressed. But it was only feasible because Hain was an established public figure familiar to the media. Hain seems to have benefited psychologically from this, becoming more able to cope with the situation. In some ways the behaviour of the police in this case contrasts markedly with police treatment of the Neville Heath sex murders 30 years earlier, where after the first murder the police prevented the publication of his photograph on the grounds that it would prejudice later identification evidence. Some have argued that this allowed him to kill again before being arrested.

The very same concept of news management could be applied to a rather different state of affairs more directly related to the legal profession than the previous example. Inherent in the law on contempt and *sub judice* rules is their potential as mechanisms of social control. 'Gagging writs', which are essentially devices intended to stifle public comment without any real intention of taking the matter to court, are also examples of this. A classic case, and perhaps the most notorious example, is the *Sunday Times/* Thalidomide affair. The detail of the legal problems involved in seeking recompense for the gross deformities suffered by many 'thalidomide children' cannot concern us at the moment. It is the events of 1972 which are more immediately pertinent. The drug Thalidomide had been on the market between 1959 and 1961 and over the years that followed a number of claims had been settled out of court. Some parents would not or could not settle in this way and litigation was continuing. The *Sunday Times* had begun to publish a series of articles on the difficulties of the children amongst other things, when the manufacturers of Thalidomide, essentially via the Attorney-General, applied for an injunction on the grounds that their case was being prejudiced. The divisional court agreed, the court of appeal disagreed, and the House of Lords agreed. The major feature in all this is not simply that the rules of contempt may operate as a gag—they are designed to do that after all—but that the gag extends to the discussion of important issues which are at most only minimally related to the case itself.

The issue of marketing and testing new drugs is probably best illustrated by disasters and, after all, the problem of children reaching adolescence having been disabled all their lives is not to be ignored despite ongoing litigation. A question which is sometimes raised in relation to civil cases such as this is whether or not it is right to artificially remove the possibility of the news media as well as anyone else giving advice to litigants. Giving advice to litigants is not an unacceptable practice as such. After all, it is part of the duties of solicitors and barristers to advise their clients about whether to go to court, settle out of court, and even whether the monetary gains that might be achieved through court action are more than outweighed by the embarrassment, undesirable publicity, time and cost involved in the action. If there is nothing intrinsically wrong with such advice, how then can it be undesirable for the news media to similarly offer advice?

The Research Evidence

It is clear in the above discussion that many of the issues raised are mainly legal ones rather than psychological ones but it is apparent also that psychological research is relevant to part of the debate. The main reason for this lies in the notion that prejudice requires that the chances of a fair trial are altered. That is, prejudicial publicity is that which materially alters the verdict of the court. For any single court case it is impossible to know whether publicity has changed its course but psychological research offers a means of testing the general hypothesis that legally defined 'prejudicial' publicity alters the verdict.

It is notable that the British Committee on Contempt of Court (1975) produced no evidence of a social scientific nature on the effects of pre-trial publicity although there was a certain amount of research available then. They did present some minor evidence from the sort of natural experiment where as a consequence of being convicted at a slightly earlier trial, the accused had received full and possibly prejudicial publicity. According to the Committee's report, in the case of the Kray Brothers:

> This is precisely the sort of material publication of which is normally prohibited by the law of contempt because of its potentially prejudicial effect. In the second trial the charge was again murder, but after being warned by the presiding judge not to be influenced by the publications the jury acquitted the defendants. Similarly the jury who recently acquitted Miss Janie Jones of blackmail charges at the Old Bailey must have been well aware that she was convicted on other charges in a previous and highly publicised trial (p. 23).

Whatever this shows, and it may well be (reversing expectations derived from the law on contempt) that juries are far wiser than the law allows, rather more formal proof is needed.

Most of the research evidence related to pre-trial publicity is American and, for what it is worth, data suggests (Eimermann and Simon, 1970) that as few as 1% of American criminal cases receive a line of publicity in the national press. In any case, the percentage of individuals pleading guilty is very high indeed—somewhere between 75% and 90% of those processed through the courts. However, this does not mean that every case has a 1% chance of being reported. Coverage is selective and certain sorts of crimes are over reported. A greater proportion have a chance of receiving publicity in the local press (the figure is as high as 17%) but it is 2½ times more likely that a crime brought before a jury will be reported.

Social scientists, in one notable case (Simon and Eimermann, 1971), gathered evidence for use by the defence in an American trial to argue for a shift in the location of the hearing. Two men had been accused of the murder of a prominent local personality. As might be expected, the crime attracted the attention of the local press and received a lot of publicity. Little, if any, of this publicity seemed prejudicial in the legal sense. But it left little doubt that the accused were vagrants and that there were witnesses. The press had not been irresponsible but there was a chance that the publicity would have a definite adverse effect on the accused. Researchers conducted a telephone survey of potential jurors a week before the trial. Of those who agreed to co-operate, approximately four-fifths had heard or read about the case and about three-fifths could provide some details. Sixty-five per cent of those who could remember details of the offence favoured the prosecution's case against the men, 27% were indifferent, and the rest unable to give any answer at all. That is, none of those exposed to pre-trial publicity thought the accused innocent! In marked contrast to this, among those who were unable to supply details of the case, 4% favoured the prosecution, 6% favoured the defence, and 53% were indifferent. If nothing is known of the case, indifference about the guilt or innocence of the accused parties dominated. It appears that awareness of details of the case affected beliefs that the defendants would receive a fair trial. More of those unable to supply details of the case thought that the defendants could expect a fair trial in that community. Although this data was presented in court as evidence that juries from that community would be biased, it was rejected. However, in what appears to be a remarkably equitable outcome, one of the two men pleaded guilty to the murder and was convicted, while the other was freed by the verdict of the jury! As with any correlational study there are many problems of interpretation. Primarily it is not known whether exposure to publicity is a correlate rather than a cause of beliefs concerning the guilt of the accused.

Experimental research has inevitably come from 'simulated' jury trials. There is no possibility of real life research on juries, which might be more desirable, so those interested have to be content with second best. In one experiment using mock or simulated juries, Kline and Jess (1966) divided the trials into two groups. In one half of the trials, the jurors received a copy of a newspaper containing a prejudicial account of the events leading up to the trial. In the remaining trials, the jurors received non-prejudicial versions of these same events. The study took place in a school of law and used real judges to direct the trial. After the evidence had been presented, the experimental and control juries all deliberated independently. No differences between the verdicts of the prejudiced and non-prejudiced juries were found. However, during their discussions, those juries which had been given the prejudiced information brought it up as a matter for discussion though nearly always rejecting it completely as a course of evidence. This rejection was largely on the basis of the judge's instructions concerning the proper sorts of evidence for the jury to consider in reaching their verdict. Those juries who did not reject entirely such evidence did not differ from the control juries in their verdicts.

Simon (1966) also used mock-jury trials but this time either presented a sensational version of a pre-trial publicity sequence of news stories, much as the popular press might present it, or a version as might appear in a conservative newspaper such as the *New York Times*. Before the trial, the respondents who had these different versions were asked to comment on the guilt or innocence of the accused. Afterwards, the subjects were exposed to a recording of an abbreviated trial consisting of an admonition from the judge, opening statements testimony from witnesses and closing instructions from the judge. Finally the jurors were once more asked to evaluate the guilt of the accused. The evidence clearly showed that pre-trial publicity had an effect on the pre-trial opinion of the jurors. First of all they were willing to make judgements about the guilt of the accused, which presumably would not have been the case without the newspaper publicity. Secondly, concerning the sensational version of the stories, those jurors who read that the accused had a previous criminal record were less likely to believe him innocent. Those who read the conservative version were inclined to have no opinion about the guilt of the accused. However, after the hearing things changed. The trial had a big effect on the percentage feeling that the accused was innocent. Whereas before the trial most seemed to think that the accused was guilty, after the trial the reverse was the case.

On the basis of the evidence presented so far, the following would be a reasonable summary:

1. Pre-trial publicity is effective in creating judgements of guilt in the minds of the reader (see also Tans and Chaffee, 1966). This is not at all surprising since the mere fact of arrest and going to court indicates guilt in the sense that most people going to court eventually plead guilty. Pre-trial publicity is prejudicial but only in the same way as being charged with a crime.
2. Jurors seem capable of rejecting pre-trial publicity, or making allowance for its effects. In this sense, pre-trial publicity is not prejudicial (though whether or not some jurors will over- or under-compensate is a moot point).

But there are one or two other studies which seem on the face of things to contradict the studies so far discussed. This contradiction is probably much less substantial than it appears. Sue, Smith, and Gilbert (1974) carried out an experiment which depended on ratings rather than mock juries. Some subjects read a transcript of a fictitious case which included a newspaper account of the discovery of the murder weapon in the accused's home. This evidence could not be presented in court because it was obtained by improper search procedures. In the other condition, a gun was found which had no bearing on the case at all. In the transcript of the trial, the judge either told the jury to disregard any pre-trial publicity or said nothing about it at all. The judge's instructions made little or no difference but the pre-trial publicity did have an effect. Where the inadmissable but relevant evidence about the gun was given, guilty verdicts were significantly more frequent than in the case where the weapon was irrelevant. It seems that the potential jurors were making allowance for the incriminating weapon even though this evidence could not be presented in court. Perhaps this is not surprising given that a legal technicality prevented the publication of these results. These findings have greater implications for court room procedure than the media, since they suggest that a fair trial is impossible once inadmissable evidence has been presented. It seems that this study on inadmissable evidence is the weakest, coming as it does from the least naturalistic of the research designs, and perhaps the most problematic of all areas of evidence.

Conclusions

John Whale (1977) makes the following points:

. . . the legal climate in which journalists work is a constantly changing one. The chief inhibitor of press freedom in the United Kingdom is the law. But the law is not carved on tablets of stone. It varies with the changes made in it by Parliament, the successive interpretations of it put forward by judges, and the use made of it by litigants (including Government); and all those variations are a distant expression of public opinion. At any time, therefore, journalists are in a state of some uncertainty about what the law is, and different editors treat it with different degrees of robustness. In the mid-1970s that uncertainty was increased by the existence of four weighty reports to the Government about aspects of press law, and the Government's slowness in deciding what to do about them (p. 143).

The four reports Whale mentions are Phillimore on contempt, Younger on privacy, Faulks on defamation, and Franks on secrecy. This amount of interest in the press is nothing new and controls have historically been extensive and to some extent damaging (Curran, 1977). The reasons for wishing to control the news media are singular and simple: to prevent the news media controlling the public. Despite the rather dampened interpretations of the potential of the mass media to effect change which have emerged out of more than half a century of mass media research, the fear of the power of publicity remains. It is no good the mass media researcher suggesting that the news media are relatively ineffective in creating and changing public opinion, since there are obvious examples of how the press may just once in a while be very effective in producing change. Watergate is a good example of this.

The issue of the relationship of the news media and the law rarely becomes important as a matter of routine. It is only when the assumed freedom of the press and freedom of the courts are satisfied in mutually incompatible ways that a major problem arises. Both these freedoms are at best relative. In some senses neither is more important than the other although the judiciary traditionally claim the prime rights. One can however imagine circumstances in which the freedom of the press to make comment is defensible particularly, perhaps, in cases in which the judiciary adopt a highly political role (e.g. Griffith, 1977). On the other hand, one can easily imagine the stream of endless, scurrilous publicity which would tip the balance away from the news media.

All of this assumes that the news media are effective in prejudicing 'justice'. The data do little to support this point of view. There is something to be said for questioning whether it is fully appropriate to apply the law on contempt to the news media. Some have argued that contempt should only apply to trials before juries (given that there are other laws such as those on libel to cope with most unfair reporting). The evidence here suggests that for the most part juries are well able to disregard the effects of pre-trial publicity. In other words, the ability to judge in this respect is much the same as that assumed of the judiciary. Since an appeal presumably would not be heard before a jury, we might have a safety net should we abolish contempt by publicity.

On the other hand, one suspects that there may well be little gained as a matter of routine by freeing the news media in this way. The press has a mixed track record in relation to the courts. The present laws on contempt may well inhibit investigative journalism but so does the economic climate and many other factors. Freeing the press may make a marginal change but probably not a very big one. It is notable that the committee on contempt sat not as a consequence of endless brushes between the news media and the courts, but as a consequence of the occasional extreme case, such as the Thalidomide litigation which raised exceptional issues.

Clearly we are getting well out of the province of the social sciences and into matters of belief and opinion, but social science has provided some reasons for re-examining the situation.

Part Five

THE MASS MEDIA AND THE SOCIAL SERVICES: EDUCATION, HEALTH AND WELFARE

12

Education by the Mass Media: Compensating for Educational Disadvantage

IT IS undeniable that people can learn from the mass media. Learning from the media is self-evident, but this is a relatively crude statement and needs qualification. People obviously do not recall everything they see on television, so what precisely do they learn? Even this would yield a relatively crude statement of the educational impact of the media. The fact that people learn things from television in no way means that the media are good for standards of education. It is perfectly possible that the time spent with the mass media might have been used effectively if given over to more educational activities. Is it a good thing that children learn about the world from television or would they have learnt more if they had read the books that were put aside in favour of television? Television may promote both learning and ignorance at one and the same time according to what yardstick is being employed.

A major problem in education is that the educational system reflects the inequality and disadvantage in society. The most deprived classes of society gain least out of education. The children of the working class, instead of being stretched to achieve their potential by education, fail in or are failed by education. In the 1960s Education and the Social Sciences became more and more concerned about the lack of achievement in the longterm of certain easily identifiable groups in the school system—girls, the working class, and blacks. Various studies had begun to show that the home had a profound influence on the performance of the child at school and entry to higher education. Motivation to achieve in school emerged as not merely intrinsic to the school but developing and accelerating from birth if not before. Middle-class mothers interacted differently and more effectively with their children; middle-class children were more exposed to books, drawing and writing materials; more middle class children went to pre-school playgroups; middle-class children lived in more 'nourishing' social and physical environments; middle-class children were not left undisciplined; middle-class children were better fed; and middle-class children were encouraged to stay at school. The inner city slum dwellers, the biggest failures of the educational system, were causing trouble in the streets.

In terms of progress through the educational system, statistics preach much the same message. The working class, the female, and the black stay in education for less time, do less well, and may even seem to respect education less. The precise interpretation of these facts is considerably in doubt. The crudest and least defensible view is that these figures only reflect the poor native ability in these classes, i.e. they do poorly because they are innately or genetically inferior. The evidence for this is, of course, hotly disputed and few, in any case, with an informed opinion would suggest that this is the complete explanation. The second part of the explanation put forward is that the home environment, particularly in the early years, has a tremendous influence on the intellectual development of the child in many ways. For example, by not providing early experiences which stimulate the child's mind sufficiently, by not interacting with the child from the first few moments of life, by not providing nutrition, by not providing a positive attitude to books and other school related aspects of early life, the family may produce an under-achieving child. The third sort of explanation revolves round an interaction between the features of the school system and features of the home. The view is that the school system, being the epitome of middle-class values, is systematically biased against black and working-class cultures. The clash of cultures, the failures of communication between the cultures, the failures of understanding between cultures all serve to switch off the working class within schools. Other explanations include the differential socialization of males and females which tends to push males into achievement, females into motherhood.

The mass media enter the equation in several different ways. The first (and in the history of mass communications research, primeval) argument is that the television (and other forms of popular culture) detracts children from intellectually satisfying activities. Thus children watch TV rather than read, viewing becomes the centre of family life instead of chatter and discussion, and TV fails to stretch the developing imagination. The viewing figures for different social classes add some apparent substance to this. Working-class children spend more time viewing and, as we have seen, do worse at school. (However, the media could also provide TV of sufficient quality to compensate the child for a lack of intellectual stimulation by his family.) One last important reason is the feeling that society would function better with a well-informed population. After all, it is one of the central tenets of democratic theory that the population has knowledge on which to base its choices.

There are clear stimuli to the concern about the impact of the mass media on education. In Great Britain, worries about the effects of television on educational standards in the mid-1950s were a manifestation of a split of opinion about the introduction of a commercial television service. Until this time, broadcasting had been almost exclusively based on a public corporation without advertising. The fear that the new service, being commercial, would shed all standards and responsibilities in favour of pure and unadulterated commercial goals has obvious implications for the educative aspects of TV—given that one is willing to assume that the mass media have considerable power to change tastes. In the late 1960s, the stimulus for the development programmes designed to educate the pre-schooler and the disadvantaged was the movement to introduce compensatory education/social action projects into the United States. *Operation Headstart* was the most famous of these. Here, special classroom teaching was given before normal entry into school. In this way the disadvantaged child might be advanced to the levels of school readiness of his middle-class, advantaged counterpart. This compensatory programme was in its turn partly stimulated by the urban unrest of the 1960s. This, of course, involved blacks living in inner city areas. The rise of black consciousness, reactions to bussing, and other familiar events all helped create a belief that the problem could be solved by compensatory education. It is not surprising that the obvious potential of the mass media to substitute for the family, to reach even the poorest homes, attracted attention.

We are not discussing the use of television in a classroom context here— that is outside our scope, but merely the use of regular transmissions in normal mass media output. Educational TV is a separate issue presenting a completely different set of contingencies compared with the mass media. The use of video in education is merely another step removed from educational TV. Its success says nothing about the educational impact of routine broadcasting.

Some Preliminary Issues in the Educational Impact of the Mass Media

A crude elitist model of the mass media suggests that viewers can be sorted out into two broad types. The first is the heavy indiscriminate user of the mass media, who will consume all the media fodder available. He consumes the superficial unchallenging products of men and companies whose sole aim is huge audiences and thereby greater profits. This type neither seeks nor receives any form of intellectual or cultural stimulation from the mass media. In contrast is the light, discriminating viewer. This type sees the mass media as a resource—turning on programmes of special interest, particularly the informative, cultural, challenging, and educational. The *commercial interests in the mass media pander to the former*, the *responsible broadcaster caters for the needs of the latter*. The choice of words is not accidental. Evidence certainly suggests that people vary markedly in the quantity of television, for example, that they consume. Perhaps 10% view for more than about 4 hours a day and perhaps another 10% view for less than about 1 hour a day (Goodhardt, Ehrenberg, and Collins, 1975). But, in themselves, such figures say no more than that there are heavy and light viewers. It is also known that there are both mass audience programmes and minority programmes. Some programmes are watched by tens of millions and some by fractions of a million. The little viewed programmes are assumed to be, and are in some ways, minority interest programmes. They are seen as the most enriching and educationally worthwhile of the products of the media. The mass audience programmes are assumed, almost by definition, to be pap. A scheme therefore offers itself—if the mass audience viewer could be encouraged to view the minority interest programme, he would be enriched and stimulated.

But this flies in the face of facts. Light viewers are not really the selective viewers that the above 'model' implies. Light viewers usually watch the most popular programmes, heavy viewers watch the unpopular ones (Goodhardt *et al.*, 1975), which is the reverse of expectations. A moment's thought shows why it happens this way. For a programme to be very popular it has to attract people who switch it on especially. A minority programme gains an audience simply from those who do not bother to switch off. According to Goodhardt *et al*:

'. . . people with a real specialist interest do not generally feel a need to follow it *on television*. Artists do not feel they need to watch art programmes; knitters, knitting programmes; or businessmen, business programmes. Specialists already know all that. Even religious people do not religiously watch all their programmes, but go to church instead' (p. 131).

Furthermore, according to the same authors' data, there is nothing of substance to show that the upper class (mainly professional and managerial) differ from the lower strata in terms of types of viewing. The upper social groups, although viewing less in general, watch the same sorts of programmes in much the same relative quantities. They watch proportionately less rather than materially differently. Of course, the upper class claim to survey interviewers that they like the more serious programmes. They may like such programmes better but do not give them a higher proportion of their time.

If, as Goodhardt *et al.* claim, people with a specialized interest in a topic have little interest in specialist programmes simply because they know it all already, this implies that the viewers of the specialist programmes have little motivation to learn since they lack strong interest. This is not a good sign that people learn a lot from the mass media. The mass media are not particularly effective at providing people with a knowledge and understanding of the world in which they live. Do not forget that Klapper (1960) used the failure of an information campaign concerning the United Nations in partial proof of the inadequacy of the effects model of mass communication research (Star and Hughes, 1951). It would be nonsense to suggest that the media do not inform in some circumstances. Indeed there is considerable evidence that people claim to use the media as a source of information (e.g. Wade and Schramm, 1969). A modern failure of the mass media to inform effectively further illustrates the need for caution.

One characteristic of the 1970s was a growing awareness of the importance of economic factors in everyday life. In modern news broadcasts the use of fairly sophisticated economic concepts is common. Such an emphasis is partly forced on the media by the changing nature of world events. Suddenly the price of oil becomes a critical fact of life affecting everyone. Do the mass media, particularly television, actually enhance our understanding of economic concepts? As politics becomes ever more enmeshed in economics, it is vital that people are sufficiently informed about such forces. Evidence provided by Adoni and Cohen (1978) suggests that understanding of economic matters is poor. Their research was carried out on Israeli adults. This was a particularly apt choice in view of the fragile Israeli economy which had inflation touching 100% a year. How well do economic ideas permeate through such a culture?

The level of ignorance was remarkable. Concepts such as balance of payments, gross national product, value added tax, and cost of living index were understood by only one-third of the population. By 'not understood' is meant they could not be explained. Such concepts are crucial and ignorance of them illustrates the lack of effectiveness of the mass media. The highest levels of understanding of economic ideas were found in males, the better educated and higher income groups. These were also related to feeling that one understands economic concepts. Watching television news was a relatively poor predictor of such subjective feelings of understanding! Irrespective of their actual understanding economic concepts, people tended to feel that the television was actually helping them to understand. There was evidence that for women watching television, economic news increased understanding. However, for men there was no correlation between watching economic news and understanding. The effects of television can be at best described as minimal if only 15% of the population understands concepts such as balance of payments.

Compensatory Education or Disadvantaging the Disadvantaged

If some sections of society are disadvantaged by the inadequacies of their home environment, the solution to the problem seems obvious. Social and educational services should be encouraged and enabled to provide whatever the home cannot. Since it is commonly accepted that the first few years of life are critical to intellectual and social development, obviously such an enterprise should begin as soon as possible. So how do we compensate for the inadequacies of the early home environment? Quite simply, by training the disadvantaged child in the skills learnt by more fortunate children. In this way the school preparedness of disadvantaged children could be brought up to the level of the rest. Many skills could be taught. However, relatively greater stress is placed on basic numeracy and literacy concepts— making children familiar with letters and numbers. *Operation Headstart* in the 1960s attempted to do just this. The aim was to provide compensatory education in socially disadvantaged areas. One of the methods used was to introduce the children to school in the summer before they actually started school. Instead of 5 years or so of encouragement in the home, 6 weeks or so in a school classroom was hoped to suffice. This compensatory education certainly worked to increase these educational skills in the disadvantaged group. It would be surprising if it did not. Unfortunately, evidence of longer-term gains in the disadvantaged group was more difficult to find. Some evidence suggests that the children merely slipped back to the levels that would have been expected had the child not received compensatory education (Howitt, 1976). Even several years after the upsurge of compensatory education there is no universal agreement on its effects. The area is a methodological morass with many pitfalls (see Campbell and Boruch, 1975). In Great Britain, Tizard (1974) produced a review of research into pre-school education. This casts some doubt on the efficiency of pre-school playgroups and similar activities. If playgroups and nursery schools provide no great contribution to the school readiness of children, how could a few short weeks before school be expected to have much effect?

In parallel with all this emerged a television programme, *Sesame Street*, which working on the salvationist principle, 'why should the devil have all the best tunes', used the techniques of commercial television to produce a programme designed to teach children the very skills which the compensatory education movement was trying to promote. *Sesame Street* used the 'puppets', the Muppets, to attract and hold the attention of pre-school children. Elaborate graphics and music added to the appeal. Just what could such a programme, with much the same objectives as the *Headstart* initiative, do to improve school readiness in the disadvantaged child? The producers of the programme (the Children's Television Workshop) had taken an unusual step. They had made arrangements for a research-based evaluation programme to check on the effectiveness of the show.

There are several issues. The first is whether this television series with strong educational objectives actually competed effectively for audiences with commercial programmes not designed to educate. The second is whether the series was effective in teaching the young viewer anything. The third is whether the series did anything to reduce the differential in educational readiness between advantaged and disadvantaged children. Audience research figures which suggest that the working class and the inner city dwellers spend much time with television gave grounds for optimism. If they devoted more time to *Sesame Street* than the middle class then some compensation for disadvantage could be expected. Great care needs to be exercised since the series may be educational without reducing disadvantage. The programme appeared in many different countries with varying degrees of local adaptation of content. In Great Britain little encouragement was given by the British Broadcasting Corporation, which would not screen it. The reason was that it was too American, too out of keeping with British culture to make it suitable for British children. In any case, the BBC had a number of programmes of its own specifically designed for pre-school children. These had much the same objectives as *Sesame Street* of stimulating the intellectual development of young children.

It might help clarify the issues involved in the evaluation of *Sesame Street* somewhat if we begin by considering a quite different enterprise, one which was designed to promote the use of books in the less literature-conscious sectors of society. In Norway in 1973, the makers of children's programmes joined forces with a book club to strengthen interest in book reading in 2–10-year-olds. Programmes were made of books which were offered for sale through the book club at the same time. The proceeds were for the benefit of refugee children. The aim was to 'even out the differences between children unfamiliar with books and children familiar with books' (p. 46) (Werner, 1975). The results offered little to show that these ends had been achieved. Income was a major factor in book purchases from the club. Higher income families were five times more likely to purchase than those with lower incomes. This was exactly as would have been expected. It reflects previous knowledge about literacy in middle- and working-class families. But income was not the only explanation of these discrepancies. There is a further, more cultural set of considerations. The educational achievement of the mother and whether or not she worked were related to purchases. In fact, the higher the mother's educational attainment, the more likely it was that books were purchased (even when income is taken into account). Furthermore, when educational level and family income are allowed for, the working mother bought more books from the club than the non-working mother. Given the tendency of girls to achieve less in the education system, it was significant that girls had fewer books bought for them. This could not be explained in terms of the differential interest of boys and girls in the books. In some social classes the girls asked for (but did not necessarily get) the books more frequently than boys. Werner concludes that the actual result of the project was quite the opposite of what had been intended. The campaign *increased* the knowledge gap between the social classes (and sexes) rather than diminished it.

Clearly it cannot be assumed that starting with good intentions to use the media for the benefit of society inevitably leads to success. The mass media are not technological soup kitchens taking nourishment to the needy. Rather than pinpointing a target, the mass media act rather like a shotgun splattering all in their path. The rich get rich. With this caution, evaluating a programme like *Sesame Street* becomes easier.

Producing an Attractive Educational Programme

Is it possible to produce a television programme which competes with commercially produced programmes for young children but which has educational objectives? This may appear to be a strange question but it is meaningful in context. American television is as dominated by commercial interests as any in the world. This applies as much to children's television as any other (Melody, 1973). The *Sesame Street* series was to be broadcast over public service networks in the USA rather than through the more dominant commercial ones. The series seemed to be effective in certain ways. First of all it managed to attract large audiences. Secondly, there was evidence that the programmes attracted and retained the attention of the audience. The earliest research on *Sesame Street* suggests very high levels of attention to the programme amongst viewers (as high as 89% of the audience at any one time). However, this was a captive audience, not children in their own homes. Distractions were therefore rare and the research might be over-estimating what would happen under more naturalistic conditions.

Levin and Anderson (1976) studied the development of attention to TV in pre-school children for whom alternative activities were available. White middle-class children were brought to a TV viewing room which contained toys and other distractions. An unfamiliar episode of *Sesame Street* was on the TV. Up to the age of 2½ years TV was largely ignored but then attention increased markedly. Four-year-olds had an attention figure of 58%, which is considerably less than the figure of 89% obtained without distractions. The authors were able to evaluate the effectiveness of various attention-gaining devices incorporated in the programme. Child characters, puppets but not animals, bright and lively music but not slow music, and adult females but not adult males were among the best attention getters. Still graphics led to reduced interest. Such studies are carried out in contexts dissimilar to the home environment. The home lacks the same element of novelty as that of being taken to some researcher's laboratory for an afternoon out. In any case, being in a strange environment might encourage the child to take the easy option of sitting back and watching television. Certainly more detailed research in the home produces startlingly different impressions of the viewing behaviour of young children. Admittedly this evidence does not deal with *Sesame Street* exclusively but is illustrative nonetheless. In a study of pre-school children in England and Ireland, Howitt (1976) observed children in their homes during the period 4 p.m. to 6 p.m. The observers were familiar visitors to the homes of the children. Relatively small proportions of children watched the television attentively. At most only about 30% of children gave full attention or watched without many interruptions. Up to half of the children would be playing outside instead of watching television. Interestingly, in Ireland (which was able to receive both programmes from the British mainland as well as Irish broadcasts) mothers reported that a relatively cheaply produced British programme (*Playschool*) was almost as attractive to children. This used essentially traditional techniques such as stories, 'toy-making', and a couple of presenters, which contrasts with the commercial razzmataz of *Sesame Street*. However, the children claimed that the latter was their favourite programme. Interestingly, except for the period when the news was broadcast, the attention levels of pre-schoolers to TV remained relatively stable. This was irrespective of whether a programme specifically for pre-schoolers was being shown or just a general children's programme. Perhaps this puts the success of *Sesame Street* into perspective.

In the final analysis, the success of *Sesame Street* has to be evaluated to include the international interest in it. Palmer, Chen, and Lesser (1976) claim that it had been seen in fifty-nine countries or territories with its original English dialogue or some form of local adaptation. That is an immense audience.

Sesame Street as a Teacher

The team behind *Sesame Street*, which included academics as well as media personnel, planned four broad objectives:

1. Symbolic processes (letter, number, and symbol recognition and use);
2. Cognitive organization (e.g. classifying and sorting objects);
3. Reasoning and problem solving; and
4. The social and physical environment.

These objectives are reasonably specific. But stating objectives and reaching them are not necessarily the same. Furthermore, if the educational objectives are achieved this may not mean that a significant contribution has been made to pre-school education. The effects may be detectable statistically without making much impact on society.

The effectiveness of *Sesame Street* in reaching its objectives has been carefully documented by several research teams. Some of the earliest research was carried out in close cooperation between the *Sesame Street* production team and Bogatz and Ball (1970, 1971). This both clarified and obscured issues. Things were obfuscated because one of the conditions in the research encouraged some of the parents and children to watch the programmes together. Toys and books and other artifacts were given to help them in their viewing. Children in the control (non-encouraged group) often watched the series but the heaviest viewers were those with this parental involvement. This makes the statistical analysis of the data rather problematic. It is very difficult to gauge whether it is viewing alone or viewing together with parental encouragement which produced increases in educational skills. According to Liebert (1976), the encouragement increased the unit costs per viewer one hundred times. This is not a desirable feature if programmes like *Sesame Street* are to be employed in poor countries.

Bogatz and Ball (1971) tried to improve on this but, according to Cook and Conner (1976), their study turned out to be flawed. Although once again it seemed that viewing with encouragement has some effect on the sorts of measures used, there was no significant difference between heavy viewers who were encouraged and light viewers who were encouraged! In fact the heavy viewers fared less well than the light viewers on the basic skills! Cook *et al.* (1975), using the same data, found that encouragement was a better predictor of learning than viewing. This reanalysis suggests that the programme was not as effective as Bogatz and Ball had first suggested. Liebert (1976) says, 'when needed corrections were made, it became apparent that the effects of viewing itself had been slight' (p. 168).

In Mexico, Diaz-Guerrero *et al.* (1975) evaluated the educational efficiency of *Plaza Sesamo*, a local version of *Sesame Street*. The research was in two phases. The first phase was an experiment out of the home context in which children at day-care centres either watched the programme or some cartoons. Assignment to experimental and control groups was at random and continued day by day, 5 days a week, until 130 programmes had been shown. Tests showed consistent improvements, particularly in skills with numbers, letters and words, and general knowledge. All changes favoured the *Sesame Street* group. This particular piece of research was supplemented by a field experiment with a larger sample of children, but in which the actual control of viewing behaviour was far less rigorous. In this experiment the results were 'generally negative'. One explanation of the difference is 'in the earlier study, more adults attending to children were present at more times, creating a subtly different atmosphere in the first experiment than in the second' (p. 154). This explanation reflects precisely the criticism of the effects of *Sesame Street* obtained in the earlier studies.

　How does one respond to this? What explanation is there of the relative failure of these programmes to stimulate without adult assistance? Howitt's (1976) data on children in Britain and Ireland suggests that the idea of television stimulating pre-schoolers in any meaningful way is rather wide of the mark. Observers recorded the response of pre-schoolers to television in their home. Although the types of response made by the children varied somewhat, the overwhelming response was merely drawing the family's attention to specific programme aspects or making remarks thereon. About one-third of children in each country made such responses. The other common responses included things like singing along, repeating words of sentences or replying to the television set, dancing, banging, clapping, moving to and fro with the music—scarcely the most educational of activities, although not to be frowned upon. Perhaps irrespective of the aims of the programme makers, the child prefers to be entertained rather than educated. Certainly the children were not rushing off making models or doing the other things suggested.

　But Liebert (1976) raises a much more important issue—that of the use of the mass media to close the culture gap, to reduce educational disadvantage. Although the producers of *Sesame Street* made no great claims in this area, it is clearly an important issue. When a certain amount of care is taken over the statistical analysis of the data from the *Sesame Street* studies, there is little evidence at all that the gap is closed. Cook *et al.*'s (1975) data suggest that the advantaged groups tend to increase their abilities more than the disadvantaged. Minton (1972) found increases only in her advantaged group consequent on watching *Sesame Street*. Salomon (1976) similarly found improvements in those already advantaged. Some may recognize the irony of a programme, which might have been a weapon in the war against deprivation, making matters worse. Liebert (1976) points out that the programme was worthwhile because it introduced new standards into American television.

None of this is very promising and in some ways the theory underlying the use of pre-school television for educational purposes over a long term is suspect. The first reason is that there is no real evidence that an early stimulus to educational development actually confers any long-term advantage in the education system whether it be television or playgroup. The second is that it is uncertain that we know the sorts of stimulation which are necessary rather than merely precocious. The third is more pragmatic. If formal compensatory education has not effectively demonstrated its worth, what chance does a televised substitute stand? Whether the failure to reduce disadvantage and the lack of clearcut evidence that *Sesame Street* is an effective teacher without adult support is a damning indictment depends very much on one's objectives. The improvements in programme quality standards it demonstrated may offset its failure to reduce educational disadvantage. Since the gap between advantaged and disadvantaged widens in school over time, the programme, had it succeeded fully, might only have served to delay the opening up of the gap.

Imaginative Play

One of the criticisms of the mass media is their influence on the creativity of children. Television exercises the dominant senses of man almost completely—the visual and the aural. The other mass media tend only to dominate either one or other of the senses. Furthermore, television tends to leave little to the imagination. Characters which could only be read about in books can now be viewed through someone else's imagination. Consequently, the question whether television can stimulate creativity or whether it dampens imagination warrants some attention, particularly so in a society where the exploratory and self-learning approaches to education are gradually replacing old-fashioned teaching. Although there is not much evidence on this, there is a little concerning relatively young children.

Singer and Singer (1976) studied the impact of the pre-school programme *Mister Rogers' Neighborhood* on the imaginative play of 3–4½-year-olds. This was an experiment consisting of four different groups of subjects:

1. One group of children watched an episode of the programme every day for a fortnight.
2. As above, but an adult was present who called the child's attention to aspects of the programme.
3. This group watched no television but spent the sessions with an adult guiding their play activity.
4. This group was the control and received no special treatment other than the routine of the nursery at which the research took place. But this was common to all the groups.

The play behaviour was rated by observers in terms of its imaginativeness. One issue was whether the child used play objects in unusual ways. Another dimension was the positive effect of the play experience. That is, to what extent the child expressed joy, elation, and liveliness in play. The results of the experiment showed that both imaginativeness and positive effect were influenced by the experimental treatments. The control group got worse, the TV alone groups improved a little, the TV group with adult did better than this, and the adult stimulating the play behaviour of the child produced the greatest improvements. Thus, although TV seemed better than nothing, it is better if an adult is there to help and encourage the child. This relative failure of TV alone to make much difference to the imaginative play of children is very much in line with Howitt's (1976) field research, which suggested that TV has no great stimulating effect on the behaviour of the child viewer.

Meline (1976) studied young adolescents but wished to compare the influence of different media. Creativity in this case was measured by a simple psychological test. The children were asked to invent new means of transport, new means of recycling waste, new means of stopping people smoking, and new improvements to cities in the future. The media used were audiovisual (videotape), aural (sound tape), or printed materials. Various solutions to the problems listed were given. The visual presentations used graphic images rather than merely 'talking heads' explaining solutions. Essentially, apart from the visual component, the presentations were identical. The results were fairly unequivocal. Solely verbal presentations (both printed and taped) produced novel ideas which were relatively free from the constraints of the original stimulus. However, audiovisual presentations were relatively poor at stimulating creative thought. The key difference is obviously not that of print versus the rest, but whether visual images are present. These seem to have an inhibitory effect on creativity. More research would be needed to know whether television programmes without this strong visual component would be effective, or whether children's story books with illustrations are worse than children's story books without illustrations. This data has some bearing on McLuhan's hot—cold dichotomy. Television is a cold medium because it dominates our thoughts, leaving us unable to explore our awareness further.

Conclusions

It is easy to point to the lack of public awareness of information which has been disseminated through the mass media as evidence of the ineffectiveness of the media as a means of educating and informing the public. At the same time this tends to assume that human learning is a much more simple process than in fact it is. Human minds do not soak up every scrap of information offered to them. Apart from books, for example, none of the mass media are suitable as reference sources to be used when the need arises. The newspapers, magazines, radio, and television provide information when they schedule it, not when the audience necessarily needs it. Consequently there may be a big gap between the audience's need for information at any one time and what the mass media provide. Much information provided by the mass media does not need memorizing because it is of little importance to the audience. Furthermore, it is difficult for the mass media to repeat material over and over again until mastery is achieved. The mass media, unlike the education system, could not be geared to individual learning needs using present technologies.

The fact that we have shown that the media serve to widen the gap between advantaged and disadvantaged members of society probably reflects this to some degree. Limited repetition may suit the advantaged, better learner, but may do little for the disadvantaged, slower learner.

13

Health, Ill Health and the Mass Media

There is some freedom of choice between sickness and health. That is the message of preventative medicine and health education. Major advances in areas like nutrition, aetiology, and diagnosis constitute a generally accepted body of knowledge which, if exploited, could help ameliorate or even stamp out disease. The links between smoking and cancer, heart and respiratory disease; the more effective treatment of breast cancer if detected early; the importance of exercise in promoting health; public hygiene: these are familiar examples. Naturally, the mass media have been a focus of attention since preventative medicine and health education require: (a) an informed and co-operative public for maximum success, (b) to reach vast numbers of people, and (c) to reach the healthy who do not have direct contact with medicine. Equally, the mass media have great utility for the ill-health educators. If consumer products advertised in the mass media are bad for the health, then the mass media become advocates of sickness. The obvious case of such bad effects of the mass media is in the advertising of cigarettes which are acknowledged to be a major cause of disease. But there are others including patent drugs, sweets, cakes and biscuits, and alcohol, for which the media are not entirely blameless. Clearly mass communication is a two-edged weapon.

The Media Promote Ill Health

Theoretically, at least, there are several ways in which the mass media could promote ill health. One is to advertise products which affect the health; a second is to neglect to publicize information which demonstrates the health risks attached to certain products; a third is to decry warnings of danger; and a fourth is to inadvertently encourage the use of products by

157

actively supporting similar but less dangerous substances. Smoking makes a good case study of these issues, drugs a further illustration.

Smoking

The public belief that smoking is harmful has a short history. Its brevity reflects the hostile response of the media to scientific evidence. By the early 1950s sufficient medical evidence was available to allow dire warnings of the effects of cigarette smoking to be issued. For example, the Medical Research Council of England and Wales announced that smokers of cigarettes may have a fifty times greater risk of lung cancer than non-smokers. This and other similar examples might have been expected to form the basis of a number of dramatic news stories. But according to Cirino (1973), who traced the press coverage of this important medical story, this was not the case. The stories were ignored or placed in obscure positions in the newspapers. There was also a singular lack of any editorial comment on the topic:

> There were no newspaper crusades to arouse the politicians to pass legislation requiring equal time and space to combat the persuasive power of cigarette commercials. There were no stories of the tragic deaths that were now known to be associated with cigarette smoking. More than 99% of the media have continued to accept advertising without demanding a warning. The media in effect have joined with the tobacco industry in opposing legislation controlling ads (p. 57).

This failure was compounded by the press almost invariably contradicting medical developments with statements from the industry that such medical evidence was inconclusive. Cirino argues that these tobacco company statements misled the reader into thinking that there were real grounds for disagreement between doctors. In fact, the only dissenters of note were doctors in the employment of the tobacco industry. This did nothing to advance the public's rejection of smoking. It is commonly known that there is a great resistance amongst smokers to giving up smoking. But without knowledge of the dangers of smoking there is no major motivation to stop. The decline in cigarette consumption in the Western world despite greater consumption of products such as alcoholic drinks is evidence that once the information was spread, tremendous changes in social attitudes occurred.

It is not too difficult to hazard a guess why the media went to such lengths to present smoking research in a bad light. The tobacco industry, which provided much advertising revenue, might have resented anti-smoking propaganda. Furthermore, reporters and editors who smoked might have preferred to believe that cigarettes are not dangerous.

Fortunately for public health the smoking and health debate is moving swiftly into history and the battle to educate, if not to protect, the public has been won. Most people now believe the health dangers of smoking. The media's role in preventing persuasive messages reaching the public is well illustrated by this example.

Drugs

The drug industry invests heavily in advertising of one sort or another. Some of this is aimed at the prescribing doctor but a good deal is directed at over-the-counter sales of patent medicines. Many of the drugs advertised are mood-altering substances—psychotropic drugs. New York Mayor John Lindsay's phrase 'wake up, slow down, be happy, relieve tension, with pills' is a powerful indictment of the contents of this advertising. Critics claim that far more is promised than the drugs in fact deliver. Stimson (1975) studied the way in which advertisements for psychotropic drugs present stress as a medical problem requiring medical rather than social treatments. He surveyed medical journals, magazines, and newspapers published in the early 1970s in Great Britain together with mailed advertisements and hand-outs produced by drug companies for doctors. The advertising of some drugs he finds wanting. He complains that descriptions of what symptoms are appropriate to particular drugs are vague. Anxiety, tension, and emotional states are poorly defined descriptions which may be applied to a range of quite unrelated problems. The actual messages of the advertisements are relatively unstructured but, for Stimson, the latent messages are much clearer. Examination of material sent to doctors showed that women were portrayed much more frequently than men. Women outnumbered men as 'suitable' candidates for the drugs by fifteen to one. Women with families were unhappy because of pressures on mothers; women without families were equally unhappy. Furthermore, the advertisements took quite 'normal' trials and tribulations of everyday life as signs for the need to use psychotropic drugs. Thus a medical 'cure' is promoted for such 'diseases' as being unable to get on with a new boss!

Stimson was more concerned about the effects of such advertising on doctors than on the lay public. Others have paid attention to the effects of the media on the audience's perceptions of health and drugs. Most of this research has related the sheer volume of exposure to the media with attitudes to and use of proprietary drugs. Of course, allowance is made for possible relevant factors such as sex, age, social class, and educational status. These, if left uncontrolled, could mislead the unwary into believing that there is a causal relationship between exposure and behaviour when in reality there is none. One study evaluated the effects of TV drug advertising on the use of proprietary drugs. The authors of this (Milavsky, Pekowsky, and Stipp, 1976) looked more deeply to see if there was a spill-over to the use of non-legal or illicit drugs. If proprietary drugs are advertised as solving life's problems, an instant sunshine, then why should this belief not extend to illicit drugs? The data showed that amount of exposure to television and amount of proprietary drugs used (including proprietary psychotropic drugs) were correlated. The relationship was not particularly strong, however. Evidence about the validity of TV exposure as an indicator of exposure to drug advertising is clearly needed. The best the authors could do was to point to the very high association between knowledge about drugs and amount of exposure to television as proof of this. There was no evidence that the acceptance of proprietary drugs advertising messages generalized to illicit drugs. The relationship was in fact a negative one—the greater the television exposure the less illicit drug use. The negative relationship can be explained in various ways. For example, one does not expect young people who are part of a drug culture to sit around watching television all day. It does not fit with the way of life. Howitt and Dembo's (1974) subcultural explanation of so-called TV effects might be relevant here.

More direct evidence, which measured actual exposure to drug advertisements, comes from a study by Atkin (1978). Adolescents were asked how often they saw drug advertisements. Controlling for age, sex, social class, and educational achievement, there was a modest correlation between exposure to drug advertisements and a number of behavioural and attitudinal variables concerning drugs and illness. Apparently such drug advertisements encouraged the belief that illness is common, that people frequently use drugs, and that drugs work quickly. Those people most familiar with drug advertisements are more concerned about becoming ill, use drugs more, and tend to approve the use of drugs in illness. Atkin explains the weakness of the relationships as follows:

> The overall lack of attitudinal impact of medicine ads may be explained by the fact that there are so many other interpersonal influences operating on attitudes toward drugs; in competition with messages from parents, peers, and teachers, the possible indirect impact of ads for aspirin or sleeping pills is bound to be restricted. For instance, there is a stronger inverse correlation for children whose parents disapprove of medicine usage than for those who have parents that support medicine taking. In addition, it is likely that children who see the most medicine ads on TV also view a greater number of public service announcements that seek to discourage drug use; these anti-drug messages may serve to counter the influence of conventional medicine ads (p. 79).

So the impact of television on the adoption of patent and illicit drugs is not to be overstated. Indeed, although there is evidence that proprietary drug advertisements work, as do those for cornflakes, nothing suggests directly that television promotes surreptitiously the use of more dangerous drugs. It is possible that too much emphasis has been placed on television in these studies since Wright (1975) provides evidence that newspapers and magazines were more useful to people seeking medical information than radio and television.

Although there is a shortage of good evidence in this area, it is worthwhile pursuing the question of drug use and the mass media further. Young (1973) believes that the media make the drug situation worse. There is something incongruous in the emphasis given by the mass media to drugs such as marijuana. This Young explains using a light-hearted scientific 'law': 'The *greater* the public health risk (measured in number of mortalities) of a psychotropic substance, the *less* the amount of information (including advertising) critical of its effects' (p. 314). In short, tobacco and alcohol cause more pain and suffering than L.S.D. and marijuana, but receive weaker criticism. The takers of 'unusual' drugs become labelled as social *deviants*. Smokers and drinkers do not. The mass media share a consensual view of the world with much of the population. This consensus defines certain groups of individuals as being apart from the rest, as being deviant. The list of deviants is long but includes strikers, students at sit-ins, prostitutes, spiritualists, illegal immigrants, agitators, foreign agitators, pimps, con-men, immigrant runners, pushers, and junkie doctors. In each case the cause, according to the consensus, is either the personal sickness of the deviant, or the corruption of the deviant by others. In the consensual view the world is bifurcated. There are the good and bad, right and wrong, the punishers and the punished, and righteousness and evil. Views outside of the consensus are difficult to hold since the consensual view is all-embracing, rigid, and powerfully structured. The big danger of the consensus is that it 'precludes a rational approach to the problem' (p. 322).

How does this explain how the mass media worsen the drug problem? Anyone would be forgiven for thinking that the antagonism of the media towards drug takers should serve to put most people off drugs for life. Clearly an additional concept is needed to clarify matters. This turns out to be that of the *amplification of deviance*. In deviance amplification, an individual (or group) becomes labelled as deviant and consequently suffers a degree of isolation from the rest of society. Nice ordinary people do not want to be involved with deviants. Because they are deviant, unwanted, they have problems in finding work and because decent people do not wish to know them they are forced more and more into the company of other deviants for friendship and social contact. As a result of this they are further drawn into deviant activities. The more deviant the individual becomes the more severe society's reaction against him. The more severe society's reaction against him, the more deviant the individual becomes. The image is of a spiral of social reaction feeding increased deviance which feeds back into social reaction. The process can go on *ad infinitum*.

For Young, the police are crucial to this spiral. The police, because of the nature of their job, are themselves isolated. They live largely where they are told to and often are prevented by circumstances and the nature of their work from getting to know how young people normally behave. The police may be familiar with how young people behave when being arrested but have little idea how the majority behave normally. As a consequence of this ignorance the police are vulnerable to media stereotypes of drug-takers. Indeed, the nature of the power relationship of the police over the drug-user is such that any direct contact between the two groups is likely to reinforce the stereotype gained from the press. The police may become keen to sort out the drugs problem by arresting more users. The intensification of police action forces the drug community to become better organized in its own defence. Feeling oppressed or persecuted by stiff sentences or harassment increases solidarity. Forced into a special community, the drug-taker's behaviour and distinctiveness from the rest of society becomes heightened and less easily ignored. The media become more convinced that they were right given the peculiarities of the estranged group of drug-takers.

Young's argument is rather elusive despite receiving some favourable if uncritical attention in the literature (e.g. McCron, 1976). One reason for this is that although it is very easy to understand that the response of the police to groups of drug-users might have a profound effect on those groups, it is harder to prove the involvement of the mass media in this process. Judging from Young's writing, the process would exist without the media. The impression is that the ideas were grafted on to a critique of the mass media rather than directly stemming from an analysis in which the media were a central focus. Certainly proof, circumstantial or scientific, that the police rely heavily on mass media images is lacking from Young's account.

The Mass Media Promote Health

A classic study in the social psychology of attitude and behaviour change is Janis and Feshbach's (1953) research on the effects of fear-arousing appeals on dental hygiene. One of three different levels of 'threat' were given to different experimental groups in a lecture-type situation. In one condition toothache was the sole consequence of poor dental hygiene, in the second condition the pain and discomfort arising was worse, and in the third the threat included cancer as well as tooth loss. It emerged that the greater the threat the greater the resistance to the message. Dental care was worst in the group exposed to strong threat messages and best in the mild threat condition. This is quite the reverse of common sense expectations. Unfortunately, the literature in this area is difficult to summarize. Some studies have found that high threat is more effective in producing change than low threat. (For a thorough review see Janis, 1967; and Levethal, 1970.)

Janis and Feshbach's study was not about mass communication as such. Nowak (1972) replicated the essence of the earlier study in a novel Swedish experiment which, unlike the Janis and Feshbach study, involved the mass media. Different TV transmitters simultaneously beamed alternative versions of the programme to different parts of the country. This was one of the rare occasions when a broadcasting organization co-operated fully with researchers to produce something akin to the random experiment beloved of experimental psychologists. The experiment itself looked at the effects of a programme about dental hygiene on the attitudes and behaviour of the audience.

One feature of the research was that professional communicators (media personnel) actually produced the programmes. The styles varied from the serious and heavy to the light and humorous. The two versions of the programme advocated the same messages and by and large shared interview and other material. Various surveys were conducted to evaluate the relative effects of the two alternative versions of the programme. A further comparison was made with the attitudes and behaviours of those who saw neither version of the programme.

It would be very convenient to say that the programmes proved to be effective and that the light and humorous version produced the most improvement in dental hygiene. However, it proved very difficult to evaluate the data from this survey. It was even more difficult to make strong claims about the effects of the programmes on knowledge and attitudes. Technically the evaluation of the effects of the programme was complicated by selective exposure and the differential interest value of the different versions. But despite the intricate care given to the research design, the findings were not unexpected and very much in line with the rather simplistic predictions that might have been made in advance of the broadcasts. Most of the effects were small. The more light-hearted, entertaining version seemed to have the greatest promise as a means of increasing knowledge about dental hygiene for the less educated viewer. The experiment is important because it shows the need to be pessimistic about the powers of the media in health education. Even professionally produced programmes broadcast at a peak viewing time do not necessarily achieve dramatic effects.

Nowak's study does not provide much encouragement to use the media in health care. Simple ideas concerning dental hygiene may already be familiar to the audience, but some health problems are not quite so straightforward. Several of the dietary causes of ill health may be beyond the grasp of an unsophisticated audience. For example, without some rudimentary biological knowledge, what use are warnings against saturated fatty acids? Here a more intensive approach is perhaps necessary, such as that used in the following community health programme.

Maccoby and Farquhar (1975) draw attention to the frightening statistics on coronary disease in Western society. Heart disease is virtually unknown in many parts of the world and is usually considered to be a product of certain excesses. The stereotype of the highly powered fat executive being most at risk is not accurate since it is those of lower social economic status who are most at risk. The researchers decided to use a semi-experimental method designed to help people change their coronary producing behaviours (largely smoking and eating fatty acids). Three communities were selected which were as similar in size and other features as practicable. The communities were surveyed to obtain baseline data on diet, exercise, and smoking. This stage was followed in two of the communities by an 8-month media campaign together with the intensive treatment of individuals at risk in one of these. The media campaign was described as follows:

> Cooperation from local TV and radio stations enabled us to convey messages using some 40 TV spots, numerous radio spots, and mini-dramas. Space was made available in local newspapers for 'doctors columns' and dietary columns. A number of printed items (a basic information booklet, a cookbook, a heart health calendar, and so on) were mailed directly to residents. Additional messages were conveyed by business cards and billboards (p. 120).

The more intensive treatment of 'at risk' individuals involved a number of principles derived from behaviour modification theory. Each subject planned and reported on his diet under expert guidance. Weight losses were recorded. Training in food preparation and good shopping habits were also included. Reduction in smoking was tackled as follows. A smoking diary was first developed for each individual who was then encouraged to cut down on consumption. Methods like going for a walk, deep breathing, use of sugarless sweets, and so forth were used when pressures or cues to smoke mounted, such as drinking coffee and being offered a cigarette by a friend. The campaign was effective. Cholesterol levels, related to heart disease, improved. Information about bad foods increased. The mass media alone did not improve 'healthy attitudes and behaviours' as much as the media and intensive treatment combined. However, according to Maccoby and Farquhar (1976) the differential almost disappeared after 2 years. The media and the community may interact to deal effectively with health issues. The best example of this concerns contraception and family planning. Whether or not one considers contraception as a health problem, in many countries most contraceptive methods are funnelled through the medical services, particularly doctors. In any case, population control (one aspect of family planning) is an important social problem in its own right. Verbrugge (1978) describes the results of a study begun in the late 1960s of the West Malaysian population policy. The main aim was to encourage the use of the contraceptive pill. Fewer than 10% of women were using any form of contraception, so the importance of such a programme is obvious. What encouraged women to seek contraception early in the campaign? Primarily this was interpersonal sources. Husbands were the most important, followed by clinic nurses and friends, then neighbours and relatives. Most had heard about family planning on the radio and about two-fifths had read something in newspapers, but the latter were not the most important sources. Things were a little more complicated than this since those getting a lot of help and support from interpersonal sources were also getting a lot from the mass media. Diversity in communication sources seems to be a key feature in early acceptance. The reports of the acceptors seem to suggest that the mass media are not very influential. Only 7% of the women claimed to have been primarily influenced by the mass media. Perhaps 'only' is the wrong word since 'only 7%' can represent an enormous number of women. Nor should it be forgotten that media represent one feature of society which is readily manipulable by planners. There is no foolproof way, for example, which by a husband could be encouraged to influence his wife. The mass media are claimed by Verbrugge to 'nourish interpersonal contacts, increasing acceptors' ability to influence eligibles. Mass media do not figure directly as an important source of information, advice, or influence in acceptance' (p. 66).

One difficulty with interpersonal communication is that it may tend to ignore issues that lack drama or interest value. So while it may be that contraception and cancer become foci of conversation, simple public health and hygiene measures may not capture the imagination. The community may draw together to proselytize on the more dramatic health issues but cannot be turned on to order despite such successes.

The Recruitment of Patients

Although virtually everyone knows where to seek help when ill, there are circumstances in which patients may need to be more actively sought. This is particularly the case when the patient is unaware of treatment opportunities or unwilling to use the normal channels because the problem itself causes embarrassment. We have already discussed psychologically-acting drugs in this chapter and with something in excess of 200 million prescriptions per year for such drugs in the United States alone there is an obvious likelihood of some abuse of such drugs. A treatment and research unit was set up at the University of Washington (the Polydrug Treatment Unit) to help people suffering from social, work, or physical problems resulting from the use of drugs. Treatment was free. In the beginning patients were obtained by referrals from social welfare agencies. They tended to be white, unemployed, and undergoing some radical change in their life. It was suspected that this method of recruitment left unreached individuals who did not come to the attention of social welfare agencies, the middle class being a case in point. Consequently, a media campaign designed to contact these 'hidden' clients was planned (Strauss, Ousley, and Carlin, 1977).

Public service advertisements were shown on the local TV stations over a 3-week period together with some publicity in local newspapers. The advertising spread the message that drug problems were not confined to young, drug-oriented groups and featured the Polydrug programme. It was explained that it provided free, confidential outpatient treatment to those misusing psychotropic drugs with the exceptions of heroin and alcohol. If the advertising had been charged at its full commercial rate instead of given free it would have cost about ten thousand dollars. This figure is a key element in any evaluation of the success of this advertising. Incoming phone calls to the Unit were recorded to obtain evidence concerning the sorts of people responding to the campaign. A mere thirty-six individuals telephoned in response to the publicity. Thirty-six people on the road to cure sounds reasonable even though relatively expensive to reach. But this is a drastic over-estimate, since twenty-five of these were not really suffering any drugs problem at all. For example, they were taking only two or three tablets of Valium a week or were merely interested in what the Unit was trying to do. This contrasts markedly with the recruits from the normal welfare channels who nearly all had a drug problem. The media campaign was not a success in terms of the range and variety of patients recruited. Few additional patients were acquired and the target population not effectively reached. The media campaign was not considered 'cost effective', as well it might as it cost in the region of a thousand dollars per recruit.

Further Considerations

Some (e.g. Walker, 1973) argue that communication is an important variable in relationships within the health professions and between professionals and clients. Communication is often made difficult in the surgery because doctors are largely recruited from middle-class backgrounds, are trained in a fairly insular social situation, and have to deal with patients with very different life experiences from their own. The consequences of this might include a fear of visiting the doctor, delaying a visit because of this, and the risk of failing to obtain treatment early enough. These communication problems are not immediately and directly pertinent to the mass media, though it could be that the medical profession obtain ideas of their working-class patients from the newspapers, etc. This possibility would lead to poor communications and understanding between doctors and patients. Likewise, one might worry if patients got their ideas about the medical profession solely from the mass media. De Fleur (1964) and De Fleur and De Fleur (1967) present some evidence that the mass media do create an impression in the young viewer that nurses are cold, impersonal and detached. McLaughlin (1975) reports a content analysis of fifteen major peak viewing time programmes dealing fictionally with the medical profession. Power and authority are primary characteristics of fictional doctors. These extend far beyond the therapeutic situation into the private lives of their patients. Doctors are also shown as irresponsible in two senses. First of all they are rarely given orders and commands by superiors and, secondly, something like 40% of treatments given were experimental, dangerous, or unproven. In nearly half of the cases the doctor pursued matters into the private lives of the patients. The doctors were not always very successful in the therapeutic situation, but they were nearly always successful in treating personal conflicts or problems: '. . . the doctor is . . . is . . . a "necessary outsider"—one who can deal objectively with the facts at hand, interpret and shuffle them, and solve all kinds of problems' (p. 183). If patients took these messages to heart they would go to doctors to resolve any crisis but a health one. But is this not a problem already faced by doctors? It is the familiar stereotype of a patient seeking a shoulder to cry on rather than medicine.

Another area where the mass media could have a role is in updating the practising doctor. With progress in most fields of science and technology being made at enormous rates, there is a likelihood that a doctor may become out of date sometime during his medical career. This need for in-service or continuing medical education is met with in various ways and by various sources. Portis and Hunter (1975) describe the use of medical education television in parts of the United States to inform doctors of advances in medical practice. They evaluated the effectiveness of a medical television programme on adolescence and found that doctors did learn something. However, they write:

'(it) can be expensive to produce, in both direct time costs and also donated time by television stations and doctors. Because of the costs involved very impressive results are expected in terms of reach and impact on the medical doctors . . . the doctors did not show a strong preference for medical television or movies over other forms of continuing medical education. And the research does not show a very strong effect of the TV program or films on medical practice. It may be that broadcast television is more useful for providing medical information to the general public than to medical doctors' (p. 170).

Perhaps this conclusion should be greeted with some relief. It might be a little disconcerting if they had found that the medical profession is best updated by the media. The idea of a TV-dependent medical profession does not inspire confidence.

Conclusions

Several ways have been presented by which the media may be a help or hindrance to promoting health. Little emerged that was indicative of an enormous role for the mass media. Certainly there are problem areas to which the media may contribute, but there are no issues which can be addressed solely by mass communication. One can speculate about a mass communication system which promotes ill health more actively and effectively than at present; one can equally see a mass communication system which meticulously teaches good health practices, enhances patient–doctor communications, aids in preventative medicine, and which recruits those needing medical help readily. There is little doubt that a mass media system designed around the needs of medicine and health could do some good. However, such a system would be expensive. We have already seen that some attempts to utilize the mass media to promote public health have been ineffective on a cost-benefit basis. The temptation to look to the mass media to solve problems which affect the mass of people may be overwhelming but careful evaluation and costing is needed. It would be paradoxical if the effectiveness of medical treatments were carefully researched while the worth of health education through the media merely assumed. There has been little in this chapter to promote such a complacent assumption. The allocation of priorities in the medical area, especially removed from the free market economy, is in itself problematic (should money be spent on immunizing thousands of people against colds or on a single heart transplant?).

14

The Mass Media and Welfare

Some social problems are so pervasive, monopolizing resources so completely, that any possibility of an 'instant' solution is very attractive. The provision of social welfare resources for the poor, the institutionalized, and the disadvantaged is yet another case in point. The range of the mass media's involvement in welfare is enormous. It stretches from ways in which the public opinion about welfare is formed, transformed, or maintained to questions of how the claiming of benefits by those eligible could be improved. The reasons why the mass media become a focus of attention amongst those responsible for welfare provision are largely the familiar ones: (a) the relatively large mass of people who use the mass media, (b) the relatively high costs or impracticality of other methods of reaching clients and eligible individuals, and (c) that the poor are assumed to be heavy consumers of the mass media. Of course the poor are not the sole target of social welfare provision. The sick, the young, and the infirm also need help.

Research has shown that the heaviest consumers of the media are the most likely to receive or need welfare provision. For example, Medrich (1979) found that households with constantly tuned in television sets had lower educational standards and income. Single parent households were well represented. That is 'those with fewer material and cultural resources and those who also often live with less privacy in crowded homes'. Others have shown similar trends (Greenberg *et al.*, 1970). And, of course, many who rely on welfare are old, sick, infirm, or housebound for various reasons, and consequently they may be highly dependent on the media as a source of entertainment and information.

The following are some of the most important ways in which the mass media have been seen to relate to welfare issues:

The Mass Media as a Cause of Social Welfare Problems

It would be unrealistic to argue that the mass media are a direct *cause* of poverty. Some might argue though that the media contribute to a cycle of deprivation which keeps people in poverty. For example, if the children of the poor rely greatly on the television for intellectual stimulation, their intellectual achievement may be lowered, and their chances of progress in work and school reduced. Only occasionally, with issues like suicide, have direct accusations against the mass media been made. The contents of the chapter on education are highly relevant to this discussion.

The Mass Media to Attract Funds for Charities

The ubiquitous nature of the media makes them attractive targets for organizations who need to recruit help from outsiders. The simplest example of this is using the media to make appeals for money. Some of these are no doubt extremely successful and, in many cases, seem to produce worthwhile incomes.

The Mass Media as a Source of Recruitment of Clients

Welfare services frequently need to reach eligible clients who often prove difficult to locate by conventional means.

The Mass Media as Opponents of Welfare Services

There is an argument which claims that the mass media, particularly newspapers, by dint of their methods of selecting and presenting news relevant to welfare, promote the view that those receiving welfare benefits are scroungers. This reinforces anti-welfare tendencies in some areas of public opinion.

The Mass Media as Definers of the Public Perception of Welfare Users

The way in which welfare users are seen may affect their treatment in society. Television and the other media may be part of the defining process.

The Mass Media Worsen a Social Work Problem

Suicide may or may not be a social problem. Its definition as such depends on a vast array of intertwining social, moral, and legal judgements. Various voluntary social welfare agencies such as the Samaritans seek to help prevent suicides. Most health and social services, as well as the prison service, have procedures designed to avoid suicide attempts by those in their care. In this sense, at least, the problem is recognized as such. One may imagine many different ways in which suicide could be influenced by the media: prophecies of unmitigated gloom, economic disaster, and the like may not help; the death of a particularly popular film or television star might create a flood of suicides out of grief (as is claimed in the case of the death of Rudolph Valentino); the promotion of the view in the media that suicide is an acceptable course of action in certain circumstances could also contribute. Very little research has been taken into this area although a number of claims have been made. For example, Phillips (1977) argues that road accidents increase just after publicised suicide stories. Motto (1967) researched the influence of the newspapers on suicide rates. He compared periods of newspaper blackouts with equivalent non-blackout periods making allowance for population increases, seasonal variations, population characteristics, and previously existing trends. No significant changes were found during the blackout periods, with one exception. This was a single significant result which showed an *increase* in suicides in the *absence* of newspapers. This clearly contradicts allegations that newspapers provide models for suicide. But with only one significant result, it is more reasonable to assume that there is no relationship between newspapers and suicide in general.

Popular opinion would have it that remorse over or imitation of the suicide of a famous personality leads to copying. Motto points out that the suicide of Marilyn Monroe in August 1962 was followed by a 40% increase in the suicide rate for that month, largely accounted for by a rise in male suicides. This however, made no difference to the annual rate. In any case, suicides of other famous people have not resulted in suicides among their followers. Motto concluded that 'the value system inherent in the manner the news is usually reported has a deleterious influence on the emotional growth of immature readers, which in turn can later be conducive to increased suicide potential' (p. 256). However, these assertions are in no way proven by the research evidence he cites. How seriously we take these data depends very much on our interpretation of suicide rates. The criticisms that apply to crime rates have parallels for suicide figures. What is and what is not a suicide is largely decided by doctors who may be acting less 'objectively' than a simple interpretation of the suicide rates imply. Nevertheless, it seems warranted to conclude that newspaper reports of suicide have no influence on published suicide rates though quite how such statistics are interpreted is a moot point.

The Mass Media as a Publicist for Welfare Services

The use of the mass media for seeking help for or recruits to the welfare services has great appeal. Advertising for donations to charity is merely the beginning. However, giving money is relatively painless and it should not be assumed that the media will assure the success of any venture. So what success would occur in appeals which require individuals to make an enormous personal contribution of time and commitment? A good example of this would be the search for foster and adopted parents for children in institutional care. It is not unusual to see advertisements seeking foster parents in the local press or even on national television advertisements. These largely seek to make the viewer or reader aware of the possibility of fostering. Sometimes, and often this is harshly criticized for the cattle market image it suggests, individual children have been featured in the media in an attempt to find particular children homes. An instance of this comes from an attempt to find foster homes for mentally retarded children. It is commonly known that it is not difficult to find couples to adopt or foster certain sorts of children (e.g. white babies), but others can be very difficult indeed to place. Mentally retarded children would require a far more intensive search. One welfare organization in Nebraska (the Lancaster Office of Mental Retardation) carried out a publicity campaign over a period of several years by means of articles in a free newspaper distributed to every household. The articles featured a child, together with his photo-graph and a written description including information about his favourite foods and toys. This approach contrasted markedly with the efforts of other local welfare agencies. For example, the Department of Public Welfare mainly used word-of-mouth recruiting techniques (i.e. largely relied on foster parents talking to friends and acquaintances) for placing non-retarded children with foster parents.

It was possible to compare these distinct strategies in this community using the results of two separate surveys (Coyne, 1978). As might be expected, those who became foster parents to mentally retarded children were more committed to fostering than the foster parents of non-retarded children. For example, whereas seventeen out of twenty of the mentally retarded group had known other foster parents or had been foster parents themselves before fostering the mentally retarded child, only nine out of twenty of the other foster parents were in this category. The mass media had a role in this since many more foster parents reported that the media had made them aware in the media based campaign than in the word-of-mouth campaign. About three-quarters of the foster parents who claimed that the mass media made them aware already knew other foster parents before they volunteered to the Lancaster Office of Mental Retardation. However, the media were ineffective in the final stages, that is when actually applying to become a foster parent. Four out of five in both samples claimed to have been mainly influenced by other people to apply.

The media have a role to play since new foster parents (those who had not been foster parents for any agency before) were more easily contacted using the mass media. But even here personal contact was important since those recruited by the mass media already had considerable contact with other foster parents. The mass media apparently activated latent tendencies concerning fostering rather than persuaded in any meaningful sense. Only those who were finally chosen to be foster parents were included in the survey. It is not known what influenced the unsuccessful applicants, but selection factors may have operated. For example, agencies may not have looked with favour on potential foster parents with no previous experience and no contact with other foster parents who might have warned about the problems involved in fostering. The effectiveness of the mass media in this context depends on whether the pool of suitable recruits is increased rather than simply in terms of the total response engendered. Indeed it is counter-productive to encourage a large number of unsuitable applicants.

In the above example we looked at the way in which the mass media recruit help for the welfare services. Probably more general is the issue of how the clients of the welfare services can be reached directly by the mass media. Welfare provisions do not always have their desired effects because of the failure of the clients, those entitled to welfare, to actually make a claim or seek help. Usually this failure is reflected in indices of take-up rates. In Britain, for example, only four out of five children eligible for free meals at school actually have them.

The Child Poverty Action Group (Meacher, 1971) sought to discover the extent to which the take-up of means-tested benefits could be increased in London through an advertising campaign. This included the circulation of leaflets, limited mass media advertising in a local newspaper, plus a little fortuitous publicity on television. People in low income areas were contacted and interviewed both before and after a publicity campaign which tried to increase the take-up of rate rebates. (Rates are a tax on property levied irrespective of the income of the occupier.) Rate rebates are available to those on low incomes in order to alleviate the burden of the tax. In the low income area only 12% of those *eligible* were actually claiming rate rebates before the campaign. This increased to 19% after the campaign. The effects of the campaign were not spread through all groups of the needy. Pensioners tended to take up the rebate entitlement more than others in any case and the publicity worked quite well on them. On the other hand, low income *families* both before and after the campaign failed to claim rebates. The campaign was effective in the sense that it actually cut the percentage of those eligible but ignorant of their rights by half. But, as we have seen, it left a lot to be desired as a means of increasing actual take-up rates. Being aware and claiming are not the same thing. Obviously the possession of information in itself was insufficient motivation to make a claim.

There are various reasons why the advertising campaign was not a complete success. First of all, the publicity failed to penetrate completely to the target population. Two fifths of the sample were unaware of the campaign. But many did not apply because they were put off by the complexity of the claims procedures, or because previous welfare claims had been rejected, or because they were afraid of officials, or because they were afraid of the social stigma of making a claim.

Neither of these studies show the media to be infallible weapons in the welfare armoury. Neither do they show that the efforts were completely wasted. Additional questions need to be asked before final judgements of the effectiveness of the media in this context can be made:

1. Were the advertisements well designed and of sufficient calibre to attract attention given the plethora of excellent commercial advertisements seeking attention?
2. What is the cost effectiveness of advertising? That is, do the media cost too much for each additional recruit? We should not forget that money and resources devoted to advertising may be subtracted from a total budget thereby taking money and resources from other worthwhile projects.
3. What is the quality of recruitment through the mass media? An advertising campaign cannot be thought of as successful if it recruits only ineligible applicants.

Friedrich (1977) claims that a media campaign about child abuse increased the willingness of members of the middle class to report cases known to them.

The Image of Welfare

Public opinion polls show a residue of antipathy to the idea of government involvement in welfare. While most people express commitment to welfare, things may not be exactly as they appear. Erskine (1975) surveyed American polls on government involvement in welfare since 1935. Throughout the history of these polls there has been a steady two-thirds to three-quarters agreeing with poll questions which imply a government obligation to basic subsistence. For example:

> Do you think our government should or should not provide for all people who have no other means of subsistence? (Asked June 1939). 69% said *should*.

Do you personally favour or oppose an all out effort by the federal government to get rid of poverty in this country? (Asked December 1969). 73% in favour.

Despite this, about a fifth of respondents were against such minimal provision in both cases. Reflecting on the results of the poll, Erskine wrote:

Such widespread and steady support for government paternalism seems incongruous considering how controversial public welfare programs have always been. This series on welfare and poverty opinion perhaps should have commenced with the criticisms, since this particular collection of questions leaves a sense of sweetness and agreement in the welfare field which everyone knows has never been the case. People wrangle about the way welfare and public work projects should be administered and distributed, but not about the obligation of government to step into the breach when needed. For example, the idea of a negative income tax has never caught on. The Nixon plan, in contrast, was obviously popular because of the President's insistence that able bodied people must work rather than accept a free ride on the guaranteed-income gravy train (p. 257).

This basic opposition has been detected by some in the mass media's presentation of welfare issues. As with other things, attitudes to government involvement in welfare are in part determined by broader political attitudes. Consequently, some would argue, it is not at all surprising that the mass media, with their basic commitment to a right wing rather than a left wing point of view, capitalism rather than socialism, should be less than entirely devoted to governmental responsibility for welfare. The ways in which this antagonism are expressed include subtle attacks on key components of the welfare system. Golding and Middleton (1978) carried out a content analysis of the manner of treatment of welfare news. They conclude essentially that the media engage in character assassination of those on welfare by highlighting the abuses of and frauds against welfare. By creating an impression that those receiving social security are no-good idlers and cheats, effectively the entire welfare system is undermined. As many as 31% of news stories in the press, radio, and television dealing with welfare and social security news were about abuses of social security; 13% involved legal proceedings in relation to social security. Headlines such as 'Big New War on Dole Cheats' and 'Pay Code Breached by Welfare Rises' simply reinforce this. While welfare provision in itself is seldom attacked, from time to time social workers come under critical scrutiny—especially when failing to prevent dramatic cases of child abuse. By publicizing sensational failures, the risk is of creating the impression that failure is the normal order of things.

All this operates through a covert and biased selection process. The more straightforward, but not altogether distinct process of stereotyping also occurs. Gardner and Radel (1978) analysed American newspapers and television in 1975, scanning for any references to disabled people. The reports, articles, or programmes were classified according to the dominant themes and images presented. About one-half of all items portrayed the disabled as a dependent person, but only about a quarter as an independent person capable of adjusting to and overcoming his disability, contributing fully to society. Roughly a tenth of items portrayed the disabled as being in some way deviant—'strange, bizarre, anti-social'. Gardner and Radel express concern that this distorted image projects ideas incompatible with modern professional thinking about welfare:

> Such stereotypes can only hinder the adjustment of these persons by denying their ability to determine for themselves their own method of coping with their handicap, and reinforcing their image of themselves as 'helpless' and 'dependent'. Hopefully, the increasing emphasis on integrating the disabled individual into the normal stream of community activities will offset the image of the disabled as essentially dependent and increase awareness of the disabled individual's ability to adjust and function successfully within the community (p. 274).

As with virtually all content analyses, the implications of this for the effects on the viewers' or readers' opinions or perceptions of disablement are conjectural. Clearly such nihilistic stereotypes may do no good given the dominance of the 'Does he take sugar?' syndrome in society. Some studies have linked such stereotypes to public attitudes.

Nunally (1961) found the public's conception of mental health rather nearer to those of experts in the field than the image portrayed in the media. The public and experts agree that the mentally ill tend not to look and act differently from 'normal' people, and that mental illness is not entirely due to organic causes. But as Nunally writes: 'In television dramas, for example, the afflicted person often enters the scene staring glass-eyed, with his mouth widely agape, mumbling incoherent phrases or laughing uncontrollably.' Steadman and Cocozza (1977–8) studied the origin and nature of the public's perceptions of the criminally insane. The public's conceptions of mental illness are rather blurred and ill-defined and there is a chance that the stigmatization of mental illness may exacerbate the rejection of those who have suffered from mental illness. It is disturbing if the mentally ill have the additional burden of discrimination originating in public misconceptions about the nature of the criminally insane. The pertinent question here is whether or not the mass media actually contribute to the misconceptions. Precise definitions of the criminally insane vary in different legal systems. Essentially the phrase refers to guilty individuals who were incapable for psychological reasons of comprehending their trial or were judged incapable of being responsible for their crimes through insanity. An additional group of the criminally insane are those transferred to hospitals for the criminally insane during a term of imprisonment.

A large sample of individuals in Albany, New York, were interviewed in 1975 in order to get public opinion data on the differences between 'most people', 'mental patients', and the 'criminally insane'. People had great fear of the criminally insane. Although 29% said that they feared former mental patients a lot, 61% said the same of former criminally insane patients. Indeed it was virtually impossible to find anyone who did not express a degree of fear of former criminally insane patients. The criminally insane were seen as violent, dangerous, and harmful. This may not be a very accurate impression at all.

Now, in terms of the actual characteristics of the criminally insane in the New York area, where the public opinion study was carried out, things are somewhat different to say the least. As one might expect with any group of criminals, some of the criminally insane had committed violent crimes including assault, murder, arson, and rape. However, the most frequent crimes committed by the criminally insane were robbery and burglary.

A clue to why the criminally insane are seen as dangerous comes from those mentioned who had been heard about through the mass media. These included the likes of James Earl Ray, Lee Harvey Oswald, the Boston Strangler, Charles Manson, Sirhan Sirhan, and Patty Hearst. In fact, no one mentioned more than once could legally be classified as criminally insane. Virtually all of the public's names of the criminally insane were murderers, kidnappers, or bombers. Whereas only about 14% of the criminally insane sample had committed murder, near enough 100% of those mentioned by the public had done so. Steadman and Cocozza claim that the media, by concentrating on the more bizarre cases, inculcate an inadequate perception of the criminally insane. This should be tempered by the observation that the media only furnished images which the public then coded as being of criminally insane individuals. The media had not stated that they were legally defined as criminally insane.

The Media Treat a Welfare Problem Favourably

It is very easy to find stereotypes in the mass media. Virtually any section of society is inevitably presented as a caricature of reality. This is especially true for remote and relatively unknown groups. Not all discussions of the role of the mass media in defining and presenting social welfare issues have adopted the critical stance we have seen so far. An important instance of these is Arnold Linksy's (1973) discussion of the image of the alcoholic in magazines over the period 1900–1966. What is impressive about this work is that Linsky tries to get deeper than most. He avoids the trap of merely counting the numbers of hicupping drunks swinging on lamp posts cartooned in the press. Instead he seeks to understand the changes in the explanations of human behaviour that have occurred during the course of this century. He is influenced by Glock's idea that almost imperceptibly and subtly man's view of human nature has changed. Largely this is from a 'free will' to a deterministic point of view. This is in keeping with the rise of the social science conceptions and decline in the moralistic tone of earlier thinking. Magazine articles over this 67-year period dealing with alcoholism were coded on two major dimensions:

(a) *Location dimension:* do the implied causes of alcoholism rest within the individual or are they environmental factors?
(b) *Moral dimension:* do the implied causes of alcoholism have strong moral overtones or are they evaluated relatively neutrally?

In terms of the location of the causes of alcoholism there was a steady move of location of causes from being outside the individual to more psychological (internal) explanations, the big shift occurring during the 1940s, although there has been a slight move back to environmental locations since. The moral dimension also changed in that period—that is to say, moral overtones to the cause have declined markedly over time in favour of a more scientific or detached attitude.

So far this considers the location and moral dimensions to be independent. It is possible to see, by combining the two dimensions, four broad theories of the causes of alcoholism: (1) *Traditional free will position:* in which the location is within the individual who through weaknesses of character or moral ineptitude chooses the drunken path (i.e. internal moral position); (2) *Social criticism position:* immoral forces outside the individual cause the alcoholism. For example, profit-seeking brewers advertising the pleasures of drink, or cruel abusive parents (i.e. external moral position); (3) *Psychological and biological explanation:* the individual has a faulty gene, faulty physiology, poor genetic predispositions, conditions poorly, etc. A scientific point of view with no direct moral implications (i.e. internal non-moralistic position) and (4) *Sociological explanation:* the cause is in the environment but no moralistic judgements implied (i.e. internal non-moral position).

These different theories of aetiology have become more or less common over the period. For example, the social criticism explanations declined from three-quarters to one-twentieth of articles while psychological and biological explanations increased from one-twentieth to over one-half of articles over the period. Similarly, suggestions of how to deal with alcoholism have changed—for example, moderation, abstinence, and prohibition decline in popularity dramatically. Linsky claims to have evidence that there has been a corresponding change in public opinion.

Conclusion

Linsky's argument, although dealing with a broad historical trend, provides an optimistic note on which to end this review of the role of the mass media in welfare. The revision of the concept of alcoholism from being moralistic to more social scientific implies much for the treatment of alcoholics. This contrasts with much of the tone of the earlier sections of this chapter in which we noted the potential of the mass media to create false impressions of welfare problems which fortunately is tempered by a tendency of the public to neglect the mass media in favour of other sources of understanding social reality. Neither did we find an overwhelming case for the suggestion that the mass media have a powerful positive role to play in attracting resources to the welfare services.

References

Abel, G. C., Blanchard, E. B., Barlow, D. H. and Mavissakalian, M. (1975) Identifying specific erotic cues in sexual deviations by audio-taped descriptions. *Journal of Applied Behaviour Analysis*, **8**, 247–260.

Abelson, H., Cohen, R., Heaton, E. and Slider, C. (1971). National survey of public attitudes toward and experience with erotic materials. In *Technical Reports of the Commission on Obscenity and Pornography*, Vol. 6 Washington, D.C.: U.S. Government Printing Office.

Adoni, H. and Cohen, A. A. (1978). Television economic news and the social construction of economic reality. *Journal of Communication,* **28**, 61–69.

Allport, G. W. and Postman, L. J. (1947). *Psychology of rumour*, New York: Holt.

Atkin, C. K. (1978). Effects of drug commercials on young viewers. *Journal of Communication,* **28**, 71–79.

Bachy, V. (1976). Danish 'permissiveness' revisited. *Journal of Communication,* **26**, 40–43.

Baggaley, J. and Duck, S. (1976). *Dynamics of television*. Farnborough, Hants.

Baker, R. K. and Ball, S. J. (Eds.) (1969). *Violence and the media. A staff report to the National Commission on the Causes and Prevention of Violence*. Washington, D.C.: U.S. Government Printing Office.

Ball, S. and Bogatz, G. A. (1970). *The first year of Sesame Street*. Princeton, N.J.: Educational Testing Service.

Bandura, A. (1962). Social learning through imitation. In M. R. Jones (Ed.), *Nebraska Symposium on Motivation*. Lincoln: University of Nebraska Press, pp. 211–274.

Bandura, A. (1965). Vicarious processes: a case of no-trial learning. In L. Berkowitz (Ed.), *Advances in experimental social psychology*, Vol. 2. New York: Academic Press, pp. 1–55.

Baron, R. A., Byrne, D. and Griffitt, W. (1974). *Social psychology: understanding human interaction*. Boston: Allyn & Bacon.

Belson, W. A. (1963). A reply to Parker's note. *Public Opinion Quarterly,* **27,** 321–329.

Belson, W. A. (1967). *The impact of television.* London: Crosby Lockwood.

Belson, W. A. (1969). Measuring the influence of television programmes and campaigns. *Advancement of Science,* **25,** 422–429.

Belson, W. A. (1975). *Juvenile theft: the causal factors.* London: Harper & Row.

Belson, W. A. (1977). *Television violence and the adolescent boy.* Press release, 19 September.

Belson, W. A. (1978). *Television violence and the adolescent boy.* London: Saxon House.

Belson, W. A. and Thompson, B. A. (1973). *Bibliography of methods of social and business research.* London: Crosby Lockwood.

Ben-Veniste, R. (1970). *Pornography and sex crime: the Danish experience.* In *Technical Reports of the Commission on Obscenity and Pornography,* Vol. 70. Washington, D.C.: U.S. Government Printing Office.

Berelson, B. (1948). What missing the newspaper means. In P. Lazarsfeld and F. N. Stanton (Eds.), *Communications research, 1948–9.* New York: Duell, Sloan & Pearce.

Berelson, B., Lazarsfeld, P. F. and McPhee, W. N. (1954). *Voting: a study of opinion formation in a presidential campaign.* Chicago: University of Chicago Press.

Berkowitz, L., Corwin, R. and Heironimus, M. (1963). Film violence and subsequent aggressive tendencies. *Public Opinion Quarterly,* **27,** 217–229.

Berkowitz, L. and Rawlings, E. (1963). Effects of film violence on inhibitions against subsequent aggression. *Journal of Abnormal and Social Psychology,* **66,** 405–412.

Blackman, J. A. and Hornstein, H. A. (1977). Newscasts and the social actuary. *Public Opinion Quarterly,* **41,** 295–313.

Blumer, H. (1933). *Movies and conduct.* New York: Macmillan.

Blumer, H. and Hauser, P. M. (1933). *Movies, delinquency, and crime.* New York: Macmillan.

Blumler, J. G., Brown, J. R. and McQuail, D. (1970). The social origins of the gratifications associated with television viewing. Mimeo. University of Leeds.

Blumler, J. G. and Katz, E. (Eds.) (1974). *The uses of mass communications: current perspectives on gratifications research. Sage Annual Reviews of Communication Research,* Vol. 3. Beverly Hills: Sage.

Bogatz, G. A. and Ball, S. (1971). *The second year of Sesame Street: a continuing evaluation.* Princeton, J.J.: Educational Testing Service.

Boorstin, D. J. (1963). *The image.* Harmondsworth, Middlesex: Penguin.

Brigham, J. C. and Giesbrecht, L. W. (1976). 'All in the Family': racial attitudes.

British Psychological Society. Scientific Affairs Board (1978). Ethical principles for research with human subjects. *Bulletin British Psychological Society,* **31.**

Brody, S. (1977). *Screen violence and film censorship—a review of research. Home Office Research Study* No. 40. London: Her Majesty's Stationery Office.

Burnham, S. (1968). Telling it like it isn't. *New York Times Magazine,* 16 September, p. 13.

Burns, A. (1972). *To deprave and corrupt.* London: Davis-Poynter.

Busby, L. J. (1975). Sex-role-research on the mass media. *Journal of Communication,* **25,** 107–131.

Bush, D. E., Simmons, R. G., Hutchinson, B. and Blyth, D. A. (1977–8). Adolescent perception of sex-roles in 1968 and 1975. *Public Opinion Quarterly,* **41,** 459–474.

Butler, D. and Stokes, D. (1969). *Political change in Britain.* London: Macmillan.

Butler, M. and Paisley, W. (1978). Magazine coverage of women's rights. *Journal of Communication,* **28,** 183–186.

Byrne, D. and Lamberth, J. (1971). The effect of erotic stimuli on sex arousal, evaluative responses, and subsequent behaviour. *Technical Reports of the Commission on Obscenity and Pornography*, Vol. 8. Washington, D.C.: U.S. Government Printing Office, pp. 41–67.

Campbell, D. T. and Boruch, R. F. (1975). Making the case for randomized assignment to treatments by considering the alternatives: six ways in which quasi-experimental evaluations in compensatory education tend to underestimate effects. In C. A. Bennett and A. A. Lumsdaine (Eds.), *Evaluation and experiment.* New York: Academic Press, pp. 195–296.

Cantril, H. (1940). *The invasion from Mars: a study in the psychology of panic.* Illinois University Press.

Carlin, J. C. (1976). The rise and fall of topless radio. *Journal of Communication,* **26,** 31–37.

Canter, D. and Strickland, S. (1975). *TV violence and the child: the evolution fate of the surgeon general's report.* New York: Russell Sage Foundation.

Chapko, M. (1976). Black ads are getting blacker. *Journal of Communication,* **26,** 175–178.

Chibnall, S. (1977). *Law-and-order news: an analysis of crime reporting in the British press.* London: Tavistock Press.

Cirino, R. (1973). Bias through selection and omission: automobile safety, smoking. In S. Cohen and J. Young (Eds.), *The manufacture of news.* London: Constable, pp. 40–61.

Clark, D. C. and Blankenburg, W. B. (1971). Trends in violent content in selected mass media. In G. A. Comstock and E. A. Rubinstein (Eds.), *Television and social behaviour*, Vol. 1. *Content and control.* Washington D.C.: U.S. Government Printing Office, pp. 188–243.

Cohen, S. (1972). *Folk devils and moral panics.* London: McGibbon & Kee.

Cohen, S. and Young, J. (Eds.). (1973). *The manufacture of news.* London: Constable.

Command Papers (1979). *Criminal statistics, England and Wales 1978.* Cmnd. 7670. London: H.M.S.O.

Commission on Obscenity and Pornography (1970). *The report of the Commission on Obscenity and Pornography.* Washington D.C.: U.S. Government Printing Office.

Commission on Obscenity and Pornography (1970). *The report of the Commission on Obscenity and Pornography.* New York: Bantam.

Committee on Obscenity and Film Censorship (1979). *Report.* Cmnd 7772. London: H.M.S.O.

Committee on Contempt of Court (1975). *Report.* Cmnd 5794. London: H.M.S.O.

Cook, T. D., Appleton, H., Conner, R. F., Shaffer, A., Tomkin, G., and Weber, S. J. (1975). *Sesame Street revisited.* New York: Russell Sage Foundation.

Cook, T. D. and Conner, R. F. (1976). The educational impact. *Journal of Communication, 26,* 155–164.

Cooper, E. and Jahoda, M. (1947). The evasion of propaganda. *Journal of Psychology, 23,* 15–25.

Courtney, A. E. and Whipple, T. W. (1974). Women in TV commercials. *Journal of Communication, 24,* 110–117.

Coyne, A. (1978). Techniques for recruiting foster homes for mentally retarded children. *Child Welfare, 57,* 123–131.

Cressey, P. G. and Thrasher, F. M. (1933). *Boys, movies, and city streets.* New York: Macmillan.

Croll, P. (1974). *The deviant image.* Paper presented at British Sociological Association Mass Communication Study Group.

Culley, J. D. and Bennett, R. (1976). Selling women, selling blacks. *Journal of Communication, 26,* 160–174.

Cumberbatch, G. and Beardsworth, A. (1977). Criminals, victims and mass communications. In E. Viano (Ed.), *Victims and society.* Washington: Visage Press.

Cumberbatch, G. and Howitt, D. (1973). Identification with aggressive television characters and children's moral judgements. In W. W. Hartup and J. Dewit (Eds.), *Determinants and origins of aggressive behaviour*. The Hague: Mouton, pp. 517–524.

Curran, J. (1977). Capitalism and control of the press, 1800–1975. In J. Curran, M. Gurevitch, and J. Woolacott (Eds.), *Mass communication and society*. London: Arnold, pp. 195–230.

Davidson, E. S., Yasuna, A. and Tower, A. (1979). The effects of television cartoons on sex-role stereotyping in young girls. *Child Development,* **50,** 597–600.

Davis, F. J. (1952). Crime news in Colorado newspapers. *American Journal of Sociology,* **57,** 325–330.

Davis, K. E. and Braucht, G. N. (1971). Reactions to viewing films of erotically realistic heterosexual behaviour. In *Technical Reports of the Commission on Obscenity and Pornography*, Vol. 8. Washington D.C.: U.S. Government Printing Office.

De Boer, C. (1977). The polls: women at work. *Public Opinion Quarterly,* **41,** 268–277.

De Fleur, M. (1964). Occupation roles as portrayed on television. *Public Opinion Quarterly,* **28,** 57–74.

De Fleur, M. and De Fleur, L. (1967). The relative contribution of television as a learning source for children's occupational knowledge. *American Sociological Review,* **321,** 777–789.

Dembo, R. (1972). Life style and media use among English working class youths. *Gazette,* **18,** 21–36.

Dembo, R. (1973). Gratifications found in media by British teenage boys. *Journalism Quarterly,* **50,** 517–526.

Dembo, R. and McCron, R. (1976). Social factors in media use. In R. Brown (Ed.), *Children and television*. London: Collier Macmillan, pp. 137–166.

Diaz-Guerrero, R., Reyes-Lagunes, I., Witzke, D. B. and Holtman, W. H. (1975). Plaza Sesamo in Mexico: an evaluation. *Journal of Communication,* 145–154.

Dohrmann, R. (1975). A gender profile of children's educational TV. *Journal of Communication,* **25,** 56–65.

Downing, M. (1974). Heroine of the daytime serial. *Journal of Communication,* **24,** 130–137.

Drabman, R. S. and Thomas, M. H. (1977). Children's imitation of aggressive and prosocial behaviour when viewing alone and in pairs. *Journal of Communication,* **3,** 199–205.

Eimermann, T. and Simon, R. J. (1970). Newspaper coverage of crimes and trials: another empirical look at the free press-free trial controversy. *Journalism Quarterly,* **47** (1), 142–144.

Elliott, P. (1974). Uses and gratifications research: a critique and a sociological alternative. In J. Blumler and E. Katz (Eds.), *The uses of mass communications*. Beverly Hills: Sage, pp. 249–268.

Elliott, P. (1973). *The making of a television series: a case study in the sociology of culture*. London: Constable.

Emery, F. and Emery, M. (1976). *A choice of futures*. Leiden: Martinuus Nijhoff Social Sciences Division.

Ennis, P. (1967). *Criminal victimization in the United States. President's Commission on Law Enforcement and the Administration of Justice. Field Survey 2*. Washington D.C.: U.S. Government Printing Office.

Eron, L. D. (1963). Relationship of TV viewing habits and aggressive behaviour in children. *Journal of Abnormal and Social Psychology*, **67**, 193–196.

Erskine, H. (1968). The polls: Negro employment. *Public Opinion Quarterly*, **32**, 132–153.

Erskine, H. (1971). The polls: women's role: *Public Opinion Quarterly*, **35**, 275–290.

Erskine, H. (1975). The polls: government role in welfare. *Public Opinion Quarterly*, **39**, 257–274.

Eysenck, H. J. and Nias, D. K. B. (1978). *Sex, violence and the media*. London: Temple Smith.

Farley, J. (1978). Women's magazines and the equal rights amendment: friend or foe? *Journal of Communication*, **28**, 187–192.

Fernandex-Collado, C. F. and Greenberg, B. S. (1978). Sexual intimacy and drug use in TV series. *Journal of Communication*, **28**, 30–37.

Feshbach, S. (1955). The drive-reducing function of fantasy behaviour. *Journal of Abnormal and Social Psychology*, **50**, 3–11.

Feshbach, S. (1961). The stimulating versus cathartic effects of a vicarious aggressive activity. *Journal of Abnormal and Social Psychology*, **63**, 381–385.

Feshbach, S. and Singer, R. D. (1971). *Television and aggression: an experimental field study*. San Francisco: Jossey-Bass.

Festinger, L. (1957). *A theory of cognitive dissonance*. Stanford: Stanford University Press.

Foreman, H. J. (1935). *Our movie made children*. New York: Macmillan.

Fox, W. S. and Philliber, W. W. (1978). Television viewing and the perception of affluence. *Sociological Quarterly*, **19**, 103–112.

Franzwa, H. H. (1974). Working women in fact and fiction. *Journal of Communication*, **24**, 104–109.

Freedman, J. L. and Sears, D. O. (1965). Selective exposure. In L. Berkowitz (Ed.), *Advances in experimental social psychology*, Vol. 2, pp. 58–97.

Friedrich, W. N. (1977). Evaluation of a media campaign's effects on reporting patterns of child abuse. *Perceptual and Motor Skills,* **45,** 161–162.

Galtung, J. and Ruge, M. H. (1965). The structure of foreign news. *Journal of International Peace Research,* **1,** 64–90.

Gardner, J. M. and Radel, M. (1978). Portrait of the disabled in the media. *Journal of Community Psychology,* **6,** 269–274.

Gebhard, P. H., Gagnon, J. H., Pomeroy, W. B. and Cristenson, C. V. (1965). *Sex offenders: an analysis of types.* London: Heinemann.

Gerbner, G. and Gross, L. (1976). Living with television: the violence profile. *Journal of Communication,* **26,** 173–199.

Gerbner, G., Gross, L., Jackson-Beek, M., Jeffries-Foss, S. and Signoriell, N. (1978). Cultural indicators: Violence profile No. 9. *Journal of Communication,* **28,** 176–178.

Gerbner, G., Gross, L., Signorielli, M. and Jackson-Beek, M. (1979). The demonstration of power: Violence profile No. 10. *Journal of Communication,* **29,** 177–196.

Glasgow University Media Group (1976). *Bad news.* London: Routledge & Kegan Paul.

Goffman, E. (1979). *Gender advertisements.* London: Macmillan.

Golding, P. and Elliott, P. (1979). *Making the news.* London: Longman.

Golding, P. and Middleton, S. (1978). Welfare abuse and the media. *New Society,* **46,** 195–197.

Goodhardt, G. J., Ehrenberg, A. S. C. and Collins, M. A. (1975). *The television audience: patterns of viewing.* Farnborough, England: Saxon House.

Goranson, R. E. (1970). Media violence and aggressive behaviour: a review of experimental research. In L. Berkowitz (Ed.), *Advances in experimental social psychology*, Vol. 5. New York: Academic Press, pp. 1–31.

Greenberg, B. S., Dervin, B., Dominick, J. R. and Bowes, J. (1970). *Use of the mass media by urban poor.* New York: Praeger.

Greenwald, A. G. and Sakumara, J. S. (1967). Attitude and selective learning: where are the phenomena of yesteryear? *Journal of Personality and Social Psychology,* **7,** 387–397.

Griffith, J. A. G. (1977). *The politics of the judiciary.* Manchester University Press.

Hain, P. (1976). *Mistaken identity.* London: Quartet.

Halloran, J. D. (1967). *Attitude formation and change.* Leicester: Leicester University Press.

Halloran, J. D. (Ed.) (1970). *The effects of television.* London: Panther.

Halloran, J. D., Brown, R. L. and Chaney, D. C. (1970). *Television and delinquency.* Leicester: Leicester University Press.

Halloran, J. D., Elliott, P. and Murdock, G. (1970). *Demonstration and communication: a case study.* Harmondsworth: Penguin.

Hartmann, D. P. (1969). Influence of symbolically modelled instrumental aggression and pain cues on aggressive behavior. *Journal of Personality and Social Psychology,* **11**, 280–288.

Hartmann, D. P. (1969). The influence of symbolically modelled instrumental aggressive and pain cues on the disinhibition of aggressive behavior. Unpublished doctoral dissertation, University of California, Stanford. Ann Arbor, Michigan, University Microfilms 65-12789.

Hartmann, P. and Husband, C. (1971). The mass media and racial conflict. *Race,* **12**, 267–282.

Hartmann, P. and Husband, C. (1972). The mass media and racial conflict. In D. McQuail (Ed.), *Sociology of mass communication.* Harmondsworth: Penguin, pp. 435–455.

Hartmann, P. and Husband, C. (1973). The mass media and racial conflict. In S. Cohen and J. Young (Eds.), *The manufacture of news: a reader.* Beverly Hills: Sage, pp. 270–283.

Hartmann, P. and Husband, C. (1974). *Racism and the mass media: a study of the role of the mass media in the formation of white beliefs and attitudes in Britain.* London: Davies-Poynter.

Herzog, H. (1944). What do we really know about daytime serial listeners? In P. F. Lazarsfeld and F. N. Stanton (Eds.), *Radio research 1942– 1943.* New York: Duell, Sloan and Pearce, pp. 3–33.

Herzog, H. (1954). Motivations and gratifications of daily serial listeners. In W. Schramm (Ed.), *The process and effects of mass communication.* Urbana, Ill.: University of Illinois Press, pp. 50–55.

Himmelweit, H. T., Oppenheim, A. N. and Vince, P. (1958). *Television and the child.* London: Oxford University Press.

Hovland, C. I. (1954). Effects of the mass media of communication. In G. Lindzey (Ed.), *Handbook of social psychology,* Vol. 2. Cambridge, Ma.: Addison-Wesley, pp. 1062–1103.

Hovland, C. I. and Janis, I. L. (Eds.) (1953). *Personality and persuasibility.* New Haven: Yale University Press.

Hovland, C. D., Lumsdaine, A. A. and Sheffield, F. D. (1949). *Experiments in mass communication.* New Haven: Yale University Press.

Howitt, D (1972). *Trash: some audience reactions.* Centre for Mass Communication Research: University of Leicester.

Howitt, D. (1976). The effects of television on children. In R. Brown (Ed.), *Children and television.* London: Collier Macmillan, pp. 320–342.

Howitt, D. (1976). *Report of pre-school children and television project.* Centre for Mass Communication Research: University of Leicester.

Howitt, D. (1976). *Report of television language project.* Centre for Mass Communication Research: University of Leicester.

Howitt, D. and Cumberbatch, G. (1971). Affective feeling for a film character and evaluation of an anti-social act. *British Journal of Social and Clinical Psychology,* **2,** 102–108.

Howitt, D. and Dembo, R. (1974). A subcultural account of media effects. *Human Relations,* **27,** 25–41.

Howitt, D. and Cumberbatch, G. (1975). *Mass media violence and society.* London. Elek Science.

Janis, I. L. and Feshbach, S. (1953). Effects of fear-arousing communications. *Journal of Abnormal and Social Psychology,* **48,** 78–92.

Jeffres, L. W. and Hur, K. K. (1979). White ethnics and their media images. *Journal of Communication,* **29,** 116–122.

Kaplan, R. M. and Singer, R. D. (1976). Television violence and viewer aggression: a re-examination of the evidence. *Journal of Social Issues,* **32,** 35–70.

Kepplinger, H. M. and Roth, H. (1979). Creating a crisis: German mass media and oil supply in 1973–74. *Public Opinion Quarterly,* **43,** 285–296.

Katz, E. (1960). The functional approach to the study of attitudes. *Public Opinion Quarterly,* **24,** 163–204.

Katz, E. and Lazarsfeld, P. F. (1964). *Personal influence: the part played by people in the flow of communications.* New York: Free Press.

Katz, E. (1971). The social itinerary of technical change: two studies of the diffusion of innovation. In W. Schramm and D. F. Roberts (Eds.), *The process and effects of mass communication.* University of Illinois Press, pp. 761–797.

Kerin, R. A. (1979). Black model appearance and product evaluations. *Journal of Communication,* **29,** 123–128.

Klapper, J. (1960). *The effects of mass communication.* New York: Free Press.

Kline, F. G. and Jess, P. H. (1966). Prejudicial publicity: its effects on law school mock juries. *Journalism Quarterly,* **43,** 113–116.

Knopf, T. A. (1970). Media myths on violence. *Columbia Journalism Review,* Spring, 1970, pp. 17–23.

Krugman, H. E. (1970). *Electroencephalographic aspects of low involvement; implications for the McLuhan hypothesis.* American Associates for Public Opinion Research; New York.

Kutchinsky, B. (1971). Towards an explanation of the decrease in registered sex crimes in Copenhagen. In *Technical Reports of the Commission on Obscenity and Pornography,* Vol. 8. Washington, D.C.: U.S. Government Printing Office.

Lang, G. L. and Lang, K. (1972). Some pertinent questions on collective violence and the news media. *Journal of Social Issues,* **28,** 93–110.

Lashley, K. S. and Watson, J. B. (1922). *A psychological study of motion pictures in relation to venereal disease.* Washington, D.C.: U.S. Interdepartmental Social Hygiene Board.

Lazarsfeld, P. F., Berelson, B. and Gaudet, H. (1948). *The people's choice.* New York: Columbia University Press.

Lazer, C. and Dier, S. (1978). The labor force in fiction. *Journal of Communication,* **28,** 174–182.

Lefkowitz, M. M., Eron, L. D., Walder, L. O. and Huesmann, L. R. (1971). Television violence and child aggression: a follow up study. In G. A. Comstock and E. A. Rubinstein (Eds.), *Television and social behavior,* Vol. 3. *Television and adolescent aggressiveness.* Washington, D.C.: Government Printing Office, pp. 35–135.

Lemon, J. (1977). Women and blacks on prime-time television. *Journal of Communication,* **27,** 70–79.

Leyens, J. P. and Camino, L. (1974). The effects of social structures and repeated exposure to film violence on aggression. In W. W. Hartup and J. Dwit (Eds.), *Determinants and origins of aggressive behavior.* The Hague: Mouton, pp. 499–508.

Liebert, R. M. (1976). Evaluating the evaluators. *Journal of Communication,* **26,** 165–171.

Liebert, R. M., Cohen, L. A., Joyce, C., Murrel, S., Nisonoff, L. and Sonnenschein, S. (1977). Predispositions revisited. *Journal of Communication,* **27,** 217–221.

Liebert, R. M., Neale, J. M. and Davidson, E. S. (1973). *The early window: effects of television on children and youth.* Elmsford, New York: Pergamon.

Lin, N. (1974). The McIntire march: a study of recruitment and commitment. *Public Opinion Quarterly,* **38,** 562–573.

Linsky, A. S. (1973). Theories of behavior and the image of the alcoholic in popular magazines, 1900–1966. In S. Cohen and J. Young (Eds.), *The manufacture of news.* London: Constable, pp. 146–155.

Longford Committee Investigating Pornography (1972). *Pornography: The Longford report.* London: Coronet.

McCombs, M. E. and Shaw, D. L. (1972). The agenda setting and function of the mass media. *Public Opinion Quarterly,* **36,** 176–187.

McCron, R. (1976). Changing perspectives in the study of mass media and socialization. In J. D. Halloran (Ed.), *Mass media and socialization.* Leicester: International Association for Mass Communication Research, pp. 13–44.

McLaughlin, J. (1975). The doctor shows. *Journal of Communication,* **25,** 182–184.

Maccoby, N. and Farquhar, J. W. (1975). Communication for health: unselling heart disease. *Journal of Communication,* **25,** 114–125.

Maccoby, N. and Farquhar, J. W. (1976). Bringing the California health report up to date. *Journal of Communication,* **26,** 56–57.

Maracek, J., Piliavin, J. A., Fitzsimmons, E., Krogh, E. C., Leader, E. and Trudell, B. (1978). Women as TV experts: the voice of authority? *Journal of Communication,* **28,** 159–168.

Meacher, M. (1971). *Rent rebates.* London: Child Poverty Action Group.

Medrich, E. A. (1979). Constant television: a background to daily life. *Journal of Communication,* **29,** 171–176.

Meline, C. W. (1976). Does the medium matter? *Journal of communication,* **26,** 81–89.

Melody, W. (1973). *Children's television: the economics of exploitation.* New Haven: Yale University Press.

Milavsky, J. R., Pekowsky, B. and Stipp, H. (1976). TV drug advertising and proprietary and illicit drug use among teenage boys. *Public Opinion Quarterly,* **39,** 457–481.

Milgram, S. (1974). *Obedience to authority.* London: Tavistock.

Milgram, S. and Stotland, R. L. (1973). *Television and antisocial behavior: field experiments.* New York: Academic Press.

Miller, M. M. and Reeves, B. (1976). Dramatic TV content and children's sex-role stereotypes. *Journal of Broadcasting,* **20,** 35–50.

Mills, K. (1974). Fighting sexism on the airwaves. *Journal of Communication,* **24,** 150–155.

Minton, J. H. (1972). The impact of Sesame Street on reading readiness in kindergarten children. Unpublished doctoral dissertation, Fordham University.

Mosher, D. L. and Katz, H. (1971). Pornographic films, male verbal aggression against women and guilt. In *Technical Reports of the Commission on Obscenity and Pornography*, Vol. 8. Washington, D.C.: U.S. Government Printing Office.

Mosher, D. L. (1971). Psychological reactions to pornographic films. In *Technical Reports of the Commission on Obscenity and Pornography*, Vol. 8. Washington, D.C.: U.S. Government Printing Office.

Motto, J. A. (1967). Suicide and suggestibility. *American Journal of Psychiatry,* **124,** 156–159.

Murdock, G. and Golding, P. (1974). For a political economy of mass communications. In R. Miliband and J. Saville (eds.), *Socialist register 1973.* London: Merlin Press.

National Advisory Commission on Civil Disorders (1968). *Report.* Washington, D.C.: U.S. Government Printing Office.

Neale, J. M. and Liebert, R. M. (1980). *Science and behavior: an intro-*

duction to methods of research. Englewood Cliffs, N.J.: Prentice Hall.

Nkpa, N. K. U. (1977). Rumors of mass poisoning in Biafra. *Public Opinion Quarterly,* **4,** 332–346.

Noble, G. (1975). *Children in front of the small screen.* London: Constable.

Nowack, K. (1972). The psychological study of mass communication effects. On the validity of laboratory experiments and an attempt to improve ecological validity. *Studies in Economic Psychology,* **82.** Economic Research Institute at the Stockholm School of Economics.

Nunnally, J. C. (1961). *Popular conceptions of mental health.* New York: Holt, Rinehart, & Winston.

O'Bryant, S. L. and Corder-Bolz, C. R. (1978). The effects of television on children's stereotyping of women's work roles. *Journal of Vocational Behavior,* **12,** 233–244.

O'Kelley, C. G. and Bloomquist, L. E. (1976). Women and blacks on TV. *Journal of Communication,* **26,** 179–192.

Palmer, E. L., Chen, M. and Lesser, G. S. (1976). Sesame Street: patterns of international adaptation. *Journal of Communication,* **26,** 109–123.

Parke, R. D., Berkowitz, L., Leyens, J. P., West, S. and Sebastian, R. J. (1977). The effects of repeated exposure to movie violence on aggressive behavior in juvenile delinquent boys: field experimental studies. In L. Berkowitz (Ed.), *Advances in experimental social psychology,* Vol. 8. New York: Academic Press, pp. 35–172.

Parker, E. B. (1963). The effect of television on magazine and newspaper reading: a problem of methodology. *Public Opinion Quarterly,* **27,** 315–320.

Payne, D. E. and Payne, K. P. (1970). Newspapers and crime in Detroit. *Journalism Quarterly,* **47,** 233–238.

Peled, T. and Katz, E. (1974). Media functions in wartime: the Israel home front in October 1973. In J. G. Blumler and E. Katz (Eds.), *The uses of mass communications: current perspectives on gratifications research.* Beverly Hills, Ca.: Sage, pp. 49–69.

Peterson, R. C. and Thurstone, L. L. (1933). *Motion pictures and the social attitudes of children.* New York: Macmillan.

Pfuhl, E. (1960). The relationship of mass media to reported delinquent behavior. Unpublished doctoral dissertation, Washington State University. Ann Arbor, Michigan: University Microfilms 61-1308.

Pfuhl, E. (1970). Mass media and reported delinquent behavior: a negative case. In M. Wolfgang, L. Savitz, and N. Johnston (Eds.), *The sociology of crime and delinquency.* New York: Wiley, pp. 509–523.

Phillips, D. P. (1977). Motor vehicle fatalities increase just after published suicide stories. *Science,* **196** (4297), 1464-5.

Pingree, S. (1978). The effects of nonsexist television commercials and perceptions of reality on children's attitudes about women. *Psychology of Women Quarterly,* **23,** 262–277.

Portis, B. and Hunter, A. D. (1975). In-service training by mass media. *Journal of Communication,* **25,** 167–170.

Richmond, V. P. and McCroskey, J. C. (1975). Whose opinion do you trust? *Journal of Communication,* **25,** 42–50.

Rogers, E. M. (1962). *The diffusion of innovations.* Glencoe, Ill.: Free Press.

Roshier, R. J. (1969). Crime and the press. Unpublished PhD thesis. University of Newcastle.

Roshier, R. J. (1971). Crime and the press. *New Society,* **468,** 502–506.

Roshier, R. J. (1973). The selection of crime news by the press. In S. Cohen and J. Young (Eds.), *The manufacture of news.* London: Constable.

Salomon, G. (1976). Cognitive skill learning across cultures. *Journal of Communication,* **26,** 138–144.

Schachter, S. and Singer, J. E. (1962). Cognitive, social and physiological determinants of emotion state. *Psychological Review,* **69,** 379–399.

Scott, J. E. and Franklin, J. L. (1972). The changing nature of sex references in mass circulation magazines. *Public Opinion Quarterly,* **36,** 80–86.

Sears, D. and Freedman, J. (1967). Selective exposure to information: a critical review. *Public Opinion Quarterly,* **31,** 194–213.

Shuttleworth, F. K. and May, M. A. (1933). *The social conduct and attitudes of movie fans.* New York: Macmillan.

Simon, R. J. (1966). Murder, juries, and the press: does sensational reporting lead to verdicts of guilty? *Transaction,* **3,** 40–42.

Simon, R. J. (1974). *Public opinion in America: 1936–1970. Chicago: Rand McNally.*

Simon, R. J. and Eimermann, T. (1971). The jury finds not guilty: another look at media influence on the jury. *Journalism Quarterly,* **48,** 343–344.

Singer, J. L. and Singer, D. G. (1976). Can TV stimulate imaginative play? *Journal of Communication,* **26,** 74–80.

Smith, D. D. (1976). The social content of pornography. *Journal of Communication,* **26,** 16–23.

Smith, S. S. and Jamieson, B. D. (1972). Effects of attitude and ego involvement on the learning and retention of controversial material. *Journal of Personality and Social Psychology,* **22,** 303–310.

Star, S. A. and Hughes, H. M. (1950). Report of an educational campaign: the Cincinnati plan for the United Nations. *American Journal of Sociology,* **55,** 389–400.

Stauffer, J. and Frost, R. (1976). Male and female interest in sexually-oriented magazines. *Journal of Communication, 26*, 25–30.

Star, S. A. and Hughes, H. M. (1950). Report of an educational campaign: the Cincinnati plan for the United Nations. *American Journal of Sociology, 55*, 389–400.

Steadman, H. J. and Cocozza, J. J. (1977–8). Selective reporting and the Public's misconceptions of the criminally insane. *Public Opinion Quarterly, 41*, 523–533.

Stephenson, W. (1967). *The play theory of mass communication.* Chicago: University of Chicago Press.

Stimson, G. V. (1975). The message of psychotropic drug ads. *Journal of Communication, 25*, 153–160.

Strauss, F. F., Ousley, N. K. and Carlin, A. S. (1977). Outreach for the middle class drug misuser. *Drug Forum, 6*, 327–335.

Sue, S., Smith, R. E. and Gilbert, R. (1974). Biasing effects of pretrial publicity on judicial decisions. *Journal of Criminal Justice, 2*, 163–171.

Surgeon General's Scientific Advisory Committee on Television and Social Behaviour (1972). *Television and growing up: the impact of growing up: The impact of televised violence.* Washington, D.C.: U.S. Government Printing Office.

Surlin, S. H. and Tate, E. D. (1976). 'All in the Family': is Archie funny? *Journal of Communication, 26*, 61–68.

Tan, A. S. and Tan, G. (1979). Television use and self-esteem of black. *Journal of Communication, 29*, 129–135.

Tannenbaum, P. H. (1971). Emotional arousal as a mediator of erotic communication effects. In *Technical Reports of the Commission on Obscenity and Pornography*, Vol. 8. Washington, D.C.: Government Printing Office, pp. 326–356.

Tannenbaum, P. H. (1972). Studies in film-and-television-mediated arousal and aggression: a progress report. In G. A. Comstock, E. A. Rubinstein, and J. P. Murray (Eds.). *Television and social behavior*, Vol. 5. *Television's effects: further explorations.* Washington, D.C.: Government Printing Office, pp. 309–350.

Tans, M. D. and Chaffee, S. H. (1966). Pretrial publicity and juror prejudice. *Journalism Quarterly, 43*, 647–654.

Tedesco, N. S. (1974). Patterns in prime time. *Journal of Communication, 24*, 119–123.

Tichenor, P. J., Rodenkirchen, J. M., Olien, C. N. and Donohue, G. A. (1973). Community issues, conflict, and public affairs knowledge. In P. Clarke (Ed.), *New models for mass communication research. Sage annual reviews of communication research*, Vol. 2. Beverly Hills:

Sage, pp. 45–79.

Tizard, B. (1974). *Pre-school education in Great Britain: A research overview*. London: Social Science Research Council.

Tracey, M. (1978). *The production of political television*. London: Routledge & Kegan Paul.

Tunstall, J. (1971). *Journalists at work*. London: Constable.

Tunstall, J. (1977). *The media are American*. London: Constable.

Turrow, J. (1974). Advising and ordering: daytime, prime time. *Journal of Communication,* **24,** 138–141.

UNESCO (1973). *Race as news*. Paris: Unesco Press.

Vebrugge, L. M. (1978). Peers as recruiters: family planning communications of West Malaysian acceptors. *Journal of Health and Social Behavior,* **19,** 51–68.

Vidmar, N. and Rokeach, M. (1974). Archie Bunker's bigotry: a study in selective perception and exposure. *Journal of Communication,* **24,** 36–47.

Wade, S. and Schramm, W. (1969). The mass media as sources of public affairs, science and health knowledge. *Public Opinion Quarterly,* **33,** 197–209.

Walker, C. E. (1971). Erotic stimuli and the aggressive sexual offender. In *Technical Reports of the Commission on Obscenity and Pornography*, Vol. 7. Washington, D.C.: U.S. Government Printing Office.

Walker, H. L. (1973). Communication and the American health care problem. *Journal of Communication,* **23,** 349–360.

Walters, R. H. and Thomas, E. L. (1963). Enhancement of punitiveness by visual and audiovisual displays. *Canadian Journal of Psychology,* **17,** 244–255.

Walters, R. H., Thomas, E. L. and Acker, C. (1962). Enhancement of punitive behavior by audio-visual displays. *Science,* **136,** 872–873.

Walters, R. H. and Willows, D. C. (1968). Imitative behavior of disturbed and nondisturbed children following exposure to aggressive and non-aggressive models. *Child Development,* **39,** 79–89.

Warner, W. L. and Henry, W. E. (1948). The radio day time serial: a symbolic analysis. *Genetic Psychology Monographs,* **37,** 3–71.

Warren, D. (1978). Commercial liberation. *Journal of Communication,* **28,** 169–173.

Warren, D. I. (1972). Mass media and racial crisis: a study of the New Bethel church incident in Detroit. *Journal of Social Issues,* **28,** 111–131.

Wells, W. D. (1973). *Television and aggression: replication of an experimental field study*. Unpublished manuscript, Graduate School of Business, University of Chicago.

Werner, A. (1975). A case of sex and class socialization. *Journal of Communication,* **25,** 45–50.

Whale, J. (1977). *The politics of the media.* Manchester University Press.

White, Streicher H. (1974). The girls in cartoons. *Journal of Communication,* **24,** 125–129.

Williams, F. (1969). *The right to know.* London: Longmans.

Wilhoit, G. C. and de Bock, H. (1976). 'All in the Family' in Holland. *Journal of Communication,* **26,** 75–84.

Wright, W. R. (1975). Mass media as sources of medical information. *Journal of Communication,* **25,** 171–173.

Young, J. (1973). The amplification of drug use. In S. Cohen and J. Young (Eds.), *The manufacture of news.* London: Constable, pp. 350–359.

Zetterberg, H. L. (1970). The consumers of pornography where it is easily available: the Swedish experience. In *Technical Reports of the Commission on Obscenity and Pornography*, Vol. 9. Washington, D.C.: U.S. Government Printing Office.

Zillman, D. (1971). Excitation transfer in communication-mediated aggressive behavior. *Journal of Experimental Social Psychology,* **7,** 419–434.

Zillman, D., Hoyt, J. L. and Day, K. D. (1974). Strength and duration of the effect of aggressive, violent, and erotic communications on subsequent aggressive behavior. *Communication Research,* **1,** 286–306.

Zillman, D., Johnson, R. C. and Hanrahan, J. (1973). Pacifying effect of happy ending of communications involving aggression. *Psychological Reports,* **32,** 967–970.

Zimet, S. G. (1976). *Print and prejudice.* London: Hodder & Stoughton.

Author Index

Subject Index

WOIVE J₂